MUSICGAMEBOOK

Cover:
Designed by Mathilde Dupuy d'Angeac and executed by Camille Dubois.

601 West 26th Street, 18th floor
New York, NY 10001 USA
Tel.: 212 989-6810 Fax: 212 647-0005
www.assouline.com

ISBN : 2 84323 827 7

Color separation: Gravor (Switzerland)
Printed by KHL Printing Co Pte Ltd, Singapore

MUSIC GAME BOOK

A WORLD HISTORY OF 20TH CENTURY MUSIC

FOREWORD BY DAVID FRICKE

With contributions by
Jean-Jacques Groleau
Thomas Mahler
Patrick Tchiakpé

ASSOULINE

FOREWORD

In this book, the story of popular music in the twentieth century is big enough to be divided into more than one hundred artists and categories, across nearly four hundred pages. But the truth, harmony, and dissonance of that time is actually two histories, a pair of wildly opposite but inextricably tangled half-centuries. There is everything that happened between the dawn of 1900 and July 4, 1954: the Impressionist reveries of Claude Debussy; the exquisite piano miniatures of Erik Satie; the birth of the recording industry and of the electric guitar; the swing and genius of Louis Armstrong and Duke Ellington; bebop and tango.

Then there is everything that happened after 7:00 P.M. on that fateful July fifth evening in 1954, when a nineteen-year-old truck driver stepped up to the microphone at the Memphis Recording Service—the original name of Sam Phillips's Sun Records studio at 706 Union Avenue in Memphis, Tennessee. Elvis Presley did not invent rock 'n' roll that night. But when he started fiddling around with a blues romp, "That's All Right," written and first recorded by Arthur "Big Boy" Crudup in 1947, the earth moved and the future took a sharp left turn into noise, ecstasy, and rapid-fire revelation. Guitarist Scotty Moore summed up the magic and wild uncertainty of that moment this way, decades later: "We just sort of shook our heads and said, 'Well, that's fine, but good God, they'll run us out of town.'"

There would have been no ten-year rush from "That's All Right" to Bob Dylan, the Beatles, and the Rolling Stones without the Cold War, the explosion of prosperity in America, the boom in teenage population and the high-speed changes in the technology and commerce of music. But there is still no adequate explanation for the speed and nerve with which everyday people made extraordinary choices and art: at Motown in Detroit and at the momentary utopia of Haight-Ashbury; in the lipstick-and-fuzzbox wonderland of glam and under British punk's rain of phlegm; at ghetto soundsystem parties in Jamaica where ska begat reggae and chanting MCs laid down the blueprint for rap; in the Bronx playgrounds where DJs scratched Chic and Kraftwerk records on tandem turntables and where anyone from the neighborhood, armed with rhyme, could rock the mic.

Ultimately, everything on both sides of that night at the Sun is connected. It is a great leap only in years between the wit and moving melodic detail of Satie's *Croquis et agaceries d'un gros bonhomme en bois* ("Sketches and Exasperations of a Big Boob Made of Wood") and the Dadaist fun and rigorously composed fusion of "Peaches En Regalia" on Frank Zappa's 1970 guitar-solo masterpiece, *Hot Rats.*

And while no one can deny that the Ramones invented punk rock as we know and love it —jackhammer guitar, teenage angst, and early-1960s song-factory classicism—I hear the same kind of fun in the machine-gun bubblegum of Jacques Dutronc's 1966 debut single "Et Moi, Et Moi, Et Moi."

The twentieth century was an amazing age to be alive: to be surrounded, challenged, and forever changed by music. I know this because I was there for most of the second half of it; because all that I experienced made me want to learn more about what came before; and because everything I know makes me want to keep moving forward.

David Fricke, Senior Editor *Rolling Stone*
March 2006

How to use this book

Game

Observation

Question

Answer

If You Like...
You Will Also Like...

Contents

Lyrics and music
Who said what?

Chuck D

Little Richard

Claude Debussy

Elvis Presley

Gilbert K. Chesterton

Ringo Starr

Janis Joplin

Miles Davis

Friedrich Nietzsche

Bryan Ferry

Richard Strauss

• *ALSO SPRACH ZARATHUSTRA* (1896), *SALOME* (1905), *ELEKTRA* (1910), *DER ROSENKAVALIER* (1911), *FRIEDENSTAG* (1938), *FOUR LAST SONGS* (1946–1948)...
• 1864–1949
BÉLA BARTÓK, ERICH WOLFGANG KORNGOLD, GUSTAV MAHLER, ARNOLD SCHOENBERG, EDGARD VARÈSE, RICHARD WAGNER, FRANZ WAXMAN

The May 16, 1906, performance of Richard Strauss's third opera, *Salome,* in Graz, Austria attracted quite a crowd. Gustav Mahler wanted to see the opera that the Imperial censors had banned. Alban Berg went with his teacher Arnold Schoenberg. A young Adolf Hitler would later claim to have been in the audience, too.

They were there to see the work that turned the last great Romantic composer into the first great Modernist. His adaptation of Oscar Wilde's scandalous Symbolist play was a shocking, thrilling work—not just for its subject matter. Strauss gave the three main characters—the flirtatious Salome, her grotesque father Herod, and the prophet whose head she demands on a platter—a complementary musical style. The opera's dissonant passages caused an uproar. It closed in New York after just one performance.

The opera form allowed Strauss to mature. Wagner's son Siegfried declared Salome a "dangerous work." The composer followed it with the one-act *Elektra* (1910), whose bloody tale of matricide was told in music so discordant that cartoonists depicted Strauss conducting an orchestra of animals. "When a mother is slain on stage, do they expect me to write a violin concerto?" asked Strauss. Strauss's involvement with the Nazis also damaged his reputation. He resigned from the State Music Bureau after refusing to take Jewish writer Stefan Zweig's name off a playbill, and his opera *Friedenstag* (1938) is seen as a veiled criticism of the Third Reich. The original power of Strauss's music is undiminished, and critics still contend with his reputation and *Salome*'s impact. Some have even dubbed him the greatest composer of the century. Strauss himself had the final word in his magisterial *Four Last Songs,* written between 1946 and 1948. And, in 1968, audiences worldwide became familiar with his work when director Stanley Kubrick used the thunderous opening of Strauss's *Also Sprach Zarathustra* (1896) for the award-winning film, *2001: A Space Odyssey.*

Drawing by Otto Böhler of Richard Strauss conducting his orchestra (c. 1910).

Who holds the record for the world's loudest band?

Claude Debussy

• *PRÉLUDE À L'APRÈS-MIDI D'UN FAUNE* (1894), *PELLÉAS ET MÉLISANDE* (1902), *ESTAMPES* (1903), *LA MER* (1905), *IMAGES* (1905, 1907, SETS ONE AND TWO, RESPECTIVELY), *PRÉLUDES* (1909–1910)...
•1862–1918
PHILIP GLASS, MAURICE RAVEL, ALBERT ROUSSEL, ERIK SATIE, RALPH VAUGHAN WILLIAMS

Claude Debussy disliked being called an "Impressionist," but his breaking of musical rules and the sheer beauty of his *Préludes* (1909–1910) for piano established him as a colorist to rank with Monet. Debussy broadened musical palettes by introducing unusual scales, writing scores that demanded new ways of playing the piano, and trying to make tone pictures of his travels and epiphanies. Literature and art influenced him as much as composers, like Alexander Borodin and Modest Mussorgsky, did. Debussy grew up with the poet Paul Verlaine and believed the floating harmony of his *String Quartet in G Minor* (1893) recreated the sensation of reading his favorite books. Educated in Paris and Rome, Debussy was open to foreign influences. He became fascinated with the percussive sound of Javanese gamelan orchestras after hearing an ensemble play at the 1889 Paris World Exhibition.

His *Prélude à l' après-midi d' un faune* (1894), based on Stephane Mallarmé's 1876 eclogue, was unprecedented in its ambiguity. The ten-minute piece suggested a dispersing dream—the sounds of a flute and subtly layered horns created an air of fantasy. At its premiere, the audience loved it so much they demanded an encore.

Debussy spent a decade working on the radical opera *Pelléas et Mélisande* (1902). Adapting Maurice Maeterlinck's static theatrical allegory about a doomed love affair, Debussy's didn't let his music overwhelm the characters. Instead, it intensified the play's psychological shades. If his nemesis Richard Wagner overwhelmed audiences with his mystic visions—an effect lampooned in the *Golliwoog's Cakewalk* of Debussy's *Children's Corner* (1906) piano suite—*Pelléas* was a vague phantasm. Critics were divided, but "Debussyism" became the talk of Paris.

He struggled to write another opera, but the *Estampes* (1903) and *Images* (two series, 1905 and 1907) continued to prove his

! Manowar (130 decibels). The title was previously held by the Who, who played at an ear-shattering 126 decibels.

Illustration by Roberto Montenegro of a character in *Prélude à l'après-midi d'un faune* (1912), the ballet by Vaslav Nijinsky. Music composed by Claude Debussy.

Left: Portrait of Claude Debussy. Paris, 1918.

skills as musical illustrator. His "harmonic chemistry" suggested Asian architecture and the sound of rippling water. The *Préludes* are as much pure music as recollections of snowscapes and sunken cathedrals, and Debussy often placed their titles at the bottom of the score, as if they were an afterthought. Debussy's delicate style belied his life and times. His wife tried to commit suicide when he left her for the singer Emma Bardac, and World War I plunged him into a profound depression. When the supreme fantasist died in 1918, his funeral cortege wound its way unheralded through Paris's bombarded streets.

Classical Romanticism

• CHARLES IVES, GUSTAV MAHLER, SERGEI PROKOFIEV, JEAN SIBELIUS, MAX STEINER, RALPH VAUGHAN WILLIAMS...
• EUROPE, UNITED STATES
• 1900S–1950S

The French poet Charles Baudelaire summed up Romanticism as "intimacy, spirituality, color, aspiration toward the infinite, expressed by every means available." This found its visual equivalent in Casper David Friedrich's 1818 painting *Wanderer Above the Sea of Fog,* with the individual triumphantly regarding the endless skyscape. The Romantic artist was free, inspired, charismatic, and often unconventional. In music, Beethoven blew apart symphonic structures and Tchaikovsky made them throb with emotion.

This nineteenth-century upheaval survived into the twentieth—and Beethoven's ambition became a touchstone for even more radical outlooks. Gustav Mahler's sprawling *Symphony No. 8* (1906) literally needed a cast of a thousand musicians and singers to perform its hymn to God. The bohemian conductor/composer believed the mountains, earth, and even the universe had songs to sing, and he obsessively tried to write them until his death in 1911.

Nationalism was also a key component of Romanticism. Jean Sibelius's tone poems celebrated Finland and its mythological sagas. Both the Englishman Ralph Vaughan Williams and the Hungarian Béla Bartók scoured their respective countrysides for folk songs to be transformed by their compositions. The insurance broker-turned-composer Charles Ives expressed his free spirit with music as eccentric and American as Huckleberry Finn leading a marching band.

Those grappling with their Romantic heritage were unimpressed. The French composer Claude Debussy complained about "frigid imbeciles riding on the backs of masters" before losing himself in small-scale

Sergei Prokofiev on the cover of *Time*. November 19, 1945.

Right:
Wanderer Above the Sea of Fog (1918) by Caspar David Friedrich, oil on canvas. (37 x 29 in.) Kunsthalle, Hamburg, Germany.

Impressionist masterpieces. Arnold Schoenberg became downright allergic to the old ways. "The juices that serve life serve also death," he hissed, and promptly invented the rigid twelve-tone system. Bartók created *Mikrokosmos* (completed in 1939) from 153 pieces that were meant to initiate the performer into the ways of the modern, while Stravinsky and Richard Strauss began to unsettle audiences with bursts of dissonance. World War II forced many of these rebels to compose in the old ways. Modernist composers like Sergei Prokofiev embraced a Romantic manner in his *War Sonatas* (1939–1944). Others fled Europe and gave up their tone poems for Hollywood soundtracks, whose patchwork majesty invited folk interpolations and high drama. Listen to the sweeping strings and grand manner of Max Steiner's *Gone with the Wind* score (1939). You can almost imagine Scarlett O'Hara standing on a precipice, high above a sea of fog.

What were Broadway impresario Florenz Ziegfield's last words?

Radio

• AMERICAN TOP 40, BBC PROMS, THE DR. DEMENTO SHOW, THE EVERREADY HOUR, FLEISCHMANN'S YEAST HOUR, GRAND OLE OPRY, LET'S DANCE, LOUISIANA HAYRIDE, NATIONAL BARN DANCE, NEW SOUNDS, PHILCO RADIO TIME, TOP GEAR...
• INTERNATIONAL
• 1890S–

! "Curtain! Fast music! Lights! Ready for the last finale! Great! The show looks good. The show looks good."

Like many inventions that shaped the century, the question of who created radio is still unresolved. One thing was certain, however. The ability to transmit sound via radio waves from one point to another allowed music to travel as it never had before. Performers no longer had to go from town to town. Instead, they entered homes or cars with the flick of a switch.

The Serbian inventor Nikola Tesla first demonstrated radio communication in 1893, although the Italian engineer Guglielmo Marconi was awarded the patent. The first audio transmission occurred on Christmas Eve in 1906. Reginald Fessenden played "O Holy Night" on his violin to ships tuned in to his Massachusetts-based signal. By the 1920s, transmitters were springing up everywhere. Radio became a mass medium.

At first, radio played live music and made its own stars. Billy Jones and Ernest Hare hosted one of the most popular American shows as a singing duo called the Happiness Boys, named after their sponsor, Happiness Candy Stores. *The National Barn Dance*, heard on Chicago's WLS, became an institution rivaled only by Nashville's *Grand Ole Opry*, where country music was mixed with skits and cornpone humor.

Records eventually replaced the live performers. Disc jockeys played records and linked them with their chatter. It was a natural fit. Audiences could hear the record, then buy it to listen to at their convenience. Variety shows hosted by crooning personalities Frank Sinatra and Bing Crosby still offered live music, but recordings offered improved fidelity and, with overdubbing, greater perfectionism. By 1948, Crosby was pre-recording his *Philco Radio Time* show on magnetic tape.

Kate Smith, one of radio's first popular female personalities, photographed with actors Bing Crosby and Morton Downey. New York, 1930.

Left:
Poster of Otto Ernst's *Radío Maxím*, 1927.

Program directors chose radio playlists that targeted specific audiences and established a station's identity. Listeners could choose between rock, oldies, country, and jazz stations . . . or something more radical. In Britain, the rise of unlicensed "pirate" radio stations, which broadcasted from ships in the North Sea, let teenage rock fans hear music the nationwide BBC network ignored. In America, DJs went "free form" with the opening of FM frequencies in the 1960s and 1970s. FM stations played music according to the DJ's tastes and moods—and were more open to experimentation. For a brief period, recording artists could make tracks longer than four minutes and get airplay.

Radio is still a potent medium. The Voice of America and the BBC's World Service have allowed Western pop music to proliferate around the globe. But the conglomeration of radio stations in the United States into monopolies, like Clear Channel and Infinity, over the last decade has had a negative effect. Stations have become more formatted, seeking a uniform sound to appeal to the broadest possible audience. Record labels have obliged by producing insipid, interchangeable music for them to play.

The Internet is the antidote to this bland conformity. Fans can use their personal computers to stream audio from stations around the world. The popularity of MP3s and the iPod have turned users into their own DJs, mixing up playlists on their handheld players. Digital satellite radio has also led to the creation of hundreds of new stations that cater toward specialist tastes and are dedicated to everything from zydeco music to jazz to hits by the decade. It's a brave new world of radio, where even the Happiness Boys can live again.

Radio:
Match each radio to its appropriate decade.

Answer

1. 1940s 2. 2000s 3. 1920s 4. 1960s 5. 1900s 6. 1970s

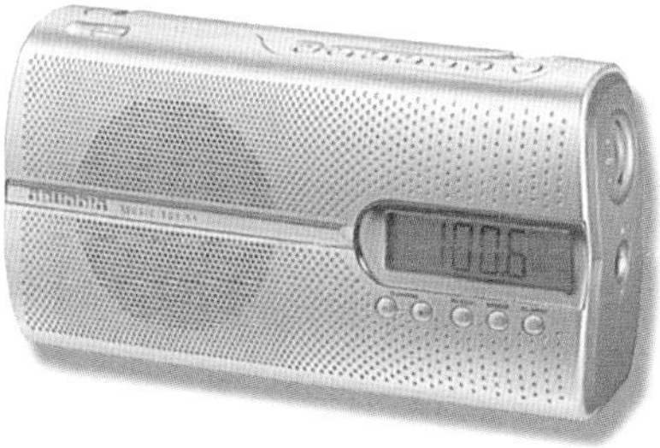

2

1

3

4

6

5

Erik Satie

• *TROIS GYMNOPÉDIES* (1888), *TROIS GNOSSIENNES* (1890), *VEXATIONS* (1893), *THREE PIECES IN THE SHAPE OF A PEAR* (1903), *PARADE* (1917), *RELÂCHE* (1924)...
• 1866–1925
GEORGES AURIC, JOHN CAGE, CLAUDE DEBUSSY, LOUIS DUREY, BRIAN ENO, ARTHUR HONEGGER, DARIUS MILHAUD, FRANCIS POULENC, GERMAINE TAILLEFERRE

Erik Satie was the great prankster of classical music. The French composer's sense of humor was so bizarre that now it's fashionable to declare him a Surrealist or Dadaist, two movements that his work managed to anticipate. What the former cabaret pianist understood better than his stuffed-shirt contemporaries was that music during the twentieth century was no longer going to be something experienced seated with intense concentration. It would be talked over, rendered half-recognizable, and sometimes flat-out ignored. So he wrote witty pieces that were meant to be misheard before they evaporated into thin air.

Satie was in a running war with contemporary practice. He wrote mostly for piano, only turning to the orchestra toward the end of his life. When Claude Debussy made Impressionistic sonic sketches of Eastern temples, Satie's piano pieces depicted a dandy preparing for a romantic conquest or a daydreamer vexed by a nagging melody. Debussy told him he lacked form, so the tripartite-obsessed, self-styled "phonometrician" wrote *Three Pieces in the Shape of a Pear* (1903). On his scores, Satie wrote little notes to the performers, as if whispering to them while they played. His music was committed to not going anywhere. Pieces like *Trois Gymnopédies* (1888) and the

Drawing by Francis Picabia for the program of *Relâche*, composed by Erik Satie. The play premiered at the Théâtre des Champs-Élysées in 1924.

Trois Gnossiennes (1890) hung suspended, virtually static in the atmosphere. Other works were determined to test his performers, and if someone was foolish enough to pay to be entertained by his music, they were in for it, too. *Vexations* (1893) was only 152 notes long, but was to be played over and over again for eighteen hours. The poor pianist was advised to prepare for "serious immobilities."

His ballet *Relâche* (1924) warned, "No performance today." Having finally learned counterpoint, Satie subjected the audience to fugues made up of distorted army songs and fragments of unrelated melody arranged in a jarring *musique concrète* style. Unsurprisingly, the opening night crowd rioted.

The poet Jean Cocteau applauded Satie's simplicity, audacity, and predilection for short pieces (*Vexations* excepted). While Cocteau called it "everyday music," Satie preferred "furniture music," anticipating the piped tunes we now hear in restaurants, elevators, and shopping malls. His use of boulevard sounds in his work would inspire composers who crossed over from pop to classical and back again, like George Gershwin and Leonard Bernstein. The neoclassicists would also revive the old songs to satirize them. Satie achieved exactly what he set out to do. His music is all around us.

Left:
Poster of the piano music for Satie's *Ragtime Parade*. Paris, 1919.

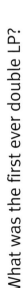

What was the first ever double LP?

French Music Hall

- JEANNE AVRIL, JOSEPHINE BAKER, BOURVIL, MAURICE CHEVALIER, JENNY GOLDER FRÉHEL, YVONNE GEORGE, YVETTE GUILBERT, MISTINGUETT, EDITH PIAF, CHARLES TRENET...
- FRANCE
- 1900S–1920S

The French music hall was cheap entertainment for the masses, Paris's equivalent of American vaudeville. Singers had to compete with acts ranging from jugglers to tango dancers, magicians, female impersonators, and comedians to make an impression. They did so with popular songs calculated to appeal to working-class audiences. This bear-pit produced some of France's most legendary entertainers.

The music hall performer had to have an act, and there were different "types." Men might sing sentimental songs or combine comic numbers with knockabout routines. They might play the seducer or rouse audiences with a bawdy army song. Women had different parts to choose from. Some played the vamp; others were not quite as innocent as they seemed or related woeful tales in a voice teetering on the edge of a dying fall. The so-called *epileptiques,* on the other hand, tore into their songs with hysterical passion.

These artists were not guaranteed an enthusiastic reception—and did anything they could to make an impression. Jenny Golder Fréhel's entire act could sometimes consist of screaming at the hostile audience, although she could also bring the house down with one of her songs about streetwalkers. The routines were as earthy as the banter. A young Maurice Chevalier made his debut singing "I Stick It in the Starch (To Keep It Stiff)." Mistinguett, who elevated Chevalier to stardom when she became his partner, would dance a *la valse chaloupée* that mimicked a pimp beating up his whore. Charles Trenet's easy demeanor stood in contrast to his fellow artists. His biggest hit was "La Mer," a song Bobby Darin translated to great success, too. After a move to New York and Hollywood, Trenet returned to France in the 1950s.

! Dave Brubeck's *Dave Brubeck Quartet at Carnegie Hall*, released in 1963.

Poster by Paul Colin for *La Revue Nègre*, 1925.

Left:
Maurice Chevalier in Paris in 1925. He came to symbolize the French music hall tradition for generations to come.

Max Beerbohm wrote that audiences went to the music halls to "be cheered up by seeing a life uglier and more sordid than their own." World War I, however, demanded something sunnier, and when the refurbished halls reopened, they offered escapist revue spectacles. These gave the same acts blockbuster treatment, with plenty of scantily clad girls thrown in. Audiences gasped at Folies-Bergère's *Coeurs en Folie* revue, which recreated a Roman chariot race. The high point of such spectacles was the show's female star, who balanced fifteen pounds of brightly colored plumes on her head.

The rise of movies brought the music hall's heyday to an end, but its stars had a talent for survival. Chevalier celebrated seventy years as a star of stage and screen and, in 1955, Mistinguett was still gyrating onstage, albeit this time to jazz. No matter how far abroad they traveled, France was their beloved home. American-born Josephine Baker proclaimed, "J'ai deux amours, mon pays et Paris." Parisian audiences loved them back.

Sheet Music:
Who wrote what?

Answer

1. Erik Satie, *Trois Gymnopedies* (1888).
2. Sergei Prokofiev, *Peter and the Wolf* (1935–1936).
3. Georges Bizet, *Carmen* (1870).
4. George Gershwin, *Porgy and Bess* (1935).

1

2

GEORGES BIZET

•

GEORGE GERSHWIN

•

SERGEI PROKOFIEV

•

ERIK SATIE

3

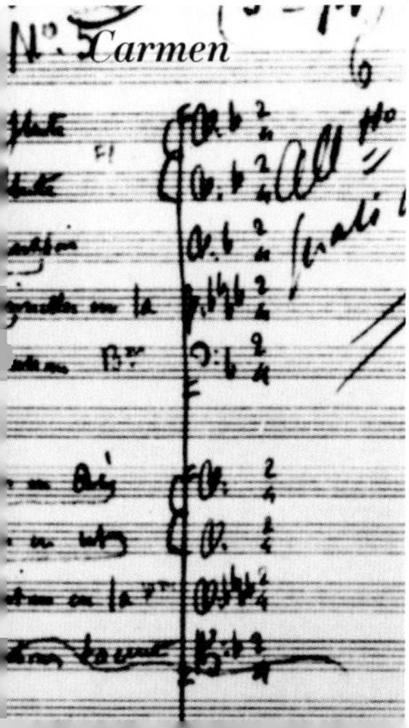

4

Berlin Cabaret

- ANITA BERBER, BERTOLT BRECHT, MARYA DELVARD, MARLENE DIETRICH, FRIEDRICH HOLLANDER, MISCHA SPOLIANSKY, CLÄRE WALDORF, FRANK WEDEKIND, KURT WEILL...
- GERMANY
- 1900S–1930S

Marlene Dietrich in a scene from Josef von Sternberg's *The Blue Angel* (1930).

Right:
Tingel-Tangel, a 1919 watercolor by Rudolf Schlichter depicting a scene from the Berlin cabaret. (21 x 18 in.) Private collection.

When most people hear the word "cabaret," they think of an image from the memorable musical of the same name: Liza Minnelli astride a chair while the MC leers from the sidelines. In fact, cabaret arrived in Germany before World War I, when author Ernst von Wolzogen and impresario Max Reinhardt both brought the anything-goes spirit of Paris's Moulin Rouge to 1901 Berlin. Audiences were entertained with comic routines and songs, and their bohemian atmosphere drew artists and curiosity seekers alike. A line from von Wolzogen's cabaret program described the jazzy music played as "klingkling, bumbum, und tschingdada!" A piano or small orchestra played accompaniment. Melodies might tweak a lewd punch line, but the songs were instant and memorable. Artists recited lyrics as often as they sang them, often with the same air of resignation Marlene Dietrich breathed into the song "Falling in Love Again" from her 1930 movie *The Blue Angel*. Wolzogen and Reinhardt's cabarets specialized in theatrical parodies, but it was in Munich that cabaret drew blood. Hypocrisy was attacked in art and song. A night at the Eleven Executioners began with men in bloodstained robes, proclaiming, "Our fun is always fierce," before singer Marya Delvard—her alabaster face and red hair glowing in the darkness—intoned suicidal thoughts. Frank Wedekind, author of the scandalous *Lulu* plays, might perform one of his gruesome songs about "murderous deeds" or *moritatem* (*mord* meaning "murder" and *tat* meaning "deeds"). Wedekind's gory Expressionism watered the ground for 1918, when a ban on public criticism was lifted. Cabaret could now say the unsayable. A young man named

Bertolt Brecht was still singing *moritaten* at Berlin's Red Grape, but license was all the rage in songs like Mischa Spoliansky's risqué "Ich bin ein Vamp!" Anita Berber danced nude and at the Eldorado, while transvestites mingled with homosexuals singing Spoliansky's "Lavender Song." The MCs who presided over the acts were precursors to today's stand-up comics, baiting the clientele with witty insults. Friedrich Hollander's "Spötterdämmerung" sensed the Babylonian end was nigh. "Tune down your much too trumpeted jokes," read the lyrics. "Give us and yourself a rest." The humorless Nazis obliged him. After 1933, cabaret's Jewish stars were shipped to concentration camps. Others took refuge in Friedrich Hollywood, where Marlene Dietrich became a screen queen and Hollander wrote music for clowns like Jerry Lewis. And the singer Brecht? Thanks to him and his accomplice Kurt Weill, the scathing cabaret spirit lived on. The success of their show *The Threepenny Opera* (1928) proved that cabaret had become high art.

What was Paul McCartney invited to do on the Beach Boys album *SMiLE*?

Igor Stravinsky

• *THE FIREBIRD* (1910), *THE RITE OF SPRING* (1913), *PULCINELLA* (1920), *SYMPHONY IN THREE MOVEMENTS* (1945), *REQUIEM CANTICLES* (1966)...
• 1882–1971
AARON COPLAND, CARL ORFF, FRANCIS POULENC, STEVE REICH, KURT WEILL

! Chew carrots on the song "Vega-Tables."

At Igor Stravinsky's premiere of the ballet *The Rite of Spring* on May 29, 1913, the cognoscenti wasted no time shrieking in horror as the chords began to clash. Impresario Sergei Diaghilev was more than a little perturbed by the melody. It sounded like two chords at war with each other, with other accents intruding and throwing the whole bruising sequence off balance. It was loud, too. "How much longer will it go on like that?" he asked. "To the end, my dear," replied the Russian composer. The bohemians in the cheap seats, however, roared their approval. The shouting match that ensued became a raucous riot, thereby ending the most famous opening night in the history of twentieth-century music.

The Rite of Spring was too much for a fashionable audience hoping for an exotic night out with Diaghilev's Ballet Russes. Stravinsky had immersed himself in folk melodies and crudely stitched them together like a Surrealist dream sequence. The thirty-year-old's savage juxtapositions suggested the confused dawn of man in which the pagan *Rite* was set. It turned out he was ahead of his time.

Stravinsky stayed in that vanguard. Born to a well-to-do family of singers in Lomonosov, he was taught composition and orchestration by Rimsky-Korsakov. *The Firebird* (1910) established his reputation, using strange scales and chordal repetition. After *The Rite of Spring*'s scandalous success, Stravinsky experimented with jazz, then renounced strings to write for both wind and percussion instruments.

Stravinsky feverishly strived to be ahead of everyone else, inventing modes as he went. The 1920 ballet *Pulcinella* was a baroque pastiche that cannibalized eighteenth-century Italian music—Stravinsky called it "neoclassicism." Escaping World War II with a move to Hollywood, he capitalized on the vogue for new symphonies by turning his rejected soundtrack offerings into *Symphony in Three Movements* (1945). By 1945, however, Stravinsky represented the old guard and was attacked by young iconoclasts like Pierre Boulez. He only fell back into fashion when

Portrait of Igor Stravinsky by Pablo Picasso, 1920. Graphite pencil and charcoal. (24 x 19 in.) Musée Picasso, Paris.

his loyal assistant, Robert Craft, encouraged him to take up atonal serialism. His greatest work in that mode, 1966's *Requiem Canticles,* had a tragic grace to it inspired by a return to Russia. After decades of reinventing himself, Stravinsky had earned the right to be nostalgic.

Detail:
Who is this?

MICK JAGGER,
from Donald Cammell and Nicolas Roeg's film,
Performance (1970).

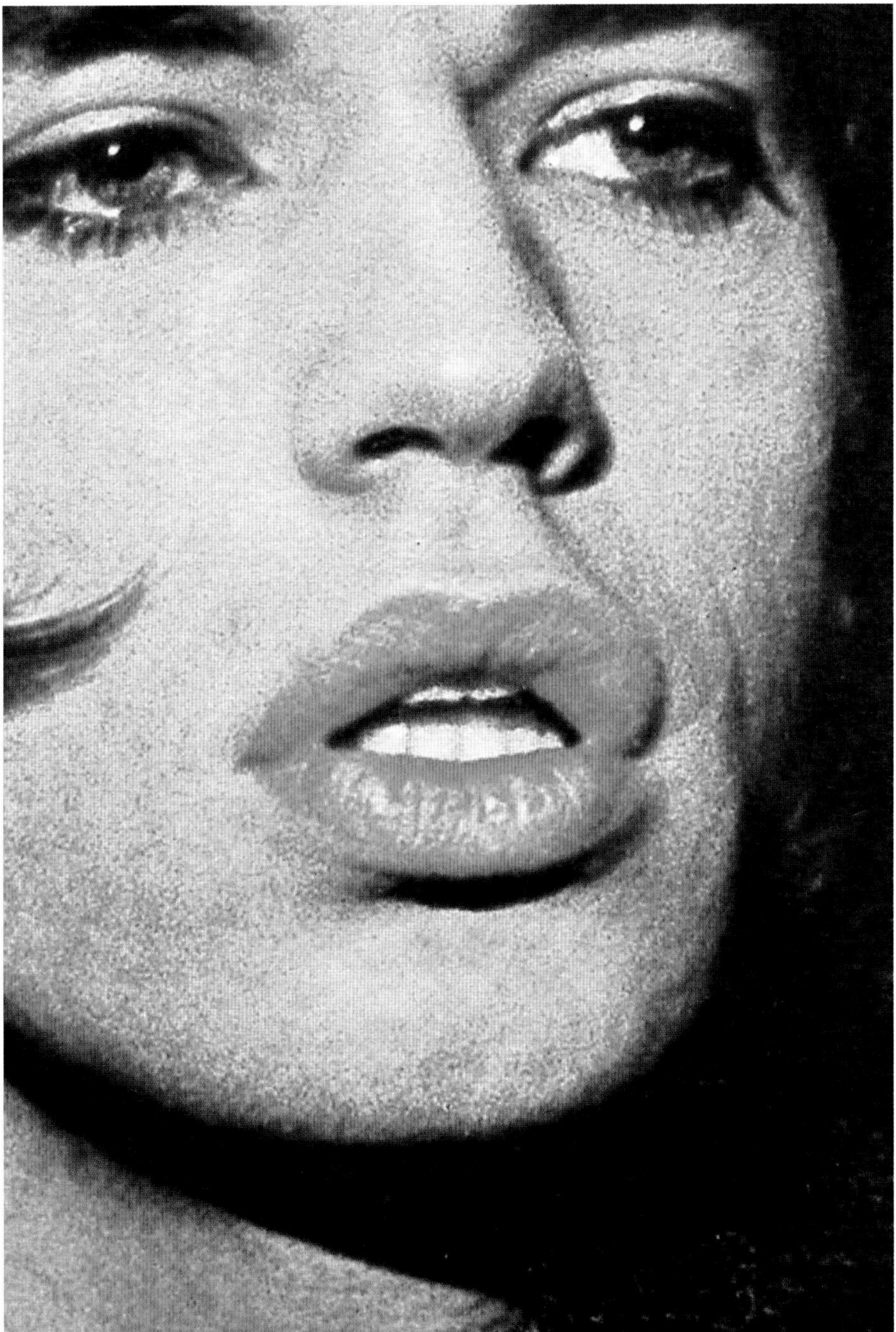

Broadway Musicals

- *SHOW BOAT* (1927), *OKLAHOMA!* (1943), *STREET SCENE* (1946), *GUYS & DOLLS* (1950), *MY FAIR LADY* (1956), *WEST SIDE STORY* (1957), *CABARET* (1966), *HAIR* (1968), *FOLLIES* (1971), *GREASE* (1972), *CHICAGO* (1975), *A CHORUS LINE* (1975), *EVITA* (1978), *CATS* (1981), *RENT* (1996), *THE PRODUCERS* (2001), *MONTY PYTHON'S SPAMALOT* (2005)...
- UNITED STATES
- 1920S–

With its bright songs, showy dance numbers, and fusion of music and narrative, the Broadway musical is such a natural-seeming art form that it's hard to understand how radical *Show Boat* seemed when it premiered at New York's Ziegfeld Theatre in 1927. *Show Boat* took the entertainment that preceded it—extravagant melodrama, lively minstrel shows, and imported operettas—and put their best elements in service of the drama. Jerome Kern let the songs tell of the journey of a vaudeville troupe adrift on the antebellum Mississippi River. The lyrics were tailormade for each character, allowing, for the first time in musical theater history, fully developed characters that teemed with vibrancy and emotionality. Audiences no longer needed showgirls for entertainment! *Show Boat* was so cutting edge that it took a while for its influence to truly to be felt. Talents like Cole Porter and Lorenz Hart continued to write witty ditties for stage revues, and Great Depression audiences demanded escapism, not art. In 1943, the musical finally achieved its apotheosis with Richard Rodgers and Oscar Hammerstein II's *Oklahoma!*—a musical in which the music and dance numbers were inseparable from its plot: a tender love story set on the Midwestern frontier based on *Green Grow the Lilacs* (1931) by Lynn Riggs. *Oklahoma!* ran for an astonishing five years, and inspired composers like Kurt Weill and Leonard Bernstein to try their hand at writing musicals. Any source material was fair game: Shakespeare (*West Side Story,* 1957), Bernard Shaw (*My Fair Lady,* 1956), kitchen-sink drama (*Street Scene,* 1946),

Poster for Andrew Lloyd Webber's *Cats* (1981).

Right: Scene from Roy Del Ruth's *Broadway Melody of 1938* (1937).

and Damon Runyon's underworld stories (*Guys & Dolls,* 1950). The songs from these musicals became popular standards, and after the charts welcomed rock music, Broadway was turned over to the psychedelic spectacle of *Hair* (1968) and *Grease*'s (1972) revivalist fare. Broadway tunesmiths displayed their own tics and traits. Stephen Sondheim's cleverly neurotic musicals were the musical equivalent of a Woody Allen movie. The Englishman Andrew Lloyd Webber preferred a broader canvas, surrounding Argentine dictators (*Evita,* 1978) and T.S. Eliot's cats (*Cats,* 1981) with brash songs and giant special effects. The team of Kander and Ebb took an acidic view of humanity in *Cabaret* (1966) and *Chicago* (1975). Other composers thrived on a smaller scale. Two of the biggest hits of recent years, *A Chorus Line* (1975) and Rent (1996), were about the theater "Gypsies" and starving performers who survived off the Great White Way's crumbs.
The irony is that an art so young is currently in danger of dying out. Once musicals were so popular that they were made into movies. By the twenty-first century, the trend has reversed itself with the success of Mel Brooks's *The Producers* (2001). Aspiring Max Bialystocks in search of a quick buck even bundled pop golden oldies into ersatz productions known as "jukebox musicals." As the song says, it's a charade that's lighter than air. But that's entertainment.

How long do the first three notes of John Cage's composition *As Slow As Possible* last?

Cole Porter

• *FIFTY MILLION FRENCHMEN* (1929), *THE GAY DIVORCÉE* (1932), *ANYTHING GOES* (1934), *DU BARRY WAS A LADY* (1939), *BROADWAY MELODY OF 1940* (1940), *KISS ME, KATE* (1948)...
• 1891–1964
GEORGE GERSHWIN, JOE JACKSON, GERTRUDE LAWRENCE, RANDY NEWMAN, STEPHEN SONDHEIM, SQUEEZE, ANDREW LLOYD WEBBER

Cole Porter (center) with Fred Astaire and Eleonor Powell, two of his favorite performers, 1940.

Right:
Portrait of Cole Porter, 1954.

Cole Porter's songs aren't just tonic—they're champagne. Dry and intoxicating, the potions this sophisticate from the American Midwest created for movies and Broadway shows represent the pinnacle of songwriting. His lyrics have been printed alongside verses by T.S. Eliot, and his melodies are models of elegance. To perform a Cole Porter number is to play a Stradivarius violin.

Born into money and a graduate of Yale and Harvard, Porter didn't have to fake his refined pose, although he cultivated an image that suggested he could toss off something like "(Let's Do It) Let's Fall in Love" between cocktails. His songs had a knowing wink, too. "I Get a Kick Out of You" scandalously mentioned cocaine, and "Anything Goes" turned a jaundiced eye on moral and sexual anarchy.

Inspired by both vaudeville and the virtuosity of poets like Byron, he crafted couplets with the force of comic punch lines. He teased his audience by stringing rhymes like "tell," "gazelle," and "hell" together. He concocted audacious internal rhymes, like "Flying on high with some guy in the sky" from "I Get a Kick Out of You." Porter took his witty use of words seriously. After reading a study that said most hit songs used the long "o" sound, he littered "You Do Something to Me" with them.

"I am the most enthusiastic person in the world," he once said. "I like everything as long as it's different."

A notorious homosexual married to a wealthy Kentucky divorcée, his urbanity masked a wide range. He wrote songs from the perspectives of cowboys ("Don't Fence Me In") and prostitutes ("Love for Sale"), while list

! A year and a half. The work, currently being performed in Germany, will take 639 years to complete.

songs like "(Let's Do It) Let's Fall in Love" and "Anything Goes" packed the entire world in them.

His melodies were as meaningful as his lyrics. A recurring refrain torments the obsessed singer of "Night and Day," while "Ev'ry Time We Say Goodbye" sighs with melancholy. He suited his songs to the conversational delivery of his favorite star, Fred Astaire, whose musical feats he praised in "You're the Top." This adaptability has made them favorites of a diverse group of singers from Ella Fitzgerald to Iggy Pop.

A fall from a horse in 1937 crushed his legs and subdued much of his spirit, but Porter experienced a revival a decade later with *Kiss Me, Kate* (1948), his hit adaptation of *The Taming of the Shrew*. He is the only composer in the world one could imagine making Shakespeare hummable.

THE MUSIC PAGES

GOSSIP AND SCANDAL

Cotton Club:
He was the leader of the New York Gopher Gang when he was eighteen, was arrested more than forty times for theft and assault by the time he was twenty-one, and was eventually charged with murder. In 1923, at age thirty, the gangster Owney Madden started the famous Cotton Club, which opened doors for Duke Ellington and then Louis Armstrong. In the heart of Harlem, this was the hot spot for the American "white aristocracy."

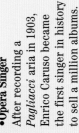

• **Off with Their Heads!**
Richard Strauss's opera *Salome* has closed in New York after just one night. The industrialist J.P. Morgan's daughter was seen visibly whitening when Salome kissed the head of John the Baptist. The *Tribune*'s critic noted of the finale: "An impulse which can only be conceived as rising from the uttermost pit of degradation is beatified." (1907)

• **Jazz and Kremlin**
"One involuntarily imagines an orchestra of sexually driven madmen conducted by a man-stallion brandishing a huge genital member." —Maxim Gorky on jazz (*Pravda*, 1928)

• **Dada Knows Best!**
Hugo Ball has opened his Cabaret Voltaire at No. 1 Spiegelgasse, Zurich. Among the entertainment on opening night: dancers wearing grotesque masks designed by painter Marcel Janco, poems recited simultaneously by up to seven speakers, and Ball himself delivering his abstract "phonetic poems," dressed as an obelisk. (1916)

• **Does Jazz Put the "Sin" in Syncopation?**
In her attack on the popular music, Anne Shaw Faulkner, head of the Music Department of the General Federation of Women's Clubs, declares "that it has a demoralizing effect upon the human brain has been demonstrated by many scientists." (*Ladies Home Journal*, 1921)

•**Opera Singer**
After recording a *Pagliacci* aria in 1903, Enrico Caruso became the first singer in history to sell a million albums.

CURRENT EVENTS AND NEWS IN BRIEF

• Muse

In her time, Lina Cavalieri, the early twentieth-century diva, was considered "the most beautiful woman in the world." Her hand in marriage was requested more than 840 times. She accepted four. Among her lovers was the Italian dictator Mussolini.

• Rhapsody in Blue

"I was summoned to Boston for the premiere of *Sweet Little Devil*. I had already done some work on the *Rhapsody*. It was on the train, with its steely rhythms, its rattle-ty-bang that is often so stimulating to a composer . . . I frequently hear music in the very heart of noise. And there I suddenly heard—and even saw on paper—the complete construction of the *Rhapsody*, from beginning to end. (No new themes came to me, but I worked on the thematic material already in my mind, and tried to conceive the composition as a whole.) I heard it as a sort of musical kaleidoscope of America—of our vast melting pot, of our unduplicated national pep, of our metropolitan madness. By the time I reached Boston I had a definite plot of the piece, as distinguished from its actual substance."

George Gershwin, 1924

George Gershwin

• *LA LA LUCILLE* (1919), *RHAPSODY IN BLUE* (1924), *AN AMERICAN IN PARIS* (1928), *OF THEE I SING* (1931), *PORGY AND BESS* (1935)...
• 1898–1937
MICHAEL FEINSTEIN, OSCAR HAMMERSTEIN, RANDY NEWMAN, NIKOLAI PETROV, STEVEN SONDHEIM, ANDREW LLOYD WEBBER

From the moment Ross Gorman played *Rhapsody in Blue's* memorable clarinet glissando in 1924, Gershwin was a composer—and America finally had classical music it could call its own. Inspired as much by the French style of Debussy as by African-American music and Jewish chant, Gershwin introduced classical music to the blues he had incorporated into popular songs like "Fascinating Rhythm." Originally it was George's brother Ira who was supposed to learn how to play the family piano, but young George had a remarkable affinity for the instrument, attending concerts and then playing back what he had heard by ear. He worked as a rehearsal pianist before having his first song published in 1918. By the following year, Al Jolson made "Swanee" Gershwin's first hit, and he wrote the score for the musical *La, La Lucille* (1919). *Rhapsody in Blue* (1924) made Gershwin a force to be reckoned with. Ravel refused to teach him, saying, "Why should you be a second-rate Ravel when you can be a first-rate Gershwin?" When Igor Stravinsky heard how much money Gershwin made from hits like "Someone to Watch Over Me," he asked if the songwriter could teach him. Gershwin continued to be inspired by the French, writing the tone poem *An American in Paris* (1928) after a trip to the city, and using real car horns in the score to recreate the sound of the capital's traffic.

Gershwin's musicals became more sophisticated, using songs to tell stories. The 1931 political satire *Of Thee I Sing,* about a presidential candidate running on the "Love" platform, won the Pulitzer Prize. Inspired, Gershwin poured his vast knowledge of black musical forms into *Porgy and Bess* (1935), the first true American opera. A financial flop, its rich songs like "Summertime" and "It Ain't Necessarily So" only became standards following Gershwin's death from a brain tumor in 1937. Only thirty-eight years old, he left behind a volume of the American songbook that embraced all the

expressive possibilities of the country's melting pot.

Scene from Vincente Minnelli's *An American in Paris* (1951), with Leslie Caron and Gene Kelly. Music by George Gershwin.

Left:
George Gershwin (c.1920).

How much did a three-day ticket to the 1969 Woodstock festival cost?

Tango

- 020, CARLOS GARDEL, GOTAN PROJECT, LITTO NEBBIA, ASTOR PIAZZOLLA, OSVALDO PUGLIESE, SEXTETO MAYOR, ANÍBAL TROILO...
- ARGENTINA, PARAGUAY, URUGUAY
- 1900S–

Portrait of the singer Carlos Gardel, the icon of tango. Album cover for *The Best of Carlos Gardel* (1998).

Right:
The world of tango as seen by an anonymous mural painter in Buenos Aires.

The tango was born in the late nineteenth century in Buenos Aires. True to its origins in South America's most cosmopolitan city, the striking dance combined a variety of influences. The word "tango" indicates African origins. The dance is related to the Cuban habanera, and the distinctive rhythm is derived from music played by slaves to amuse their masters in the Dominican Republic. This truly mongrel art form is constantly evolving, with offshoots including ballroom tango, show tango, and even Finnish tango.

The sharply syncopated music is dominated by an oversized accordion called a *bandoneón*. The improvised movements of the closely embracing dancers can appear sudden and violent. The legs of each dancer weave and dart around one another like feints from the knife fights common among the Argentinean *gauchos*. It is a dance of frustrated desire, reflected in the thrashing bodies of the dancers and the agonized lyrics of its greatest songs. Condemned by the Pope and the Queen of England, tango attained global notoriety after Rudolph Valentino put a rose between his teeth and tangoed in Rex Ingram's *Four Horsemen of the Apocalypse* (1921). Carlos Gardel became the genre's first superstar when he began putting lurid lyrics to the tango melodies—his first hit was about a pimp pining for a beloved whore. Through touring, movies, and a slick Continental image, Gardel became a superstar fêted in Madrid and Paris until his untimely death in a 1935 plane crash.

Superseded by the fox-trot and the Great Depression, tango waned until the Argentinian maestro Astor Piazzolla applied jazz and classical elements to what became known as "nuevo tango." Piazzolla used orchestras, electronic jazz ensembles, and sudden tempo shifts to make music for listening to—not dancing—and

!

$24.

enraged tango purists. But works like "Balada Para un Loco," about a madman wandering Buenos Aires, became classics of their kind. Piazzolla made his point: tango's greatest strength is its ability to absorb other styles. Groups like Litto Nebbia and 020 play "tango rock" and the French-Argentine musical ensemble Gotan Project have created electronica tangos. For those who prefer their tango traditional, there are successful touring shows like *Tango Argentino*. In over a century, tango has gone from belonging to Buenos Aires to finding its place in the world.

The Birth of Jazz

• SIDNEY BECHET, BIX BEIDERBECKE, BUDDY BOLDEN, RED BROWN, SCOTT JOPLIN, JOE "KING" OLIVER, NEW ORLEANS RHYTHM KINGS, ORIGINAL DIXIELAND JAZZ BAND, KID ORY...
• UNITED STATES
• 1900S–1920S

Jazz is not something that can easily be put into words. As the great trumpeter Louis Armstrong once remarked, "If you have to ask, you don't know." The pianist Keith Jarrett claimed jazz didn't exist except when it was actually happening. While the music is immediately recognizable, putting your finger on it is an entirely different matter.

Academically speaking, a jazz band is defined as a musical ensemble that plays syncopated rhythms and bends notes to a lower pitch than those found in the major scale. These are called "blue notes." In the early days, this sort of tweaking was called "ragging" a tune. Musicians subverted the melodies with their playful spirit. This freedom also allowed members of the band to improvise, and musicians found new ways to make their groups swing harder.

Jazz can be played by almost anything. Jazz instrumentalist Alice Coltrane (John Coltrane's wife) played the harp, for example. Traditionally, however, it is associated with brass instruments, like Armstrong's trumpet, and reed instruments, like Sidney Bechet's saxophone. These instruments descended from those used by the funeral bands that played in New Orleans. It was in this Louisiana port city that jazz formed at the beginning of the century.

New Orleans bands played blues, ragtime, minstrel songs like "Swanee," and European music, all of which they gave their own individual spin to. The demand for entertainment in Storyville, the city's red-light

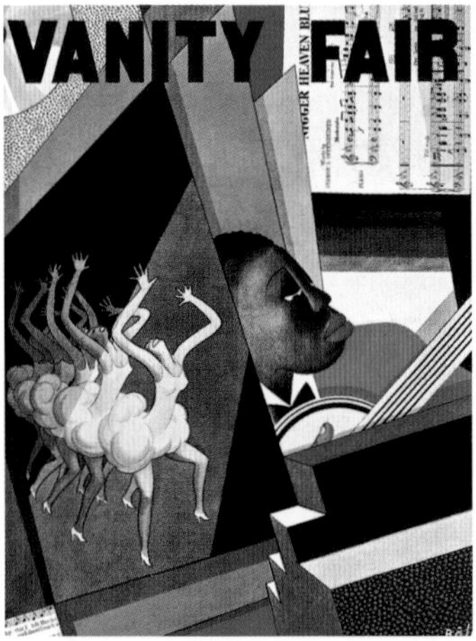

(top)
King Oliver and his Creole Jazz Band in San Francisco, 1921.

(bottom)
Cover of *Vanity Fair* (January 1928), with an illustration by Bolin.

Right:
The New Orleans Rhythm Kings in Chicago, 1923.

district, attracted educated black musicians from around the region. Buddy Bolden transposed blues music for his popular brass band, whose players "variated the melody" of the songs to fit the setting, whether it was a whorehouse or a society ball, throwing in blue notes and playing in the distinctive growl associated with the blues genre.

Jazz did not grow up in a vacuum—the music spread rapidly to other cities. In New York, musicians played ragtime's syncopated rhythms with a more rollicking feel, making their left hand "stride" from the upbeat to the downbeat on the piano. Pullman train porters who supplemented their income by importing records from region to region helped spread the sound, and when Storyville was closed by the government in 1917, New Orleans musicians headed north and west.

Cornetist King Oliver and trombonists Kid Ory and "Red" Brown relocated to Chicago. Brown's band was the first to be called a "jass" band ("jass" being a slang term for "semen"). The word first appeared on record in 1909, but "jass" became "jazz"when pranksters crossed out the "j" on posters; to avoid the embarrassing result, the "s" was changed to "z." In Chicago, these musicians trained others, and encouraged their friends back home, including the young Louis Armstrong, to join them.

When Prohibition was declared in 1919, jazz became the music of choice in the speakeasies. A new generation of stars emerged. Bechet and cornetist Bix Beiderbecke made the instrumental solo jazz's hallmark. The 1920s became known as the Jazz Age. The first original art form to develop in America had quickly found its feet.

Who wrote the song "Look at Your Game Girl," later covered by Guns N' Roses?

Delta Blues

• JOHN BILLINGSLEY, JOHN LEE HOOKER, SON HOUSE, ELMORE JAMES, SKIP JAMES, ROBERT JOHNSON, CHARLEY PATTON, MUDDY WATERS...
• THE AMERICAN SOUTH
• 1920S–1930S, 1960S

! Charles Manson, who killed film director Roman Polanski's first wife, Sharon Tate.

People like to call the Mississippi Delta "the land where the blues was born." It stretches from outside Memphis to Vicksburg, Mississippi, a fertile plain dotted with plantations at the turn of the century. There, gospel and West African folk came together, creating a new hybrid form of the blues, and its practitioners—who sang of their people's hardship—were well-received. The sound of the Delta is of a heavy rhythmic acoustic guitar and impassioned call-and-response vocals. The performers and their rare recordings of this haunting music have assumed mythic status.

To have seen the Delta bluesmen play when the music flowered during the 1920s and 1930s was an entirely different experience from hearing them on record. Backed by a string band, they would have to be ready to play anything enthusiastic juke joint audiences demanded. Their repertoire included blues, ragtime tunes, and gospel favorites. Charley Patton, a dandified showman regarded as a founding father of the Delta Blues, enlivened his concerts with comic vocal asides. A song like his "A Spoonful Blues" might be made from several different melodies, and he growled them in a hoarse voice that could draw a crowd from the farthest corner of the fields. Patton was often thrown off plantations because his singing distracted other workers.

The Delta blues is chiefly associated with Robert Johnson, a spectral figure who outdid Patton in popularity. His supernatural ability to sing, play guitar, and write songs—that later became standards—was attributed to a midnight deal he struck with the devil. Johnson's songs did little to

(top)
Impromptu performance with guitars and tambourines on the banks of the Mississippi. *On the Mississippi,* 1906.

(bottom)
Cover of the album *Blow My Blues Away, Vol. 2*. The compilation was recorded in 1967–1968 by George Mitchell.

Left:
Portrait of Robert Johnson (c. 1930).

dispute this story. He sang of "Hellhounds on My Trail" in a voice wary of imminent damnation, his fingers picking out both a sparse melody and on the guitar's bottom strings, a boogie bass line. The legend was sealed when he died in 1938 after being poisoned by the jealous boyfriend of a woman he had flirted with.

Patton and Johnson's music was rediscovered by folk scholars who tracked down surviving Delta bluesmen in the 1960s. Son House was one such musician. When he was found living in upstate New York, he actually had to be taught how to play guitar again The rerecordings of his 1930s hits became important historical documents. Later, a handful of Robert Johnson songs that survived on crackly 78 rpm records were covered by the Rolling Stones and Cream, British bands long enamored with their dark allure.

Composers: *Who composed the classical songs for these films?*

Answer

1. *Excalibur*: Carl Orff, *Carmina Burana*.
2. *Death in Venice*: Gustav Mahler,*Symphonies No.* 3 and *No. 5*.
3. *Shine*: Sergei Rachmaninov, *Concerto for Piano No. 3*.
4. *Manhattan*: George Gershwin, *Rhapsody in Blue*.
5. *2001: A Space Odyssey*: Richard Strauss, *Also Sprach Zarathustra*.

EXCALIBUR

1

Death in Venice
25th ANNIVERSARY AWARD
DVD
WARNER BROS. PRESENTS
A FILM BY
LUCHINO VISCONTI

2

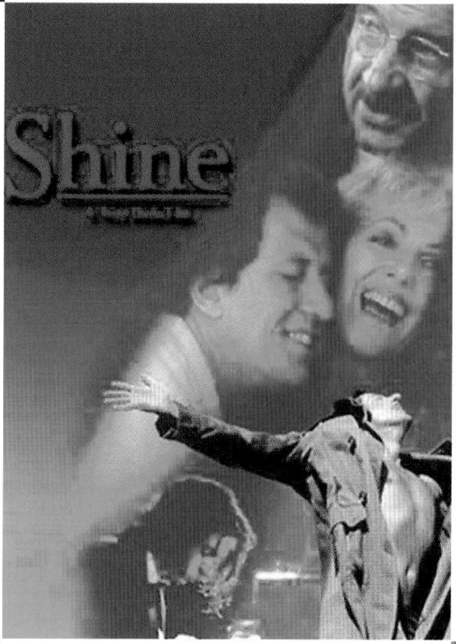
Shine

3

WOODY ALLEN
DIANE KEATON
MICHAEL MURPHY
MARIEL HEMINGWAY
MERYL STREEP
ANNE BYRNE
MANHATTAN
w.moviegoods.com

4

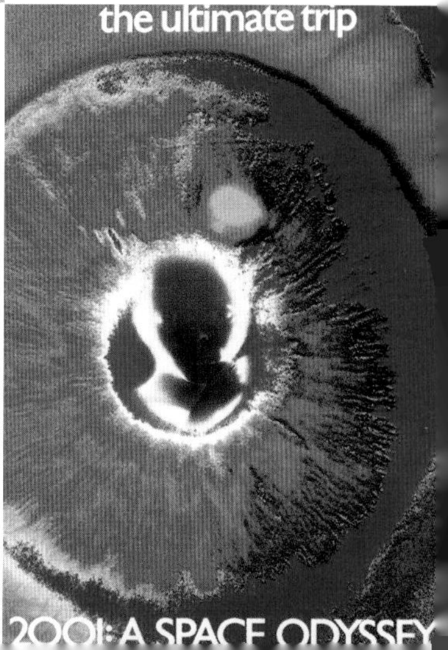
the ultimate trip
2001: A SPACE ODYSSEY

5

Louis Armstrong

• *AMBASSADOR SATCH* (1955), *PORGY AND BESS* (1957), *PARIS BLUES* (1960), *HELLO, DOLLY!* (1963), *WHAT A WONDERFUL WORLD* (1970)...
• 1901–1971
BIX BEIDERBECKE, CAB CALLOWAY, MILES DAVIS, DIZZY GILLESPIE, LOUIS JORDAN, WYNTON MARSALIS, LOUIS PRIMA

Louis Armstrong when he was just starting out (c. 1920). The Hot Five with (from left to right) Armstrong, Johnny Saint Cyr, Johnny Dodds, Kid Ory, and Lil Hardin.

Left:
Portrait of Louis Armstrong with his famous trumpet, during his European and African tour, 1945.

It's tempting to speculate how the course of musical history might have changed if an overexcited eleven-year-old Louis "Satchmo" Armstrong hadn't fired a pistol into the air on New Year's Eve in 1912. He was sent to reform school. There, they taught him to play the cornet. If he hadn't taken to the instrument, Armstrong might never have left New Orleans to become jazz music's first celebrity and greatest ambassador.

Armstrong had an irrepressible personality—exactly the kind of person who might try to draw attention to himself with a gun shot—and in his 1920s recordings with the Hot Five and Hot Seven ensembles, he made the solo jazz's calling card. Armstrong didn't play the melody, but rather used it as an excuse for virtuosic flourishes. The opening fanfare of 1928's "West End Blues," for instance, invigorates his early mentor King Oliver's shuffle. Armstrong alternates long phrases with flashy pyrotechnics and sudden swoops into the higher registers. Here, the player became as important as the song, which he transformed with his personality.

That persona was one of pure joie de vivre, and Armstrong's effervescence was key to making him a star. With an electric smile and dapper style, he could charm anybody. As early as 1927, he was singing, too, in an extraordinary croak that stood out among the slick vocalists of the Roaring Twenties. Armstrong's voice

was his second instrument. He often abandoned lyrics to "scat," wordlessly teasing the melody in the same way he did with his trumpet.

Armstrong was a performer for all seasons. He could seamlessly complement Bing Crosby or Jimmie Rodgers, and during the 1950s became a favorite foil for Ella Fitzgerald, another singer who had elevated scat into an art form. Europe received him so rapturously in the mid-1930s that he stayed there for three years, his fans back in the U.S. sending old recordings into the charts. With the decline of swing music after World War II, Armstrong settled into being a bona fide entertainer. He appeared in Hollywood films, sidling up to Grace Kelly in Charles Walters's *High Society* (1956) or trading trumpet blasts with Paul Newman in Martin Ritt's *Paris Blues* (1961). In 1963, "Hello, Dolly!" became a surprise No. 1 hit and he was rediscovered.By 1968's "What a Wonderful World," his voice seemingly girdled the planet. Satchmo had become the sound of the universe.

What British band did guitarists Eric Clapton, Jeff Beck, and Jimmy Page all play for?

Chicago Electric Blues

- WILLIE DIXON, BUDDY GUY, HOWLIN' WOLF, ELMORE JAMES, JIMMY REED, MUDDY WATERS...
- UNITED STATES
- 1940S–1960S

Between 1910 and the 1960s, America experienced the Great Migration. Poor Southern blacks moved north to urban industrial centers like Chicago and Detroit. They left to escape racism and find employment, and they brought the Delta blues with them.

One such pilgrim was Howlin' Wolf, six feet thee inches and three hundred pounds of the blues. Wolf had worshipped at the feet of the growling bluesman Charley Patton, and destroyed his voice with whisky in order to sound like him. He was different than the rest. Wolf came to Chicago with a kick-ass electric band and a contract from Chess Records in his pocket. "I'm the only one drove out of the South like a gentleman," he recalled.

Down South, the blues were traditionally played by a string band. However, Chicago's displaced Delta community took up electric instruments, following the lead of Howlin' Wolf and his contemporary Muddy Waters—a singer-guitarist with the voice of Moses, if the Old Testament prophet had been born in Mississippi. In the late 1940s and 1950s, a blues band might feature an electric guitarist and harmonica player along with bass, drums, and a piano. Saxophones were optional, although horn sections were popular in Chicago's west side.

The amplified instruments were soon playing lengthy solos. Guitarist Hubert Sumlin didn't even strum

! The Yardbirds.

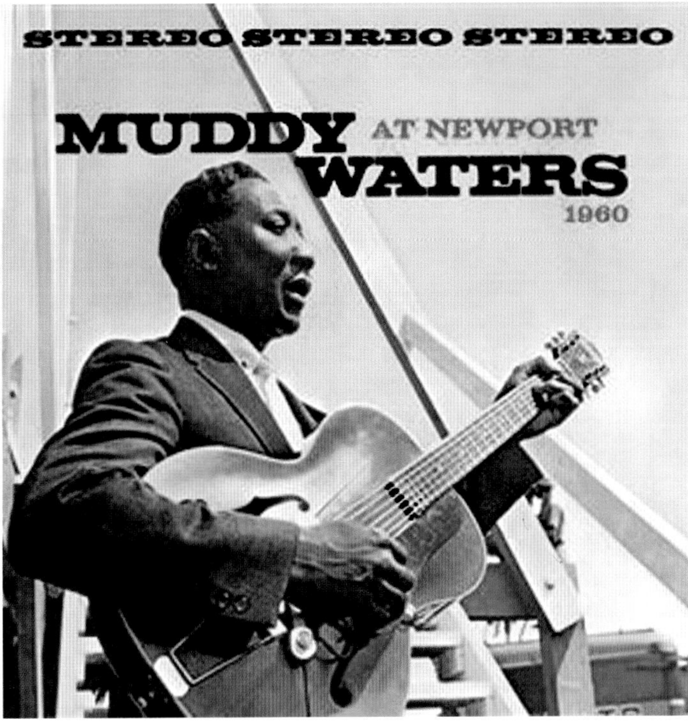

Cover of Muddy Waters's *Muddy Waters At Newport* (1960).

Left:
The sign for Blue Chicago, one of Chicago's most famous clubs.

chords. He played bombardments of single notes behind Wolf's bone-rattling screams. The competition between these showy entertainers was fierce. Waters's band became known as the Headhunters because of the way they blew rival bands off stage. When Bo Diddley swiped his distinctive beat for "I'm a Man," Waters stole it back for the song "Mannish Boy."

Chicago became home to professional blues songwriters. Writing for the Chess Records stable, Willie Dixon penned more hits than anyone before or since, including blues staples like "Hoochie Coochie Man," and "Smokestack Lightnin.'" Dixon had a flair for leering innuendo. His little red roosters and wang dang doodles belonged to backdoor men looking for their woman's spoonful. Jimmy Reed was just as prolific. His songs, like "Bright Lights, Big City," were simple riffs that could be played by anyone, and were.

Fans included British groups like the Rolling Stones—who took their name from Muddy Waters' "Catfish Blues," and tracked down their idol only to find him painting a recording studio ceiling—and Led Zeppelin, whose "Whole Lotta Love" bore enough resemblance to Dixon's "You Need Love" for the recording label, Chess, to sue them. Without the Chicago blues, rock would be a very poor cousin indeed.

Billie Holiday

• *AN EVENING WITH BILLIE HOLIDAY* (1953), *LADY SINGS THE BLUES* (1954), *MUSIC FOR TORCHING* (1955), *LADY IN SATIN* (1958), *FINE AND MELLOW* (2002)...
• 1915–1959
MILDRED BAILEY, RUTH BROWN, BETTY CARTER, ARETHA FRANKLIN, MACY GRAY, KATIE MELUA, ANITA O'DAY

Cover of *Lady Day: The Best of Billie Holiday* (2001), released by Sony.

Right:
The American jazz singer Billie Holiday in England, 1954.
2001, Sony.

When "Lady Day" Billie Holiday would sing "Strange Fruit," the entire Café Society in downtown New York would come to a halt. The registers would stop ringing. The waiters would stand perfectly still at the back of the club. The lights would go down except for a single spotlight, which picked up Holiday's face from the darkness. She would sing, "Strange fruit hanging from the poplar trees . . ." and when she finished, the audience wouldn't know whether to applaud or run. Initially, Holiday didn't like the song much, but she squeezed every last painful drop out of it. She knew how true its lyrics were—after all, she confronted racism throughout her life. "I've lived songs like that," she once said. For example, Holiday grew tired of having to use the back entrance to get into clubs while the rest of her white bandmates were welcomed through the front. Even though she had been one of the first black singers to appear with a white band—Artie Shaw's group—she left the band in 1938, disgusted.

Her voice was pinched and had a limited one-octave range. But she was one of jazz's greatest vocalists because she treated every song as a personal monologue and, in the process, turned jazz songs into blues laments. She had had a difficult life: raped at age eleven, she also claimed to have worked as a teenage prostitute. Boyfriends and husbands beat the often heroin-addled singer in addition to ripping her off. When Holiday sang "God bless the child that's got its own"—a line from her most famous composition—she meant it.

She was also a brilliant vocal technician who never let a song get the better of her. As a struggling singer in 1930s Harlem, Holiday tired of the bottom-drawer material she had to sing. To breathe life into them, she playfully phrased the lyrics behind the beat and used her voice to mimic the horns of Louis Armstrong and Lester Young. She developed a sense of timing and phrasing that could make "I've Got My Love to Keep Me Warm" swing even as drugs destroyed her voice. Holiday flourished as a unique vocalist in an era of homogenized singers, personalizing whatever she

took on. Her version of George Gershwin's "I Loves You, Porgy" became definitive—even Nina Simone performed it as if she were channeling Holiday's spirit. She died with seventy cents in the bank after being put under house arrest for drug possession. Twenty-eight years later, U2 released the hit song, "Angel of Harlem," a tribute to one of the great legends of music.

Who began her career on *The Mickey Mouse Club?*

The Divas

- MARIA CALLAS, LINA CAVALIERI, GERALDINE FARRAR, MARY GARDEN, DAME NELLIE MELBA...
- AUSTRALIA, FRANCE, ITALY, SCOTLAND, UNITED STATES
- 1900S–1970S

Before the birth of cinema, the biggest stars owned the opera stage. Even for fans who couldn't afford to hear them, the sopranos were the epitome of beauty and glamour. They became the earliest stars of the mass media—making records, appearing on printed postcards, and in the shadows of the first movies. These women were the divas, and their larger-than-life existence gave birth to modern celebrity. The gossip and stories about these singers inevitably overshadowed their considerable music abilities. Geraldine Farrar is now best known for allegedly singing "he had a highball" during a duet with an inebriated Enrico Caruso. In 1906, however, her decision to sing an aria from Gounod's *Roméo et Juliette* while reclining onstage in a nightgown provoked a national debate. The celebrity of Farrar and contemporaries like Lina Cavalieri was such that they could appear in silent movie adaptations of the roles that made them famous without irony. The tightly corseted Cavalieri was photographed so many times, she became known as the world's most beautiful woman. Women had to be outgoing to make their names on the stage. This, along with their enormous fame, accounted for the divas' temperament—Dame Nellie Melba once shoved aside a tenor who tried to take a bow alongside her. The divas were notorious for demanding the finest fabrics for their costumes and lavish backstage signs of appreciation. Their fans ate up each juicy detail, from the whispered affairs to the endless retirement tours and sudden "vacations," which covered up rehab stints or hidden illnesses, mental or physical. The last true diva of the old school was Maria Callas, a soprano possessed of an unsurpassable force of will. Determined to join the ranks of the great opera beauties, the pudgy

! Britney Spears.

Maria Callas at the exit of La Scala in Milan, c. 1950. The fate of the last great diva resembles some of the heroines she played.

Left: The diva Geraldine Farrar in the title role of *Mignon* (1866), the famous opera written by Louis Ambroise Thomas.

Greek forced herself to lose seventy pounds, and threw herself into her roles with unprecedented authority. Her voice divided audiences. Yet the thrill of listening to her was in the reckless pursuit of emotional truth—Callas often missed a note, but never let what made her characters tick escape her. Callas's dramatic life overshadowed her indelible performances as the suicidal singer Tosca, the murderess Medea, and the druid priestess Norma. An affair with shipping heir Aristotle Onassis passed into legend, and she conducted a running battle with her peers and her audience. "When my enemies stop hissing, I shall know I'm slipping," she once proclaimed. They hissed a hoarse Medea in 1961, and Callas sang the line, "Cruel man! I gave everything to you!" to the crowd, shaking her fist. They applauded her then, but she died alone in Paris. A diva to the last, Callas was a figure bigger than anyone she portrayed.

Photography: *Who photographed which singer?*

Answer

1. RICHARD AVEDON for *Je m'appelle Barbra by* Barbra Streisand (1967).
2. MARIO TESTINO for *Ray Of Light* by Madonna (1998).
3. DAVID LACHAPELLE for *Rainbow* by Mariah Carey (1999).
4. ANNIE LEIBOVITZ for *Born In The USA* by Bruce Springsteen (1990).

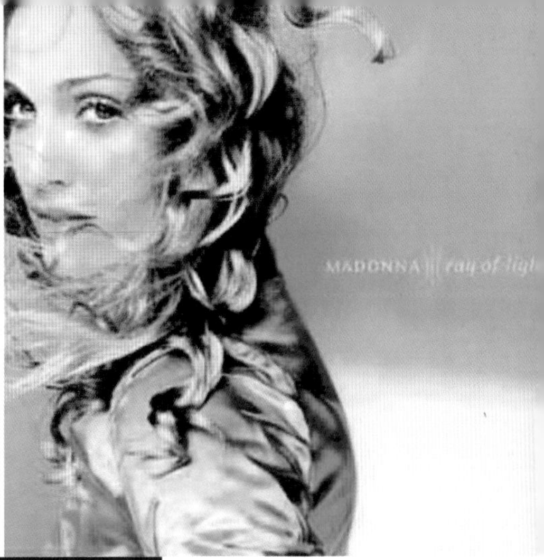

1

2

RICHARD AVEDON

•

DAVID LACHAPELLE

•

ANNIE LEIBOVITZ

•

MARIO TESTINO

3

4

Conductors

• LEONARD BERNSTEIN, SERGIU CELIBIDACHE, ARTHUR FIEDLER, WILHELM FURTWÄNGLER, HERBERT VON KARAJAN, SIMON RATTLE, SIR GEORGE SOLTI, LEOPOLD STOKOWSKI, ARTURO TOSCANINI, BRUNO WALTER...
• EUROPE, UNITED STATES
• 1900S–

Rehearsal with Nikisch, 1912, Richard Jack, oil on canvas (60 x 84 in.), Tate Gallery, London. The Hungarian conductor Arthur Nikisch (1855–1922) leading the London Symphony Orchestra during a rehearsal at Queen's Hall in Edinburgh, Scotland.

Right:
The famous conductor Arturo Toscanini leading the New York Philharmonic, using the traditional baton (c. 1938).

The conductor has not always commanded the respect that he does today. Hector Berlioz used to lurk offstage in case the man with the baton took any liberties with his work, and nineteenth-century composers like Beethoven and Mendelssohn saw fit to conduct their music themselves. Since then, the humble conductor has assumed almost mystical status. A great conductor doesn't just wave a stick. He (and it's usually "he") is both impresario and educator:interpreting the score, advocating new music, and reviving forgotten composers.
A conductor traditionally makes his way to leading an orchestra via the opera house, but some have made more spectacular debuts.

Arturo Toscanini became an overnight sensation after stepping in for a conductor in Brazil and leading *Aida* (1886) from memory.
In 1943, the young American Leonard Bernstein substituted for a sick Bruno Walter at such short notice that he conducted the New York Philharmonic in a gray business suit—an event that made the front pages.
As a musical director, a composer is charged with turning the orchestra into a group of world-class performers and then drawing an audience. During the 1930s and 1940s, an influx of European émigrés into America helped elevate Midwestern orchestras to the front rank. Homegrown conductors like

Bernstein became an anomaly. These conductors developed trademarked sounds, like the "free" breathing and bowing of instruments in Leopold Stokowski's Philadelphia Orchestra or the fine polish that Herbert von Karajan brought to the works of everyone from Bach to Stravinsky. Some conductors treated their scores with a liberality that Berlioz would not approve of. The temperamental Toscanini freely conducted the works at whatever tempo he deemed right. Stokowski would re-orchestrate masterpieces to his liking and dramatically toss scores to the ground to demonstrate their superfluity. Sergiu Celibidache was famous for playing Bruckner so slowly that he appeared to stop time.

Other conductors have become indelibly associated with their favorites. Bernstein established Gustav Mahler's reputation and told anyone who would listen that Aaron Copland was the greatest living composer. Sir George Solti effortlessly commanded Wagner's godly battalions. Wilhelm Furtwängler preferred momentary inspiration to over-rehearsed elucidation, and recorded Beethoven's Fifth Symphony twelve separate times.

LPs and CDs commemorated great performances, and broadcasting gave classical music an unprecedented reach. Beginning in 1937, the Toscanini-led NBC Symphony Orchestra brought the classics into a nation's living rooms, and Stokowski appeared in Disney's *Fantasia* (1940). Bernstein's televised *Young People's Concerts* of the 1950s and 1960s gave him a primetime platform to educate audiences in the delights of Stravinsky. Arthur Fiedler's Boston Pops appeared on television so many times that they became America's orchestra.

Younger conductors now leap to fame through television documentaries, as Britain's Simon Rattle did with his series on modern music, *Leaving Home* (1996). Pierre Boulez and Michael Tilson Thomas have become reliable connoisseurs of modern music and what Thomas's popular program calls *American Mavericks.* Conductors have gone from a composer's despised enemy to their most valuable friend.

?

Who holds the record for the most Grammys won in a single year?

Country Roots

• BOB WILLS AND HIS TEXAS PLAYBOYS, THE CARTER FAMILY, VERNON DALHART, LEFTY FRIZZELL, BILL MONROE, JIMMIE RODGERS, ERNEST TUBB, HANK WILLIAMS...
• UNITED STATES
• 1920S–1950S

! Michael Jackson and Carlos Santana. They both won eight Grammys in 1984 and 2000 respectively.

Country has become the music of America because it's about ordinary people. It's the sound of the lonely souls in Edward Hopper's paintings or the downtrodden of John Steinbeck's novels. Its terrain of loss, hardship, and sometimes booze is one that everyone can identify with, even if they find steel guitars and emotional vocals not to their taste.

It began with immigrants who had settled in the Appalachian hills and the Deep South. Dances were the best way for the far-flung farming class known as hillbillies to socialize. String bands played British folk songs on the fiddles, gradually adding bass and washboard rhythm. This "old-timey" sound turned up in 1924 on Vernon Dalhart's "The Wreck of Old '97," the first million-selling country single. Trains like the Old '97, which linked those distant communities, would become a key part of country mythology.

In 1927, the singer Jimmie Rodgers and the Carter Family recorded their first sides in Bristol, Tennessee, for Victor Records. Rodgers wrote original songs about the folks and hobos he met working on the railroad. He made up for his rudimentary guitar with a thrilling yodel on songs like "In the Jailhouse Now" and "T.B. Blues." The Carter Family—jack-of-all-trades A.P., wife Sara, and sister Maybelle—sang folk songs in matter-of-fact harmony. Maybelle's thumb picked out the bass melody on the guitar as her fingers brushed the rhythm.

Both became stars. "Spit 'er up, Jimmie, and sing some more," audiences cried when Rodgers's tuberculosis got the better of him. A.P. Carter combed the countryside for material, rescuing tunes that

formed the backbone of country music—blues, religious songs, folk ballads, and "Will the Circle Be Unbroken," a song whose message of continuity made it country's enduring anthem.

Nashville, the site of a weekly radio broadcast known as the *Grand Ole Opry,* soon became the capital of country music, and it attracted stars like Alabama's Hank Williams and the Texans Ernest Tubb and Lefty Frizzell. Williams and Tubb were stalwarts of honky-tonk, and played in and about the cheap dancehalls that gave the rough-and-tumble style its name. Before his death at age twenty-nine, Williams added songs like "I Saw the Light" and "Cold, Cold Heart" to the canon. Frizzell sang long melodic lines in a gin-clear tenor. Drawing out his vowels, he gave country vocals their distinctive twang.

The circle grew. Bob Wills & His Texas Playboys even played a jazz variant known as Western Swing. During the 1940s, mountain musicians like Kentucky fiddler Bill Monroe started playing the traditional songs fast and furious. With his dexterous instrumentals and haunting vocals that captured a "high lonesome sound," he helped create what became known as bluegrass. Youngsters like Elvis Presley were captivated. Eventually, Presley's transformation of country into rock 'n' roll would threaten the music's dominance.

Bob Wills & His Texas Playboys in the 1980s.

Right: Often performing with his wife Ramona (left), Louis Marshall Jones started playing music under the name "Grandpa" at age twenty-two. Nashville, Tennessee, 1974.

Contemporary Country

• CHET ATKINS, CLINT BLACK, GARTH BROOKS, KENNY CHESNEY, PATSY CLINE, DIXIE CHICKS, BOB DYLAN, THE FLATLANDERS, GEORGE JONES, WYNONNA JUDD, TOBY KEITH, TIM MCGRAW, WILLIE NELSON, GRAM PARSONS, DOLLY PARTON, KENNY ROGERS, SHANIA TWAIN, TRISHA YEARWOOD, DWIGHT YOAKAM...
• UNITED STATES
• 1950S–

Right:
Dolly Parton performing at New York's Lincoln Center. March 9, 1987.

Country has been an important ingredient in rock 'n' roll since Elvis Presley cut bluegrass musician Bill Monroe's "Blue Moon of Kentucky" at one of his earliest sessions. But rock nearly killed the genre. Country stars, like vocalist George Jones, were made to sing rock 'n' roll and didn't like it. They didn't have much choice. By the 1960s, Capitol Records had dropped all its country artists.

Chet Atkins decided to save country music. The self-taught Tennessean had revolutionized guitar playing by throwing away the pick and playing supple patterns with three fingers. He had played on records by Hank Williams and arranged Presley's "Heartbreak Hotel." As a producer, he attempted to arrest country's decline by eliminating traditional instrumentation like the steel guitar and the fiddle. With Owen Bradley, he fashioned a slick "countrypolitan" sound for stars like Patsy Cline that charmed audiences. It repulsed traditionalists, too, although to this day Cline's "Crazy" is the most played song on U.S. jukeboxes.

Country survived, but the music had broken away from its traditional sound. In California, the Bakersfield Sound rose in resistance, turning to rock guitars and heavy beats and mixing hillbilly swing and gospel into a raucous whole. In Texas, ornery cusses like the Flatlanders and Willie Nelson—the man who wrote "Crazy"—became known as outlaws for eschewing the Nashville Sound. Others surrendered to countrypolitan.

It was rock musicians, though, who rose above the infighting. Bob Dylan used country music to address Nixon's America with *Nashville Skyline* (1969). Groups like the Byrds and the Eagles delighted in the subtle tones of steel guitars and emotionally charged storytelling. Florida songwriter Gram Parsons described his country experiments as "Cosmic American Music," and shared his enthusiasm with the Rolling Stones.

The South's economic renaissance gave birth to the urban cowboy, making it easy for entertainers like Dolly Parton and Kenny Rogers to cross over into the pop charts with songs written by the Bee Gees. New traditionalists and alt.country performers took up the sounds of

honky-tonk and punk in their search for integrity. Meanwhile, "hat acts"—a term popularized in the 1990s used to describe an up-and-coming musician who wore a cowboy hat—maintained a popular stranglehold with their soap-opera looks and simplistic vocal stylings. Today, country musicians recognize the importance of drawing on other genres of music. Megastar Shania Twain's producer husband, for example, worked for heavy-metallers Def Leppard, and her male equivalent, Garth Brooks, is a longtime fan of Billy Joel. Country music has always been a vehicle for people to share their pain, be it personal and intimate or, like Toby Keith's post-9/11 anthem "Courtesy of the Red, White, and Blue (The Angry American)," politically charged and brash. Whatever the song, country's voice still demands to be heard.

What is the most expensive music video ever made?

Twentieth-Century Opera

- JOHN ADAMS, LORD BENJAMIN BRITTEN, CLAUDE DEBUSSY, GEORGE GERSHWIN, PHILIP GLASS, GIACOMO PUCCINI, RICHARD STRAUSS...
- EUROPE, UNITED STATES
- 1900S–1999

By the 1900s, Richard Wagner had changed the definition of "opera." The German composer thought opera was a work of art in its own right, a *gesantkunstwerk*—something that assaulted every sense, preferably over the course of several hours. So much for the notion of opera as an evening's entertainment. Every composer who came after Wagner had to wrestle with this new definition. Not all did so successfully. Opera tackled big and difficult themes, but with the rise of new media, lost its preeminence in mainstream popular culture.

Wagner's cosmos-spanning music mythology was not for everyone. Giacomo Puccini worked in the versimo style, which privileged realistic settings. The Italian's music was still Romantic at heart, and perfectly suited to the gorgeous lamentations of *Madama Butterfly's* (1904) abandoned heroine. Richard Strauss also indulged a Wagnerian mood in his beloved *Der Rosenkavalier* (1909), but horrified audiences with his other violent operas. Still, he was on to something. After all, the dominant mode of the modern era was tragedy, not comedy and he, along with other composers, sought to reflect the drama of this provocative time. Alban Berg's atonal *Wozzeck* (1917), for example, told the story of a victimized soldier who killed his unfaithful girlfriend in a jealous rage, then died himself.

It wasn't all *Sturm und Drang*. Debussy's subtle *Pelléas et Mélisande* (1893) showed composers that opera could create acute psychological portraits.

! Michael Jackson's "Scream" cost over $7 million.

The Three Tenors (from left to right): Plácido Domingo, José Carreras, and Luciano Pavarotti, in concert in Monte Carlo. Conducted by Zubin Mehta, June 1994. Their performance was a success worldwide and contributed to the genre's popularity.

Left:
Scene from the opera *Wozzeck,* by Alban Berg. This performance took place in 2000 at the Betty Nansen Teatret in Copenhagen.

Followers like Benjamin Britten made serious efforts to analyze the misunderstood. After finding success with 1945's *Peter Grimes,* the English composer continued to be inspired by the antiheroes of Melville's *Billy Budd* (1951) and Thomas Mann's *Death in Venice* (1973). Used to transforming cheap stories into art, opera entered a dialogue with other masterworks.

Composers incorporated new musical styles into their work, too. Gershwin introduced blues and jazz to *Porgy and Bess* (1935). The Who's "rock opera" *Tommy* (1969) found the British band bashing through the story of a deaf, dumb, and blind "pinball wizard." Opera was still highly regarded, but Broadway and LPs, which brought the concert hall into ordinary homes, eroded its popularity. Leonard Bernstein was fine writing hit musicals like *West Side Story* (1957), but his operatic works like *Candide* (1955–1989) were poorly received. The famous 1957 cartoon "What's opera, Doc?"—with Bugs Bunny as Brunhilde—said it all. The public who once embraced Mozart and Verdi now saw opera as the pretentious interest of a privileged elite.

Minimalist composers have flourished in the form, experimenting with its theatrical possibilities. Philip Glass's *Einstein on the Beach* (1976) did away with a storyline in favor of a prismatic portrait of the Nobel winner. In director Robert Wilson's hands, it was closer to a performance art piece than anything Wagner might recognize.

John Adams also used opera to understand recent history. *Nixon in China* (1985), based on the president's 1972 visit to the Communist country, brought the American composer to mainstream attention. With his controversial *The Death of Klinghoffer* (1990), opera was still trying to make sense of the world's real-life drama.

Masks off!

Who's hiding behind these women?

Answer

The Rolling Stones pose in drag as publicity for the song „Have You Seen Your Mother, Baby, Standing in the Shadows", from the album *Between the Buttons* (1966). They are (left to right): Brian Jones, Keith Richards, Mick Jagger, Charlie Watts, and Bill Wyman in the wheelchair.

Musicals

• *THE JAZZ SINGER* (1927), *AN AMERICAN IN PARIS* (1951), *SINGIN' IN THE RAIN* (1952), *FUNNY FACE* (1957), *PORGY AND BESS* (1959), *THE UMBRELLAS OF CHERBOURG* (1964), *THE SOUND OF MUSIC* (1965), *THE YOUNG GIRLS OF ROCHEFORT* (1967), *SATURDAY NIGHT FEVER* (1977), *GREASE* (1978), *ALL THAT JAZZ* (1979), *MOULIN ROUGE!* (2001)...
• LEONARD BERNSTEIN, ARTHUR FREED, GEORGE GERSHWIN, MICHEL LEGRAND
• 1927–

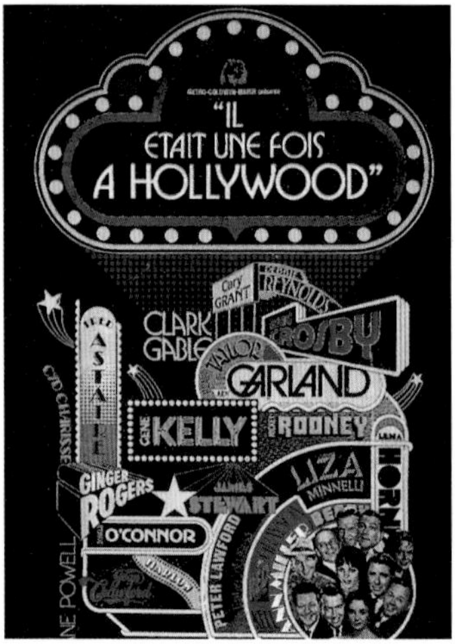

The Jazz Singer (1927), a film that includes several short musical passages, marked the first appearance of music in film. Ever since, the role of music has only continued to grow within the movie-making industry and the formidable Hollywood machine, which inaugurated the era of its own type of musical.

On the brink of bankruptcy, Warner bought the music rights from General Electric Western and produced *The Jazz Singer*. It was a stunning success that captivated the whole country. From that moment on, Broadway composers began to make their way to Hollywood. For the price of a movie ticket, a worker in Boston or a farmer in Oklahoma could finally treat themselves to the musical spectacles that had made Broadway famous.

Hollywood began to mass-produce musicals, although they were still rather static, due to the primitive film cameras, which had to be enclosed in soundproof boxes. It took the arrival of Ruben Mamoulian and Ernst Lubitsch for things to change. A successful theater producer, Mamoulian introduced the movement that had been lacking in the Hollywood productions, and Lubitsch sorted out the sound problems through post-synchronization.

Unlike Broadway comedians who were simultaneously singers and dancers, movie actors needed to be trained for the demands of the new media. Hollywood "made" studio artists by writing songs to suit their voices. From one day to the next, a second-rate actor became a star in the eyes of the American public, and as a consequence, the entire world. Hollywood quickly became a star-making machine.

Gene Kelly in the most famous scene from the movie *Singin' in the Rain* (1952), directed by Stanley Donen and Gene Kelly.

Left:
Poster for *That's Entertainment* (1974). Today, this fabulous saga of Hollywood's musical golden age is available on DVD worldwide.

?

Whose screen test report read, "Can't sing. Can't act. Slightly balding. Can dance a little"?

Busby Berkeley, known for positioning his camera in such a way as to film his dancers' legs on a larger scale, met Arthur Freed, a composer and producer, who went on to give music a central role in his films. During the 1940s, Vincente Minelli collaborated with George Gershwin on *An American in Paris* (1951). The nonchalant genius of Fred Astaire, the charm of Judy Garland, the triumphant professionalism of Stanley Donen or Gene Kelly are some of the magical names that mark the history of musicals. The marriage between cinema and music has spanned several generations. Imagination seemed to run dry in the 1950s, and little by little, the machine ran backwards: Broadway even staged successful revivals of film versions of its musicals. During the 1960s, European producers, such as Jacques Demy and Michel Legrand, who were world-famous for *The Umbrellas of Cherbourg* (1964) and *The Young Girls of Rochefort* (1967), came to the fore. Musicals became popular

!

Fred Astaire's.

Vincent Minelli surrounded by posters for his films (c. 1962).

Left:
(top)
Scene from the musical *West Side Story* (1961), directed by Robert Wise with music by Leonard Bernstein.

(bottom)
Poster for the movie *The Umbrellas of Cherbourg* (1964), directed by Jacques Demy and starring Catherine Deneuve and Nino Castelnuovo. The score was Michel Legrand's first big hit.

again with *The Sound of Music* (1965), followed by many expensive, mega productions. Apart from a few enormously popular hits—*Saturday Night Fever* (1977), *Grease* (1978), *All That Jazz* (1979), and *Moulin Rouge!* (2001)—none has truly recaptured the glory days and success of Hollywood's glorious musical past.

Film:
Who played whom in what movie?

Answer

1. Angela Bassett played Tina Turner in Brian Gibson's *What's Love Got to Do with It* (1992).
2. Gary Oldman played Sid Vicious in Alex Cox's *Sid & Nancy* (1986).
3. Diana Ross played Billie Holiday in Sidney J. Furie's *Lady Sings the Blues* (1972).
4. Kurt Russell played Elvis Presley in John Carpenter's TV movie *Elvis* (1979).
5. Forest Whitaker played Charlie Parker in Clint Eastwood's *Bird* (1988).
6. Sean Penn played Emmet Ray—a fictional character based on Django Reinhardt—in Woody Allen's *Sweet and Lowdown* (1999).
7. Jamie Foxx played Ray Charles in Taylor Hackford's *Ray* (2004).
8. Lou Diamond Phillips played Ritchie Valens in Luis Valdez's *La Bamba* (1987).
9. Val Kilmer played Jim Morrison in Oliver Stone's *The Doors* (1991).
10. Bette Midler played Mary Rose Foster—a fictional character based on Janis Joplin—in Mark Rydell's *The Rose* (1979).

?

?

?

?

?

?

?

?

?

?

Duke Ellington

• *DAYBREAK EXPRESS* (1947), *ELLINGTON UPTOWN* (1953), *ELLINGTON AT NEWPORT* (1956) *AND HIS MOTHER CALLED HIM BILL* (1959), *DUKE ELLINGTON AND JOHN COLTRANE* (1962)...
• 1899–1974
COUNT BASIE, CAB CALLOWAY, ELLA FITZGERALD, QUINCY JONES, GLENN MILLER, SUN RA

It's worth noting that as well as being the most important American jazz composer, Edward Kennedy "Duke" Ellington was a brilliant manager. The son of a White House butler, he led his big band for half a century—an extraordinary feat of diplomacy and command. He played piano, but the orchestra was his true instrument. Ellington wrote songs, suites, concertos, musicals, and movie scores, all with his band in mind. Everything was tailored to the strengths of his musicians and their individual voices. To play in Ellington's band was to be a color on a master's palette.

Members came and went, but the band rarely failed him. In 1956, as bebop threatened to make this icon of swing and his big band passé, tenor saxophonist Paul Gonsalves unleashed a solo at the Newport Jazz Festival, which nearly started a merry riot and landed Ellington on the cover of *Time* magazine. All of the Duke's men made his notes speak. When he arrived in New York in 1923, Bubber Miley provided his Washingtonians with their trademark "growl" by imitating a blues singer's wail on his trumpet. In 1926, Miley and Ellington's "jungle" band was joined by Joe "Tricky Sam" Nanton, whose "yah yah" trombone sound was but another unique voice.

A celebrated residency at Harlem's Cotton Club the following year made Duke a star. It also forced the composer to stretch himself. One signature song followed another, like 1926's "East St. Louis Toodle-Oo" and "It Don't Mean a Thing If It Ain't Got That Swing" (which gave the jazz style its name). "Black and Tan Fantasy" from 1929 wittily played homage to jazz's cemetery roots with a snatch of Chopin's funeral march.

At the Cotton Club, the dapper Duke wrote music for dances and bluesy mood pieces while experimenting with tonality. On 1931's "Mood Indigo," the traditionally low trombone and high clarinet switched places. Beginning with "Creole Rhapsody," his music expanded in form until the hits took up both sides of a 78 record. Critics began to notice, and Ellington's ambition legitimatized jazz. He could be as comfortable

Right:
Duke Ellington surrounded by fellow musicians, 1943.

playing Carnegie Hall or a "sacred concert" in a cathedral, as on the nonstop tour to promote his music. Duke let his work live, too. He re-recorded earlier pieces to see what they sounded like with fresh musicians playing them, and arranged them in longer thematic works that he called "suites" or "tone parallels." He was an egalitarian icon, arranging Tchaikovsky for his band as he performed with the new breed of John Coltrane and Charles Mingus. And although his orchestra is no longer around, his music and performances remain one of the true triumphs of twentieth-century art. Ellington's legacy continues to inspire countless musicians the world over.

? How many pairs of eyeglasses does Elton John own?

Bebop

• ART BLAKEY, MILES DAVIS, DIZZY GILLESPIE, PERCY HEATH, THELONIUS MONK, CHARLIE PARKER, BUD POWELL, MAX ROACH...
• UNITED STATES
• 1940S

A brave soul once asked Miles Davis to explain the history of jazz. He replied, "Louis Armstrong. Charlie Parker." Along with trumpeter Dizzy Gillespie, the saxophonist Charlie Parker was the architect of bop, or bebop, so called because of the distinctive two-note phrase played to introduce solos or end songs. Bop was music by musicians for musicians. Putting the emphasis on small ensembles, fast tempos, and improvisation, it took jazz away from the dance bands and gave it an air of intellectual seriousness.

Bop was born in the 1940s, when a strike by the American Federation of Musicians prevented players from going into the studio to record. Instead, they congregated at post-concert jam sessions in the small clubs lining New York's West Fifty-second Street. As the musicians tried to wow each other with their instrumental prowess, they began to depart from the melody and improvise around a song's chords or harmony. Parker, nicknamed "Yardbird," had moved to New York from Kansas City in 1940, and quickly made an impact. He played flawless solos faster than a speeding bullet. Gillespie was one of the few who could keep up with him, and they dazzled their peers when they played in unison. The pair turned tunes inside out. In 1945, when the recording ban was lifted, bop emerged fully matured. Audiences were baffled.

Cab Calloway, who fired Dizzy from his band for throwing spitballs, called it "Chinese music." A soloist would play the chorus of a melody, and then use the chords as a springboard to leap into frenetic solos. Parker recycled pop chord structures for compositions like "Ornithology," and the harmony from Gershwin's "I Got Rhythm" became so popular it got its own name, "Rhythm Changes."

How did it work? As each musician in the combo—usually a quintet with a piano and two horns—soloed, the drummer held down the rhythm with his ride cymbal, and the bassist played what became known as a

Four thousand.

Portrait of saxophonist Dexter Gordon by Herman Leonard, in New York, 1948.

Left:
(top)
Cover of Charlie Parker's *Bird and Diz* (1997), released by Polygram Records.

(bottom)
Dizzy Gillespie at the piano, surrounded by Miles Davis and the Heath Brothers. Bop City, San Francisco, 1949.

"walking" bass line. Listeners wondered where the bit they could hum along with had gone, unaware that new melodies were being made right before them. "Don't play the saxophone," advised Parker.
"Let it play you."
Yardbird played. Gillespie took notes, and showed others how to do it. The solo became an autobiography—musicians didn't play someone else's tune, but whatever they felt. Bop let musicians speak their own language. It was an innovation everyone had to grapple with. The emphasis on individualism meant bop quickly split into subgenres. Art Blakey played more soulful hard bop while Davis pioneered the laid-back "cool" style. And composers like Thelonius Monk used Bird's example to explore jazz's limitless possibilities.

Odd One Out:

Which of these singers never sang Edith Piaf's "La vie en rose"?

Answer

The odd one out is Celine Dion.
Ute Lemper covered the song on her album *Illusions (Songs of Dietrich and Piaf)* (1993).
Dalida covered the song on her album *Il Silenzio* (1965).
Cyndi Lauper covered the song on her album *At Last* (2003).
Madeleine Peyroux covered the song on her album *Dreamland* (1997).

Ute Lemper

Dalida

Cyndi Lauper

Celine Dion

Madeleine Peyroux

Umm Kulthum

• *AMAL HAYATI* (FROM SONO), *ENTA OMRI* (FROM SONO), *LA DIVA* (EMI ARABIA, 2001), *THE CLASSICS* (EMI ARABIA, 2001)...
• C.1904–1975
AMINA, ASMAHAN, SLIMANE AZEM, OFRA HAZA, NUSRAT FATEH ALI KHAN, LATA MANGESHKAR, YOUSSOU N'DOUR, WARDA

When the Egyptian singer Umm Kulthum performed, there was no telling when the concert might end. Singing in Arabic, her interpretative skills were such that the crowd demanded she repeat a single line or phrase over and over again. She caressed the lyrics with her high, androgynous voice like a lover, coaxing new meanings from them. With orchestral interludes giving her time to recover, a song like Kulthum's "Enta Omri/You Are My Life" could suspend an audience in rapture for hours.

Kulthum was a marvelous anomaly. Her muezzin father had taught her how to recite the Koran and sing religious songs, even though both acts were taboo for women at the time. She would accompany her family's takht ensemble around the Nile Delta dressed as a boy so as not to attract censure. Moving to Cairo in 1923, she became popular by performing regularly on Egyptian National Radio. As a result, her voice was heard around the Middle East. Cities would stop when she came on air.

In Cairo, Kulthum exchanged her boyish peasant look for the glamorous Western dresses worn by the well-to-do women she initially sang for. Kulthum was a savvy media operator, producing her own live appearances and rarely speaking to the press. She became the muse of the Arab Nationalist Gamal Abdel Nasser, who regularly scheduled his radio speeches to occur after her monthly ENR concerts.

She worked with a variety of collaborators. The poet Ahmed Rami supplied her with secular songs of love and longing. Composer Muhammad al-Qasabji backed her with Western instruments like the violoncello and the double bass. By the 1940s, she moved from romantic songs into Egyptian styles, commissioning Riyad al-Sunbati to compose a repertoire of neoclassical songs based on *qasa'id* (classical Arab poetry). In the 1950s, she turned to younger composers to write new love songs for her.

Musicians used to joke that "all her lovers could verify that she

Hand-colored portrait of the icon Umm Kulthum, from the book *Azzedine Alaia* by Michel Tournier, Juan Gatty, Azzedine Alaia, and Martine Barrat.

was a virgin," but the truth was Kulthum controlled her image so severely no one knew much about her. She was said to have been betrothed to an uncle of King Farouk, and her marriage with Dr. Hasan al-Hifnawi, a skin specialist, was allegedly a sham. Despite her private nature, there was no doubting the raw feeling expressed on her records—where songs often took up two sides of an album. Her support of the Nationalist cause following the Egyptian Revolution of 1952 and the Six-Day War only made her more beloved. When she died, her Cairo funeral drew four million mourners.

What album did soul singer Marvin Gaye record to pay his wife's alimony?

Edith Piaf

• *LIVE AT CARNEGIE HALL* (1957), *LA VIE EN ROSE* (1974), *TU ES PARTOUT* (2002, U.S. RELEASE), *MÔME DE PARIS* (2004, U.S. RELEASE)...
• 1915–1963
CHARLES AZNAVOUR, JEFF BUCKLEY, UTE LEMPER, YVES MONTAND

The sardonically titled *Here, My Dear.*

9It is impossible for anyone to hear Edith Piaf's voice and ask, "Who is this?" The personality and life of France's greatest *chanteuse* are inextricably tied with her *chansons,* songs expressly tailored to reflect her public triumphs and disappointments. If there's anything to wonder, it's how such a sound of raw passion could come from a frame so frail.

Born Edith Giovanna Gassion, she was raised by her paternal grandmother, who ran a brothel in Normandy. From the age of three to seven, she was blind and, according to legend, the local prostitutes prayed for the ill Gassion's sight to return. Like a miracle, it did. She was singing on a Pigalle street corner in 1935 when nightclub owner Louis Leplée discovered her and refined her rough edges for the stage. Leplée named Gassion *La Môme Piaf* or "The Little Sparrow," put her in her trademark black dress, and invited Maurice Chevalier to her opening night performance.

Piaf preferred the company of pimps and it rubbed off. When Leplée was later shot to death, she was the prime suspect. Love, death, and tragedy surrounded Piaf and her material reeked of it, thanks to her longtime association with Marguerite Monnot, who penned her earliest hits. She also cultivated aspiring songwriters as lovers. She sang what she knew. "L'Accordéoniste" is a song about a prostitute who loses her lover and in "Les amants d'un jour" she details the tragic end of their tryst—the prostitute commits suicide. In life, as in her songs, death inevitably followed ecstasy. In 1949, the great love of her life, boxer Marcel Cerdan, died while flying to see her in New York. As always, her heartbreak fueled incredible art. Monnot wrote "Hymne à l'amour" in Cerdan's memory, and it became one of Piaf's biggest hits.

No matter what befell her, Piaf counseled perseverance and no regrets. She sang for the Nazis, but refused to remove the provocative "Où sont-ils mes petits copains?" from her repertoire. She survived car crashes and addictions, and even when she could barely stand, performed

Edith Piaf, 1960. With her famous black dress and tragic voice, she represents the classic rags-to-riches myth: the street kid who became France's most popular singer.

gut-wrenching shows where she threw her entire body and soul into each note. The Sparrow's power was undeniable. Her protégé Charles Aznavour later said that the day of her funeral was the only time the traffic stopped in Paris.

Crooners

• PAUL ANKA, TONY BENNETT, MICHAEL BUBLÉ, NAT KING COLE, HARRY CONNICK, JR., BING CROSBY, JAMIE CULLUM, SAMMY DAVIS, JR., JULIO IGLESIAS, DEAN MARTIN, NEIL SEDAKA, FRANK SINATRA, ROD STEWART, RUDY VALLÉE...
• UNITED STATES
• 1930S–

The crooner's sound—a smooth and velvety whisper in your ear—was only made possible with the invention of electric amplification. Before, a singer had to make sure he was heard at the back of the hall, and he projected his voice accordingly. With radio and microphones, he could make it sound like he was warbling to you and only you. This simple adjustment created a revolution in pop singing.

The model crooner was Bing Crosby, who tailored his baritone to the microphone. He sang to it as though it were a woman and, in doing so, became an immense star. His easy-going "bubu-bu-boo" sound might be more familiar than any of his records, bar the best-selling *White Christmas* (1942). Crosby sold thirty-five million copies of the Christmas carol, and applied a scatting vocal technique he learned from the jazzman Louis Armstrong to all manner of material. Whether it was holiday music, patriotic anthems, show tunes, or Hawaiian ballads, his ability to turn anything into a hit made him a key scribe of the American songbook. Those who imitated him—like Frank Sinatra, who made the girls scream with the way he seemed to kiss the microphone—had to be able to match his relaxed versatility.

The popularity of the crooners coincided with radio's dominance of broadcasting through the 1940s and 1960s. These untutored

Julio Iglesias, the Spanish singer known worldwide, onstage at London's Royal Albert Hall, 1982.

Right:
The Rat Pack: Dean Martin, Sammy Davis, Jr., and Frank Sinatra. The three crooners are seen here in the wings at Carnegie Hall in 1967, after a fund-raiser for Martin Luther King, Jr.

singers used their voices to suggest individual personalities. Each interpreted the standards taken from Broadway shows and Hollywood movies in their own distinct manner. Dean Martin took the ease of Crosby to extremes, sounding nearly comatose at times. Nat King Cole's husky voice was so inviting that white

audiences easily embraced him even as hotels refused him a room. The rock era helped kill off the crooner, as music became more excitable and success depended on musicians being able to write their own material. Paul Anka and Neil Sedaka stayed successful by penning their own middle-of-the-road standards, while the interpretative genius Tony Bennett proved to be Crosby's flexible equal as he worked with contemporary artists like Elvis Costello and k.d. lang. The success of younger singers like Harry Connick, Jr. and Michael Bublé proves that the crooner's debonair image still has its appeal, and the pianist Jamie Cullum has found success by transforming rock songs into standards with smart arrangements. Even aging rockers like Rod Stewart have found that donning the crooner's bow tie and tux is a good career move.

?

Which minimalist composer held down jobs as a taxi driver and a plumber?

Doo-Wop

• THE CARDINALS, THE CLEFTONES, DION AND THE BELMONTS, THE DRIFTERS, THE FIVE KEYS, THE FIVE SATINS, THE FLAMINGOS, THE IMPRESSIONS, THE INKSPOTS, THE LARKS, THE MILLS BROTHERS, THE ORIOLES, THE PARLIAMENTS, THE PENGUINS, THE PLATTERS, THE RAVENS...
• UNITED STATES
• 1950S–1960S

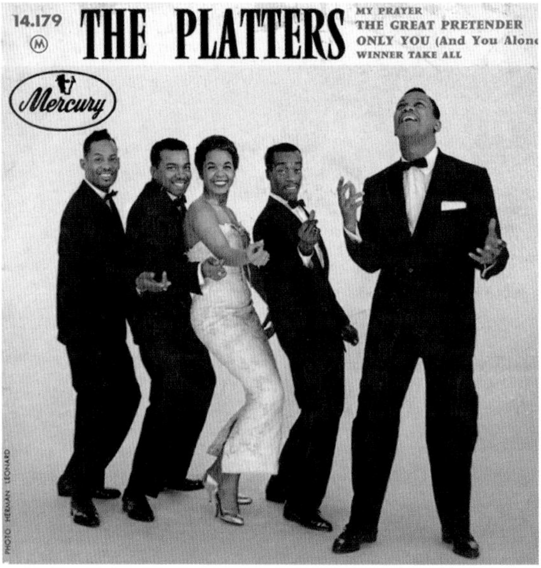

Doo-wop was born out of necessity. At the start of the 1950s, musically inclined teens in the New York and Los Angeles ghettos began congregating on street corners. Unable to afford instruments, they used their voices to approximate their musical sounds. The kids imitated their parents' records, but added to them the same fresh adolescent angst that coursed through rock 'n' roll.

The Mills Brothers could be considered doo-wop's godfathers. The four siblings (and sometimes their barber dad) from Piqua, Ohio, became nationally renowned in the 1930s for their ability to mimic trumpets, trombones, and tubas. Hits like "Paper Doll" came with a label declaring, "No musical instruments or mechanical devices used in this recording other than one guitar." Along with the Ink Spots, their harmonic genius opened a world of possibility for the young wannabe singers who followed them. Behind a lead singer, the others crooned harmonic gibberish. Hence the name: "doo-wop."

From 1951 to 1961, America fell for doo-wop. The charts looked like an aviary—populated with groups like the Cardinals, the Orioles, the Penguins, and the Ravens. Discerning ears heard the differences. Dion and the Belmonts had authentic grit in their throats. The Cleftones were upbeat roof-raisers. The Five Keys were jazzy sophisticates. Some doo-woppers had two contrasting lead singers—one satin smooth, the other asphalt rough—or shook up their recordings with sudden falsetto outbursts.

! Philip Glass.

Doo-wop's vitality came from the musicians' ability to express the adolescent experiences of inner city Italian- and African-Americans. When Dion sang about "Runaround Sue" or "The Wanderer," he sang about the very real here-today-and-gone-tomorrow life his neighbors lived. Other songs dealt with young love in the city, turning tenements into a landscape where Romeos and Juliets hid. Teenagers in love held each other tight "In the Still of the Night," fled "Under the Boardwalk," and discovered roses in "Spanish Harlem." Fast, funny songs like "Yakety Yak" presented the adult world as entirely alien to young minds.

Its romantic side made doo-wop the make-out music of choice for 1950s teens. The Platters were an instant aphrodisiac. Tony Williams's soaring tenor could have made the phone book sound like a Neruda sonnet. His group wrenched every last bit of emotion out of poetry like "The Great Pretender," "Only You (And You Alone)," and Jerome Kern's "Smoke Gets In Your Eyes." They became the first black group to top the pop charts in 1956 with "My Prayer," a song made famous previously by the Ink Spots.

The arrival of the Beatles, whose harmonies owed plenty to doo-wop's sophistication, rendered doo-wop music redundant.

Teenagers started saving up for guitars. But the canniest doo-wop stars became musical forces. The Impressions recorded some of the 1960s' most powerful Civil Rights anthems. The Parliaments became Parliament, the craziest funk crusaders of the 1970s. And doo-wop resounded in the hits of Motown's finest. They may be oldies now, but something about doo-wop keeps it forever young.

Above:
Portrait of the Penguins (c. 1955). Their biggest hit was "Earth Angel" in 1954.

Left:
Cover of a 1958 single by the Platters. Mercury Records.

Album Covers:

Can you name the artists whose work was used for these album covers?

Answer

1. Shusei Nagaoka for Earth, Wind & Fire's *All 'N All* (1977).
2. René Magritte for The Jeff Beck Group's *Beck-Ola* (2004).
3. Keith Haring for NYC Peech Boys's *Life Is Something Special* (1982).
4. Salvador Dalí for Jackie Gleason's *Lonesome Echo* (1955).

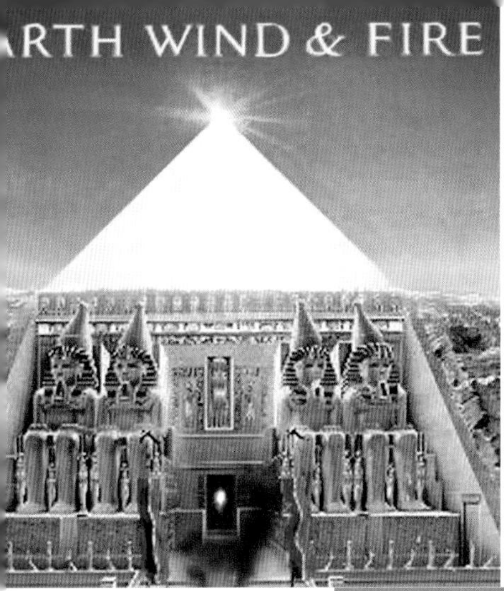

1

2

SALVADOR DALÍ

•

KEITH HARING

•

RENÉ MAGRITTE

•

SHUSEI NAGAOKA

3

4

Record Labels

• THE "BIG FOUR": EMI GROUP, SONY BMG MUSIC ENTERTAINMENT, UNIVERSAL MUSIC GROUP, AND WARNER MUSIC GROUP; INDIE LABELS: DEATH ROW RECORDS, MATADOR RECORDS, MAVERICK RECORDS, RIGHTEOUS BABE RECORDS, SUB POP RECORDS...
• UNITED STATES
• 1901–

Named after the paper sticker in the middle of a phonograph record, a record label creates, markets, and distributes recorded matter—and often is responsible for developing the careers of the musicians who play on them.

The earliest record labels were record player manufacturers who realized they could make even more money creating the music these phonographs were supposed to play. One of the first was Columbia, which began selling both phonographs and discs in 1901. Their main rival was the Victor Talking Machine Company, whose logo was a famous image of a dog listening to a phonograph's giant speaker. Each owned factories that pressed their records, and had representatives out in the field searching for singers and songwriters. These talent-spotters would become known as A&R, standing for "artists and repertoire."

Traditionally, smaller local labels were the earliest to discover trends and talent. In the early 1920s, New York's OKeh sold "race records" to the under-served African-American population. In Chicago, the Chess label became synonymous with blues music. Memphis's Sun Records boasted a rockabilly roster that included Elvis Presley, Johnny Cash, and Jerry Lee Lewis. In the 1980s, Creation became known for its jangling Britpop. Finding great music wasn't a problem, but distributing it was. Many independent labels signed deals with "majors" like Columbia to get their product into stores. Others were simply swallowed up in mergers, friendly or otherwise. Some labels grew with the popularity of their music. Atlantic began as a jazz label in the late

Collection of singles produced by different labels. At the end of the twentieth century, the advent of audio cassettes and CDs was the swan song of the vinyl record album. Its success had lasted a full century.

Right:
Advertisement for Gramophon and Victor Company: *His Master's Voice* by Mark Barraud, 1899.

1940s, but by the 1960s was the home of Aretha Franklin and Led Zeppelin. Barclay Records became one of the biggest labels in France through its canny marketing of American hits and by launching yé-yé icons. Bob Marley helped transform the reggae label Island from an operation run out of the back of mogul Chris Blackwell's car to a worldwide imprint. Once they became successful, artists asserted their freedom to jump from one label to another, and fortunes depended on their movements.
In spite of an explosion of independent labels during the punk era, a decade of consolidation in the 1990s left nearly three-quarters of the global market in the hands of four corporate giants—EMI Group, Sony BMG Music Entertainment, Universal Music Group, and Warner Music Group. However, the labels' industrial model has been overturned by the new digital format of the MP3, which allows users to freely "trade" pre-recorded music on the Internet. Unable to control distribution, these once-mighty behemoths look very vulnerable. They may one day go the route of the stickers that gave them their name.

?

What is the best-selling album of all time?

Movie Soundtracks

- BURT BACHARACH, JOHN BARRY, GEORGES DELERUE, DANNY ELFMAN, BERNARD HERRMANN, MAURICE JARRE, ERICH WOLFGANG KORNGOLD, MICHEL LEGRAND, ENNIO MORRICONE, SERGEI PROKOFIEV, ERIC SERRA, SHIGERU UMEBAYASHI, FRANZ WAXMAN, KURT WEILL, JOHN WILLIAMS...
- INTERNATIONAL
- 1908–

! The Eagles' *Their Greatest Hits 1971–1975*, which overtook Michael Jackson's *Thriller* in 1997.

A knife rips a shower curtain. A shark's jaw tears through the sea. These cinematic scenes are purely visual. Yet, accompanied by music onscreen, they are unforgettable. The connection between sound and image allows the audience to feel intense emotions. Because of this, audiences don't go into a movie theater with the same expectations as they do a concert hall. Here, an audience member doesn't just listen to music; he or she experiences it. Film was never entirely silent. Well before the talkies, silent films were accompanied by a musician, usually a pianist, who filled pauses or accented drama with his own improvisations. *L'Assassinat du duc de Guise* (1908) by André Calmettes and Charles le Bargy was screened while Camille Saint Saëns's music was playing in the theater. It was the first real collaboration between image and sound. In the heyday of silent film, D.W. Griffith had music specially composed for his mega production *Birth of a Nation* (1915). He even hired the Los Angeles Philharmonic Orchestra for the premiere. With the emergence of talkies in 1927, directors worldwide borrowed from classical music. It was only a few years later that sound was synchronized for the length of the entire film. The first great success was undoubtedly German director Georg Wilhelm Pabst's *Threepenny Opera* (1931), which brought together Bertold Brecht's script and Kurt Weill's music. But certainly the most important film of the period in which music played a leading role was Sergei Esenstein's *Alexander Nevsky* (1938), with music by Sergei Prokofiev.

In the 1930s and 1940s, Hollywood took advantage of the influx of artists fleeing the Nazi regime. Milks Rosa, Franz Waxman, Max Steiner, and Richard Hageman brought a romantic touch to the popular dramas of the time and enchanted audiences everywhere.

In 1941, Orson Welles asked Bernard Herrmann to compose

Dimitri Tiomkin leading his seventy-five-person orchestra for King Vidor and William Dieterle's *Duel in the Sun* (1946).

music for *Citizen Kane* (1941). The trumpet solo that opens the film will forever be a part of film noir history. Bernard Herrmann later collaborated on Martin Scorcese's *Taxi Driver* (1976), another cult classic. Like many other genius composers (from Erich Wolfgang Korngold and Franz Waxman to Maurice Jarre and Burt Bacharach), Herrmann devoted all his talent to Hollywood, which provided him with a long and rich career in return.

Films like *Easy Rider* (1969), *Saturday Night Fever* (1977), and *Grease* (1978) presented musical trends that corresponded to a particular audience. The soundtracks took Hollywood's more traditional music world off guard. Nevertheless, large orchestral compositions are clearly what American musical film does best. The success of John Williams, Steven Spielberg's favorite musician, or John Barry, whose name is synonymous with that of James Bond, serve as prime examples.

Distinguished works in musical composition were also produced in Europe. The composer Michel Legrand first enjoyed success with Jacques Demy's

Movie Soundtracks

The Umbrellas of Cherbourg (1964), in which every line of dialogue is sung. From that point on, Legrand contributed to every cult film, including Robert Mulligan's wonderful *Summer of '42* (1971). He also worked closely with directors like Jean-Luc Godard, Agnès Varda, Yves Allégret, and Joseph Losey. With Georges Delerue, who worked with French New Wave directors, melody reached new heights. Music was no longer used to illustrate or accentuate. Instead, it was in constant dialogue with the script and the director's intentions. In François Truffaut's *Jules and Jim* (1961), music evolved with the characters. The film included gems like "Le Tourbillon," a song that showcased Jeanne Moreau's captivating voice. In 1970, Francis Lai, another major composer in French film, gained international recognition with his original score for *Love Story* (1970), a film by Arthur Hiller, for which he won an Academy Award. The Italian Ennio Morricone made his mark in the unforgettable Spaghetti Westerns made in the 1970s with his fellow countryman Sergio Leone. *The Good, the Bad and the Ugly* (1966) and the cult classic *Once Upon a Time in the West* (1968) demonstrate the idea that music is just as important a dramatic element in films as is a tautly written script.
But there is one team in European film that stands out in particular: Federico Fellini and Nino Rota. Listening to the director's vision, Rota created unique soundtracks that brought out the master filmmaker's fantasy world. With a strange and apparent simplicity, he dutifully completed Fellini's works, using the expressive wealth of instruments often used by small local orchestras.
With the 1980s, there emerged a new sound with Eric Serra, who contributed to the amazing films of Luc Besson, in particular *The Big Blue* (1988). His work influenced an entire generation of musicians and filmmakers.
More recently, the haunting music of Shigeru Umebayashi has magnificently illustrated the dense and wonderfully aesthetic world of the great Hong Kong director Kar Waï Wong. *In the Mood for Love* (2000) is one of his most beautiful works.

Cover of the album *Movie Masterpieces* (2004), by Ennio Morricone. The Morricone collection includes music for Sergio Leone's *The Good, the Bad, and the Ugly* (1966); Leone's *Once Upon a Time in the West* (1968); Henri Verneuil's *The Sicilian Clan* (1969); Roman Polanski's *Frantic* (1988); and Roland Joffé's *Mission* (1986).

Which Soviet premier owned a Scopitone jukebox?

Johnny Cash

• *JOHNNY CASH WITH HIS HOT AND BLUE GUITAR* (1957), *SINGS THE BALLADS OF THE TRUE WEST* (1965), *LIVE AT FOLSOM PRISON* (1968), *LIVE AT SAN QUENTIN* (1969), *AMERICAN RECORDINGS* (1994)...
• 1932–2003
JUNE CARTER CASH, LEONARD COHEN, BOB DYLAN, MERLE HAGGARD, WAYLON JENNINGS, KRIS KRISTOFFERSON, NEKO CASE AND HER BOYFRIENDS, WILLIE NELSON, CARL PERKINS, UNCLE TUPELO

Nikita Khrushchev.

Known as the Man in Black, Johnny Cash became an outlaw country hero, thanks in part to his resonant bass rumble and his own run-ins with the law. Cash could sing with tremendous command, riveting the listener with the tritest lyrical narrative and introducing a cruel kind of ambiguity to the most innocuous love song. His prophet's voice was as timeless as his music, with its distinctive "boom chicka boom" rhythm. He outgrew the country genre to become an American icon.

That outlaw reputation was based on one of Cash's earliest songs, "Folsom Prison Blues," written while he served in the air force during the Korean War. It's the story of a convict who, as in many a country song, hears a train whistle blowing. He envies the people free to travel anywhere, but Cash gives his lament a twist. The prisoner "shot a man in Reno, just to watch him die." The line drew appreciative whoops when he played at the Folsom and San Quentin prisons, shows commemorated on an electric pair of late-1960s live albums.

While Cash's dark clothes and granite demeanor gave such sentiments resonance, he originally auditioned for Sun Records as a gospel artist and would later leave the Memphis label after they spurned his religious direction. It was just one of the many contradictions of Cash's life. While Cash sang of God, he was born to raise hell. While addicted to the amphetamines that saw him through his three-hundred-shows-a-year schedule, he was arrested for burning down a California forest and trying to smuggle drugs across the Mexican border in his guitar case.

His biggest hits drew on his character's unfathomable depths. In "Ring of Fire," he is awed like a poet on the edge of love's arena, while

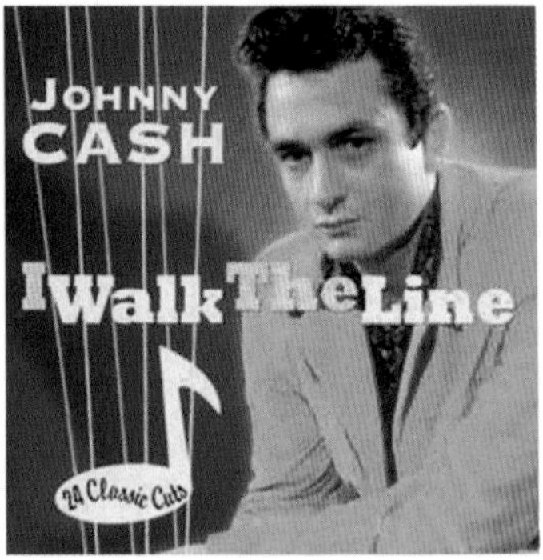

Johnny Cash in Will Zens's *Road to Nashville* (1967).

Left: Cover of the Johnny Cash album *I Walk the Line* (1956).

mariachi horns blow. In the popular song, "I Walk the Line," he explains, "I keep a close watch on this heart of mine." Cash was best at introspection, but his fascination with America's history led him to create a series of 1960s concept albums in which he sang about trains, Indians, and even the Grand Canyon, in a voice with the stately grandeur of the Oklahoma River.

A country giant who was uneasy with the Nashville establishment, he was one of the first to record the songs of Bob Dylan and Kris Kristofferson, who later joined him in the 1980s supergroup, the Highwaymen. He featured bands like the Who on his 1970s TV show. Cash's love for music in all its diversity contributed to his final renaissance during the late 1990s, when he recorded the songs of Beck, Neil Diamond, and U2. His version of Nine Inch Nails' "Hurt" became his last testament when he died at age seventy-one. In a voice that bore decades of scarring, he sang, "I focus on the pain/The only thing that's real."

Lyrics and music
Who sang what?

Little Richard, “Tutti Frutti”

David Bowie, “Ziggy Stardust”

Fred Astaire and Ginger Rogers,
“Cheek to Cheek”

The Beatles, “A Day in the Life”

Stevie Wonder,
“I Just Called to Say I Love You”

Chet Baker, “Let’s Get Lost”

Guns N’ Roses, “Sweet Child O’ Mine”

Madonna, “Material Girl”

Judy Garland, “Somewhere over
the Rainbow.”

David Bowie, “Heroes”

Classical Mavericks

- PIERRE BOULEZ, JOHN CAGE, ARNOLD SCHOENBERG, KARLHEINZ STOCKHAUSEN...
- INTERNATIONAL
- 1900S–

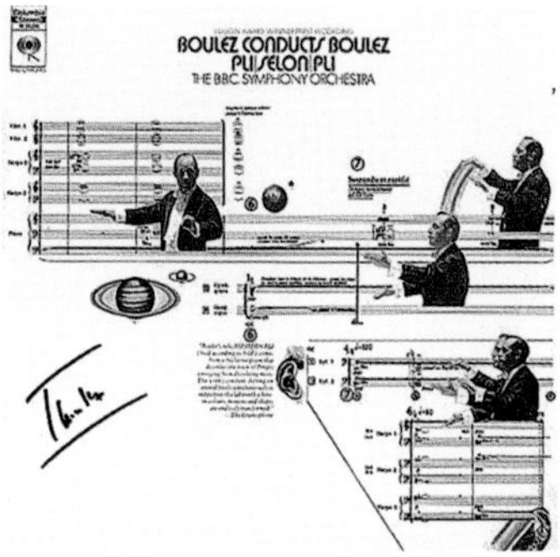

Composer Pierre Boulez and his music. Cover of *Pli Selon Pli* (1957–1962). Version produced with the BBC Symphony Orchestra.

Right:
(top)
Portrait of the composer Karlheinz Stockhausen, 1971.

(bottom)
John Cage, composing in 1949.

With the birth of the twentieth century, the music landscape changed radically. Music, which had traditionally been about creating beauty, suddenly became "difficult" and lost its popularity. Igor Stravinsky and Aaron Copland broke new ground and opened doors for new experiments. Arnold Schoenberg, a pioneer, declared, "If I have to commit musical suicide, I might as well make the best of it."

Schoenberg hated the word "atonality" and said he was only looking for different tonalities. He shunned the major and minor chords heard in popular music in favor of the twelve-tone chromatic scale. Without a home key, each chord was as equally important as the other. His twelve-tone system required the composer to select "twelve tones which are related only with one another." The tones were put in a sequenced "tone row," and each had to be played once before they could be repeated. Despite this systematic restriction, the music Schoenberg wrote was more traditional than expected. To the untrained ear, the atonal piano pieces might sound like a ball bouncing along the keys. He instructed his confused public to try to hear "colors, smells, lights, sounds, movements, glances, and gestures" in the music and, if one listens closely—and has a keen imagination—they are indeed there, waiting to be discovered. Schoenberg was keenly studied by the German Karlheinz Stockhausen and his French comrade Pierre Boulez. Wielding a venomous pen, Boulez dismissed his teacher Messiaen's "brothel music" and branded anyone who ignored Schoenberg as "useless." Stockhausen eventually broke with Schoenberg's "serialism" and with tradition—his *Gruppen* (1956), for example, needed three orchestras

to perform it. Other pieces like *Gesang der Jünglinge* (1955–1956) didn't even need instruments, just a tape recorder and studio know-how. Soon, Stockhausen was playing with the tension between musician and instrument, instrument and technology, and fragments and the whole piece. *Zyklus* (1959) allowed the soloist, surrounded by an array of instruments, to start from any part of the spiral notebook in which the score was written.

If Stockhausen enjoyed antagonistic musical tensions, his American comrade John Cage—another Schoenberg student—was inspired by the *I Ching* to let chance guide his work. His most famous "compositions" are nothing of the sort. The "music" in *Imaginary Landscape No. 4* (1951) is whatever is broadcast by twelve radios during the performance's duration. Even more radical was *4'33"* (1952) whose three movements are performed without playing a single note. Instead, any number of performers sit still for the time specified in the title. The "non-performance" consists of the surrounding ambient noise. If Schoenberg suggested music could only be made with certain elements, Cage trumped him. Music, he suggested, comes from everywhere.

What did the crowd throw at Iggy Pop during the last Stooges concert in 1973?

Glenn Gould

• *GOLDBERG VARIATIONS* (SONY RELEASE, 1990), *BACH: CONCERTOS FOR ORCHESTRAS NOS. 1–5, 7* (SONY RELEASE, 1992), *THE GLENN GOULD EDITION—BACH: THE WELL-TEMPERED CLAVIER, BOOK 1* (SONY RELEASE, 1994)...
• 1932–1982
VLADIMIR FELTSMAN, MURRAY PERAHIA, ANDRÁS SCHIFF

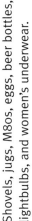

! Shovels, jugs, M80s, eggs, beer bottles, lightbulbs, and women's underwear.

Canadian pianist Glenn Gould represented a revolution in playing and brought classical music to a new audience. When this supreme interpreter of J.S. Bach declared at age thirty-one that he was retiring from the stage, he had already altered the way musicians, musical performances, and recording practices were seen by aficionados. He became a star with his 1955 debut, a recording of J.S. Bach's then-obscure *Goldberg Variations,* though he was also made famous by his unusual playing style. He didn't so much hit the keys as pull them down, sitting low in the seat to give his fingers greater freedom of movement. Sometimes his eyes were level with the keyboard. It was an incredibly precise way of playing, and Gould's technical flair showed in the brisk tempos with which he attacked the work. He didn't knock the stuffing out of the piece as Romantic pianists did. Instead, he treated each note as an atom that formed a greater whole. He gloried in Bach's innovative counterpoint, and the world heard the Baroque god with new ears.

The spotlight fell on a very odd pianist, and hipsters and jazz musicians loved him for his eccentric manner. Gould was a hypochondriac who wore mufflers and mittens even in the height of summer, and hummed as he played. Sprawled over a piano lid, he once delivered a lecture he later explained was really an art "happening." Gould didn't shy from slamming composers like Schubert and Fauré (whose work he considered "junk"), although his way with the pantonal Arnold Schoenberg delighted audiences when he toured the Soviet Union.

He likened the concert hall to the Roman Coliseum, and described the studio as letting him "make music in a more direct, more personal manner." He recorded without preconceptions and let his imagination go wild as he ran through piece after piece. Believing Bach's music could be approached like a collage of parts and tempos, he spliced dozens of recorded takes into a single performance. Toward the end of his life, he revisited the

Goldberg Variations, playing the opening theme nearly twice as slow as the 1955 version. Critics cried foul, but he theorized about releasing different recordings and letting the listener assemble from those the ultimate version. Although Gould's attention in his seclusion turned toward making contrapuntal radio documentaries of overlapping voices and late-night phone calls to his friends, he never stopped thinking about music. He couldn't. Gould had made the performer as much a part of the piece as the composer.

Glenn Gould: composer, performer, and iconoclast, 1955.

Frank Sinatra

• *SONGS FOR SWINGIN' LOVERS* (1955), *COME FLY WITH ME* (1957), *ONLY THE LONELY* (1958), *NICE'N'EASY* (1960), *SEPTEMBER OF MY YEARS* (1965)...
• 1915–1998
PAUL ANKA, TONY BENNETT, JAMIE CULLUM, BOBBY DARIN, NEIL SEDAKA, SCOTT WALKER

Poster for Tim Whelan's *Higher and Higher* (1943), starring Frank Sinatra, Barbara Hale, and Michèle Morgan.

Right:
Frank Sinatra singing "As Time Goes By" in the early 1940s.

One of Frank Sinatra's greatest hits was "The Song Is You." This crooner from New Jersey, however, could make any song his. He performed a tune like Marlon Brando recited Shakespeare. Graduating from teen idol to "saloon singer," Sinatra immortalized the American standard, defined an era of cool with his ring-a-ding style, and helped invent the modern album along the way.

Francis Albert Sinatra started as a band singer, delighting his bobbysoxer fans with his way of caressing the microphone, pulling it close to his lips when he sang. Though he constantly strived to perfect his form, by 1952, he had no record, film, or radio contract and the press noted that The Voice had cracked into The Gargle. Sinatra was washed up—a rising star no more. Sinatra's new label, Capitol, paired him with Nelson Riddle. The trombonist-turned-arranger who loved Debussy and Ravel became a key figure in Sinatra's comeback. The duo began to reinvent old standards on a series of groundbreaking albums. Instead of being a random collection of hit songs, each disc pursued a self-contained theme. The crooner grew into an interpreter. His voice resonated with a whisky-rich bass. Having won an Oscar for Fred Zinnemann's *From Here to Eternity* (1953), he turned songs into monologues, bouncing notes around or letting them take off to create strong emotional effect. Riddle provided perfect accompaniments. He held back when Sinatra let loose, emphasized dramatic moments, and made Porter, Gershwin, and Rodgers sound up-to-the-minute.

From the mid-1950s to the 1960s, Sinatra alternated dance-oriented albums like *Songs for Swingin' Lovers!* (1955) with introspective material. *Only the Lonely* (1958) introduced the signature song, "One for My Baby (And One More for the Road)," with Sinatra—who pursued a doomed relationship with actress Ava Gardner—wallowing in the quarter-to-three mood.

As rock 'n' roll threatened to make him redundant, Sinatra goofed off with his Rat Pack and made albums with diverse partners like jazz giant Count Basie and Brazilian songwriter Antonio Carlos Jobim. In 1965, he released *September of My Years.* His voice was the most recognizable in the world and his life so well known that a song like "My Way" needed no justification. Even when he recorded a series of duets with young fans like U2's Bono, the Chairman of the Board's legend loomed over all. He was buried with a bottle of whisky, a packet of Camels, a lighter, and a roll of dimes.

?

Who said "We're more popular than Jesus now?"

Miles Davis

• *BIRTH OF THE COOL* (1949), *KIND OF BLUE* (1959), *IN A SILENT WAY* (1969), *BITCHES BREW* (1969)...
• 1926–1991
CHET BAKER, JOHN COLTRANE, CHICK COREA, BILL EVANS, HERBIE HANCOCK, JIMI HENDRIX, JIMMY OWENS, SANTANA, SLY AND THE FAMILY STONE

! The Beatles' John Lennon in *The Evening Standard* (1966).

Miles Davis was like a shark. The American trumpeter could never stay still or play in a manner that conformed to audiences' expectations. He cruised jazz's shoals, moving from virtuosic bop to laidback "cool" to jazz-rock fusion via the modal jazz of his masterpiece, *Kind of Blue* (1959). And he could be as lyrical or funky as he needed to be.

The young St. Louis musician learned at the feet of the greats. In 1944, he sat in with saxophonist Charlie Parker and trumpeter Dizzy Gillespie. Both were beginning to play fast and fluid solos based on chords, not melodies. Davis would absorb this new style, known as "bop" or "bebop," when he moved to New York to play with Parker.

The first band he set up on his own was an unusual nine-piece: trumpet, alto sax, baritone sax, trombone, French horn, tuba, piano, bass, and drums. The nonet recorded twelve tracks in 1949 that, when they were released in 1957, would become known as the *Birth of the Cool*. Using musical arrangements from Gil Evans, Davis gave bop a softer tone. Tunes like "Boplicity" had their own warm laid-back aloofness.

After shaking a heroin addiction that drove him to pimping, Davis began playing with a harmon mute, which gave his trumpet the smoky after-hours tone that would be his career's one constant. In 1955, he assembled a group that included John Coltrane on sax. The group gave Davis freedom to play extended slurred passages, and freedom was what he needed.

Kind of Blue married simple blues pieces to impulsive solos that continue to delight with each fresh listen. The quintet of Davis, Coltrane, pianist Wynton Kelly, bassist Paul Chambers, and light-fingered drummer Jimmy Cobb improvised around modal structures—leaving bop's reliance on chords behind. The album became ubiquitous in cafés and "best of" lists alike.

In the late 1960s, Davis's new quintet—now including pianist Herbie Hancock and bassist Ron Carter—began using electric

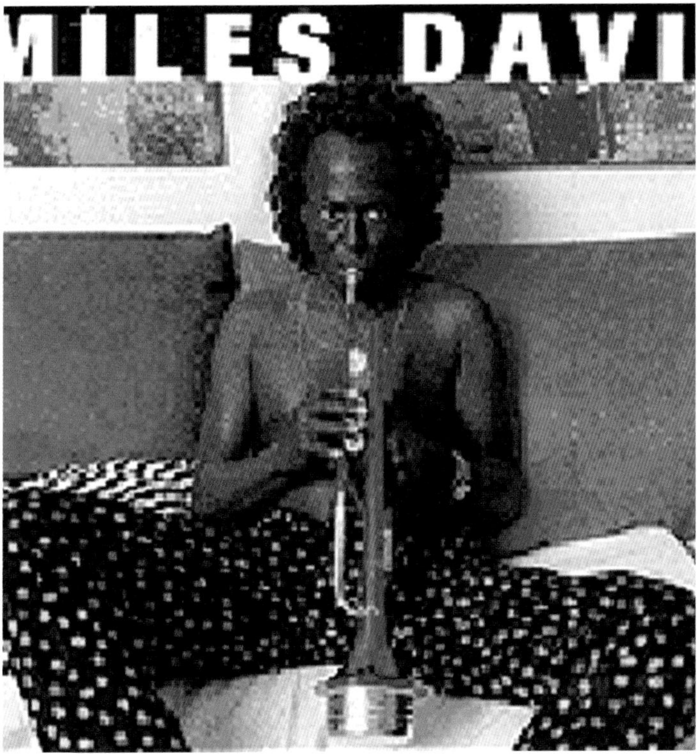

Cover of the Miles Davis album *Doo-Bop* (1991), released posthumously.

instruments. Davis's *In a Silent Way* and *Bitches Brew* (both 1969) created pieces stitched together from hours of studio performances that combined jazz and rock. Davis began to use a wah-wah pedal on his trumpet. Sometimes he would only play organ. Jazz "heads" were confounded as he became more extreme. To fans of guitarist Jimi Hendrix and funkateer Sly Stone, the forty-six-year-old Davis was the hippest thing around.

When he came out of retirement in 1981, Davis astounded again.

He began to treat pop hits like Cyndi Lauper's "Time After Time" with the reverence of "Someday My Prince Will Come." He even became nostalgic, performing some of Gil Evans's arrangements at a 1991 Montreux appearance. By the time of his death, he was experimenting with jazz.

Who Doesn't Fit In?

Who never sang for a James Bond movie?

Answer

The correct answer is Sting.
Shirley Bassey was on the soundtrack for Lewis Gilbert's *Moonraker* (1979).
a-ha was on the soundtrack for John Glen's *License to Kill* (1989).
Dionne Warwick was on the soundtrack for Shane Black's *Kiss Kiss, Bang Bang* (2005).
Paul McCartney was on the soundtrack for Guy Hamilton's *Live and Let Die* (1973).
Paul McCartney, with the Wings, was on the soundtrack for Guy Hamilton's *Live and Let Die* (1973).

Shirley Bassey

Sting

A-Ha

Dionne Warwick

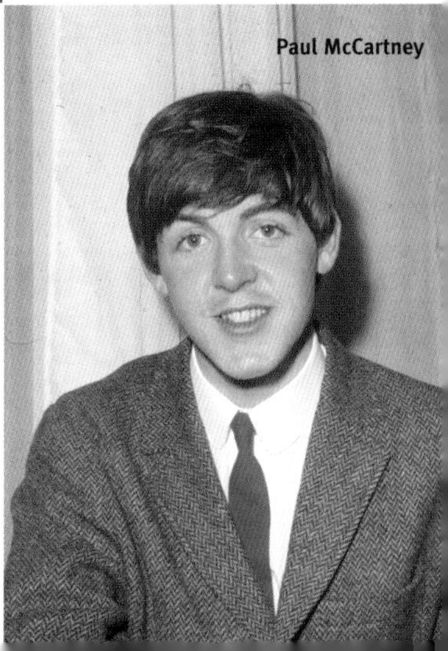
Paul McCartney

James Brown

• *LIVE AT THE APOLLO* (1963), *COLD SWEAT* (1967), *LIVE AT THE APOLLO* (1968), *SEX MACHINE* (1970), *THE PAYBACK* (1973), *HELL* (1974)...
• 1933
BEASTIE BOYS, GEORGE CLINTON, THE ISLEY BROTHERS, MICHAEL JACKSON, THE METERS, THE NEPTUNES, PARLIAMENT, PRINCE, SLY AND THE FAMILY STONE

James Brown on stage (c. 1970).

Right:
James Brown in 1973.

Musicians have long used the term "funk" to describe a hard-driving groove they associate with making love. James Brown built a whole sound from it—of back-and-forth vocals delivered with a sermon's intensity and rhythms whose clipped guitars, tense drums, and deep bass make you move your feet. It earned him the deserved title of Soul Brother Number One.

The funky sound—first heard on 1964's "Out of Sight"—was a long time in the making. Brown was an ex-boxer from Georgia who preferred music to getting clobbered. His first hit was 1956's "Please Please Please," a fraught ballad that is still in his repertoire. He led his group, the Famous Flames, on an endless tour of the American South's "chitlin" circuit. Brown, ever the performer, wowed audiences with his screaming vocals and manic dancing. The energy of these full-tilt routines were captured on his first hit album *Live at the Apollo* (1963).

"Out of Sight" and its follow-ups "Papa's Got a Brand New Bag," and "I Got You (I Feel Good)" arrived after years of honing the interplay

between the star vocalist and his well-drilled bands. Brown whooped, grunted, or chanted the title slogans over sleek grooves and horns that blasted jazzy riffs. The sound transformed soul the same way the Beatles altered pop. Brown became an African-American figurehead. When Martin Luther King, Jr. was assassinated on November 4, 1968, the so-called "Funky President" walked the streets calming the rioters before cutting the Black Power anthem, "Say It Loud, I'm Black and I'm Proud."

Brown was already recording longer, rawer tracks like "Cold Sweat," and the defection of his band in 1969 couldn't stop him. With new recruits Bootsy and Catfish Collins playing liquid bass lines and spiky guitar chops, he toughened his sound further on singles like "Get Up (I Feel Like Being a) Sex Machine."

The brothers Bootsy and Collins left to join Parliament and Funkadelic, bands that explored the freakier end of funk's spectrum. Brown faltered as disco took over and the punishing schedule of over three hundred shows a year caught up with The Hardest Working Man in Show Business.

Mr. Dynamite spent time in jail after leading police on an interstate car chase, but his reputation was rescued by hip-hop, where MCs rapped over Brown jams like "The Payback" and "Funky Drummer." A new generation of fans discovered Brown, who is probably playing somewhere right now. Well into his sixth decade of making music, he's still getting on the good foot.

?

What was Elvis Presley's favorite sandwich?

Soul

• ERYKAH BADU, RAY CHARLES, SAM COOKE, D'ANGELO, ARETHA FRANKLIN, MARVIN GAYE, OTIS REDDING, USHER, STEVIE WONDER...
• UNITED STATES
• 1950S–

Soul is an African-American style of music that takes the full-throated sound of gospel and applies it to secular songs. Born out of R&B in the 1950s, it was popularized through the Motown label's stream of teen-friendly hits and a Southern variant that wallowed in very adult heartbreak. The divide prevails today. An uneasy truce exists between pop idols like Usher and inventive "neo-soul" artists, who sample old grooves and embrace wild flights of poetic fancy over an album's length. R&B was the more acceptable name given to "race music" in the late 1940s. It was a swinging African-American music played by small saxophone-led combos schooled in jazz and blues. Both Sam Cooke and Ray Charles freely mixed gospel melodies and vocal stylizations with their R&B repertoire. This combination of the Saturday night sound of R&B with Sunday morning's religious fervor became soul music. Borrowing from gospel's tradition of personal testimony, soul is like an earthier version of opera. It's all about the voice. A singer might croon like Smokey Robinson or shout like James Brown. The investment in the song can lead singers to flutter around the scale, embellishing each note with acrobatic trills. Sixties singers like Otis Redding and

! Peanut butter and banana.

Aretha Franklin didn't need to show off. Their vocal grit told the whole story.

Those voices explored every cranny of the heart, from love's first bloom to sex, cheating, despair, and heartache. Whatever the feeling, soul artists made listeners feel it, too. Soul was a sympathetic kind of music; the singers experienced joy and pain as intensely as their audience did. Soul marched with the Civil Rights Movement, too. Curtis Mayfield wrote anthems like "People Get Ready," then recorded *Superfly* (1972), a harrowing analysis of ghetto life. But no matter how deep it became, soul never forgot the rhythm. This was protest music you could dance to.

The more articulate it became, the more things soul had to say. In the 1970s, it went from being a singles to an album medium. Motown star Marvin Gaye's *What's Going On* (1971) was a sequenced lament about the state of the world that inspired scores of imitators, including tours de force from Sly Stone and Prince. Other singers preferred to use the album format to create a soundtrack to an evening's lovemaking. Again, Gaye led the pack with the self-explanatory *Let's Get It On* (1973).

Soul was a broad sonic church. Detroit's Motown was a slick pop-soul plant. Memphis's Stax label left in the raw and funky edges. In the late 1960s, Stevie Wonder began experimenting with synthesizers,

whose contemporary sound became the perfect setting for the sexless falsettos of 1980s stars Michael and Janet Jackson. Hip-hop had its impact, too. Now soul songs are as likely to feature samples and a guest rapper on the bridge as a hip-hop tune is to have a chorus sung by a visiting R&B artist.

(top)
Ray Charles next to his piano, 1956.

(below)
Aretha Franklin during an interview, 1968.

Left:
Soul greats illustrated by Guy Peellaert (in 1973). From left to right: Isaac Hayes, Curtis Mayfield, Richie Havens, Roberta Flack, Sylvester Stewart, Taj Mahal, and Marvin Gaye. Jimi Hendrix can be seen in back.

Free Jazz

• ALBERT AYLER, PETER BRÖTZMANN, ORNETTE COLEMAN, JOHN COLTRANE, SUN RA, CECIL TAYLOR DEREK TAYLOR...
• INTERNATIONAL
• 1950S–

Cover of *Free Jazz* (1961), the album of the quartet formed by Ornette Coleman, Don Cherry, Scott LaFaro, and Billy Higgins.

Right:
John Coltrane at Concertgebouw in Amsterdam. October 26, 1963.

Free jazz was jazz's ultimate break from convention. In the past, soloists observed certain rules—they played a melody or followed the song's chord structures. In free jazz, the only framework a performance might have was the predetermined order in which soloists would play, following hand signals given by an ensemble leader. It was a recipe for pure noise that allowed the instrumentalists to hold musical conversations with one another, exchanging freshly coined ideas and themes. Pianist Lennie Tristano recorded pieces without prearranged melodies, harmonies, or rhythms in 1949. Cecil Taylor played a form of free jazz in the 1950s, precisely hitting his piano like he was

playing a drum kit. But it was saxophonist Ornette Coleman's album *Free Jazz (A Collective Improvisation)* (1961) that gave the genre its name. The first extended free improvisation LP was two sides of spontaneity.

Free jazz let soloists express their true personalities through unfettered playing, although it could sometimes feel like long-winded "over-blowing." Bassist Charles Mingus would hum a tune to his players and let them interpret the melodies in their own way—although God help the musician who played something the short-tempered genius didn't want to hear. John Coltrane seized on "The New Thing" in his search for musical transcendence. His *Giant Steps* (1959) privileged the instrumental solo over ensemble work and his saxophone's so-called "sheets of sound" became much more free with each subsequent recording.

Audiences were wary of what critics called "energy music," but its commitment to musical liberty reflected the Civil Rights struggle in America during the 1960s. The lack of rules meant its followers could do whatever they liked with it, too. Bandleader Sun Ra even claimed to have written "free jazz" compositions for his Arkestra that were more impulsive than anything the free jazzers could make up on the spot.

Musicians in other genres also embraced free jazz. Sixties rock bands like the MC5 and Velvet Underground covered Sun Ra's pieces and played their guitars as if they were in one of Coleman's anarchic ensembles. The genre's lawlessness has attracted as many fakers as masters, but the furthest end of the musical spectrum is still marked "free jazz."

By 2005, how many songs did the record industry estimate were illegally downloaded per year?

French Songs

• BARBARA, GILBERT BÉCAUD, GEORGES BRASSENS, JACQUES BREL, JACQUES DUTRONC, EDDY MITCHELL, LÉO FERRÉ, SERGE GAINSBOURG, JUIETTE GRÉCO, JOHNNY HALLYDAY, CLAUDE LANZMANN, GEORGE MOUSTAKI, EDITH PIAF, MICHEL POLNAREFF, SERGE REGGIANI, CHARLES TRENET...
• FRANCE
• 1930S–

Although the category is general and wide, French *chanson* does stand apart from popular English and American music in that it pays special attention to lyrics.
Although it dates back to Chrétien de Troyes, the first known French *trouvère,* French chanson grew popular in the period between the world wars. Music hall artists like Maurice Chevalier, Charles Trenet, and, of course, Edith Piaf, are now known worldwide.
After World War II, Paris's Saint-Germain-des-Prés neighborhood bustled with young, free-spirited music lovers. They filled smoky basement lounges where "Rive Gauche chanson" reigned.
Juliette Gréco, an icon of the times, sang lyrics by Sartre and Queneau, while Boris Vian was both suavely nonchalant with "J'suis Snob" and political with "Le Déserteur."
Reaching a wider audience, Gilbert Bécaud, aka "Monsieur 100,000 volts," electrified the Olympia theater in 1954. By the end of the exciting concert, chairs were broken and some women were on the verge of fainting. For Charles Aznavour, however, the road to success was longer. His scrawny build and husky voice was mocked at first. But later, he enjoyed international fame, which culminated in his 1958 concert at New York's Carnegie Hall.
In the 1960s, the huge success of English and American pop spawned *yé-yé* in France. Meant for teenagers, the genre is often considered silly, but there were a few mavericks who became lasting influences. Aside from the inescapable Serge Gainsbourg,

! 28 billion.

Jacques Dutronc and his partner, Claude Lanzmann, developed a kind of rock that had both a French style and was sarcastic. Michel Polnareff, an exceptional songwriter, wrote elaborate masterpieces like "Le Bal des laze" and tearjerkers like "Tous les bateaux, tous les oiseaux." He went on to become a Swinging London icon.

At the opposite end of pop, there's the more traditional vein of French *chanson*, which comes out of cabaret. It's a genre that outlives trend, but is ruled over by a holy triumvirate: George Brassens, Jacques Brel, and Léo Ferré. Brassens mocked conformity in all its forms with his clean guitar, clear voice, and gruff but tender songs. Ferré was a poet and Debussy lover. Brel in theatrical, misogynistic splutter could sing the likes of "Amsterdam," but could also produce heart-wrenching gems like "Le plat pays" and "Je suis un soir d'été." In their wake, Serge Reggiani and George Moustaki had repertoires that were both tender and cheeky. Jean Ferrat advocated revolution with his song "Potemkine," Claude Nougaro combined swing with playful language, and Barbara showed vulnerability at the piano. The 1970s sparkled. Pioneer rock stars Johnny Hallyday and Eddy Mitchell had taken hold of France and the best of the best

could be heard on Maritie and Gilbert Carpentier's television show. Claude François and Dalida topped the charts and both turned to disco. Other major figures included Michel Sardou, who cried out "Le France" and "Je suis pour." Joe Dassin, certainly the most endearing of the group, dreamed aloud of America and was successful abroad as well.

In this context, there were some singers who were like a breath of

(top)
Eddie Barclay with two of his stars, Charles Aznavour and Jacques Brel. January 25, 1965.

(bottom)
Cover of a 1964 Juliette Gréco single (released by Trianon).

Left:
French singer Georges Brassens on stage in Paris, 1960.

French Songs

The former top-model Carla Bruni is now a big name in contemporary French music. She's seen here with her guitar, 2002.

Right:
Michel Berger in concert, April 1986.

fresh air; they include Jacques Higelin, the energetic and wild singer, known for "Pars"; William Sheller, the unique performer with classical training, known for "Symphoman"; Renaud, who sang about urban life and social revolt with songs like "Laisse béton"; Alain Bashung, the king of alliteration and songs with complex lyrics like "Gaby, oh Gaby"; and the frenetic, energetic rock group Téléphone, known for "La Bombe Humaine." Alain Souchon and Laurent Voulzy were also among the top talent. Souchon was a fragile and shy eternal teenager, who wrote unforgettable lyrics, and Voulzy was a fine composer/arranger, who was heavily influenced by the Beach Boys. They proved once again that a song can be both popular and good.

The 1980s were ruled by Jean-Jacques Goldman. Fans loved him whether he was singing himself or composing for others; "Laura," one of his songs, was made popular by Johnny Hallyday in 1985. In the same vein inspired by California rock, there was also the more delicate Michel Berge. A Pygmalion and partner of France Gall, this duo enjoyed great success starting in the 1970s. But Berge, a

French version of Elton John, had to wait ten years before having a hit as a singer with the song "La groupie du pianiste."

During the same period, the short-lived punk movement would leave a lasting impression on both Etienne Daho, the elegant face of a French new wave, and emerging alternative rock (with bands like Les Béruriers Noirs, La Mano Negra, Les Wampas, and Les Rita Mitsouko). Noir Désir, who also carried on the rebel spirit, delighted audiences with *Veuillez rendre l'ame à qui elle appartient*. Combining the subtleties of the French language with a dark and powerful rock, this group was hugely popular. At the dawn of the 1990s, Patrick Bruel got it all right with "Casser la voix." Then came the bellowing voices of a string of slightly indistinguishable female singers, like Patricia Kaas and Lara Fabian. Dominique A, Autour de Lucie, and Jean-Louis Murat preferred a more simple approach and opened the way for a generation of singers to come, like Louise Attaque.

The early years of the new century were marked by new blood on the scene, a plethora of thirty-something music talent. Wanting to do more than just make sophisticated concept albums (*Rose Kennedy* in 2001 and *Négatif* in 2003), Benjamin Biolay also enjoyed writing for Henri Salvador, Juliette

Gréco, and Françoise Hardy; M. played the pop-rock-funk card with *Je dis aime* (2001); Sanseverino drew inspiration from gypsy jazz with *Le Tango des gens* (2001); Vincent Delerm opted for simple piano and was able to say it all in a few words with *Vincent Delerm* (2003); and the very Michel Houellebecq-like Philippe Katerine bared his heart with his quirky lyrics in *Robots après tout* (2005). Women weren't far behind. Prolific Keren Ann's *La Disparition* (2002) and model-turned-musican Carla Bruni's *Quelqu' un m' a dit* (2002) brought an intimate folk style to the scene. Whether singing about past love, fleeting time, or the charms of a misty café window, the French chansons' futures are secured. At the risk of contradicting the great Juliette Gréco, there is life after Saint-Germain-des-Prés.

Who did Stevie Wonder write his song "Isn't She Lovely" for?

Elvis Presley

• *ELVIS* (1956), *ELVIS PRESLEY* (1956), *FOR LP FANS ONLY* (1959), *ELVIS IS BACK!* (1960), *FROM ELVIS IN MEMPHIS* (1969), *THAT'S THE WAY IT IS* (1970)...
• 1935–1977
THE BEATLES, EDDIE COCHRAN, BOB DYLAN, BUDDY HOLLY, CHRIS ISAAK, WANDA JACKSON, LED ZEPPELIN, JERRY LEE LEWIS, RICKY NELSON, CARL PERKINS

! His infant daughter Aisha Zakia. You can hear her gurgling on the track.

Elvis Presley is the king of rock'n' roll and no one has ever dared dispute the title. Historians date the music's birth from the 1954 summer night in Memphis's Sun studios when he, guitarist Scotty Moore, and bassist Bill Black began messing around with an Arthur Crudup song called "That's All Right, Mama." Presley had been trying to record something all day but couldn't nail it. Now he gave the song a laid-back, sexy touch. The band vamped behind him with a distinctive shuffle that would take

over the world. Sun Studios manager Sam Phillips once said if he could find a white man who sang with a black feel, he'd make a million dollars. The boy from Tupelo, Mississippi, was that man, but he achieved so much more. Bob Dylan said, "Hearing him for the first time was like busting out of jail." His sneering voice and hip Beale Street style was in sync with a young generation who wanted more than the Frigidaire conformity of the 1950s. Presley mapped their future, rattling cell doors with "Jailhouse Rock" and pointing the way to the desolate flophouse at the end of lonely street, "Heartbreak Hotel." Presley shook America like an atom bomb. Television cameras only shot him from the waist up when he performed. What was going on below the belt-line—a pelvic shimmy that drove girls as wild as his lascivious voice with the sneering lip—was truly dangerous. Other TV shows tried to dress him in tuxedos. There was something about this hillbilly

dandy with the black feel that needed taming.

Presley's fortunes mirrored that of the music. His conniving manager Col. Tom Parker packed him off to the army, where they shaved his hair. When Presley came back, he went to Hollywood and appeared in a series of awful movie vehicles, somehow turning the soundtrack dross into hits. The Beatles eclipsed him, and Presley narrowly avoided becoming a total anachronism with a 1969 TV "comeback" special. Dressed in black leather and purring "Guitar Man" and "One Night," he was dangerous all over again.

It was a long fade. The resurrected Presley was interred in Las Vegas and turned into a bloated caricature of himself. He sang bizarre medleys, the gospel he grew up on, bombastic supper club material, and made the occasional good song like "Suspicious Minds." His worshippers could never let Presley surrender the throne. Even after death his kingdom lives on.

Elvis and the apostles of rock as seen by Guy Peellaert in 1974. From left to right: Vince Taylor, Tommy Steele, P.J. Proby, Billy Fury, Tommy Sands, Rick Nelson, Elvis Presley, Tom Jones, Eddie Cochran, Terry Dene, Ritchie Valens, Fabian, and Cliff Richard.

Left:
Elvis Presley at NBC studios, 1969.

THE MUSIC PAGES

GOSSIP AND SCANDAL

Savage Slur! Josephine Baker has returned to Paris after a disastrous tour of the United States. Calling her "a St. Louis washer-woman's daughter," the *New York Times* sniffed, "In sex appeal to jaded Europeans, a Negro wench always has a head start." (1936)

• **Straight Talk with Igor Stravinsky!**
On Pierre Boulez's *Pli Sélon Pli*: "Pretty monotonous and monotonously pretty."
On Maurice Ravel: "The most perfect of Swiss clockmakers."
On Olivier Messiaen's *Turangalîla-Symphonie*: "Little more can be required to write such things than a plentiful supply of ink."
On Heitor Villa-Lobos: "Why is it that whenever I hear a piece of music I don't like, it's always by Villa-Lobos?"
On Franz Liszt: "The tone poems can survive only by constantly renewed neglect."
(M.D. Calvocoressi, *"Musicians Gallery: Music and Ballet in Paris and London,"* Faber & Faber Publisher, 1933.)

• **Censure!**
The Central Committee of the Communist Party has charged Dimitri Shostakovich and Sergei Prokofiev with encouraging "formalist distortions and

anti-democratic tendencies" in their music. (1948)

• **Gold Record**
Frank Sinatra received a gold record for "All or Nothing at All." The title reached No. 2 on the charts. The song had previously failed in 1939, selling only eight thousand copies. (1943)

• **Obituaries**
"The Empress of the Blues" Bessie Smith has died aged forty-one after a car wreck in Mississippi. She bled to death after being sent her to a "blacks only" hospital miles away. Her white manager survived after treatment at a nearby hospital. (1937)

CURRENT EVENTS AND NEWS IN BRIEF

• A Sensitive Note

Pablo Casals, one of the best performers of the century, brilliantly played J. S. Bach's cello suites at a French classical music festival. Afterward, he plunged back into self-imposed silence and exile. The strike continued until Spain was liberated from the Franco dictatorship. (*Flair*, 1950)

• Modesty

Settling in the United States at the end of his life, Arnold Schoenberg—pioneer and inventor of contemporary music—said the following to an admiring student, "I'm not a teacher, we're doctors and teachers as much as we are nothing." (1940)

• Dining with Duke

Duke Ellington's appetite is legendary. One reporter recorded a breakfast in which he ate two steaks, two helpings of fried potatoes, a salad, a bowl of tomatoes, a lobster, and coffee, followed by a dessert of pie, ice cream, Jell-O, and cheese, topped by pancakes, waffles, syrup, and biscuits. One band member recalled he once ate thirty-two sandwiches between sets. (1944)

• Come out Swinging! Celebrated band leader and clarinetist Benny Goodman thrashed drummer Chick Webb at "the music battle of the century." Over twenty thousand people crowded Harlem's Savoy Ballroom to witness the King of Swing triumph in the battle of the bands. (1937)

The Birth of Rock 'n' Roll

• CHUCK BERRY, BILL HALEY AND HIS COMETS, EDDIE COCHRAN, BO DIDDLEY, FATS DOMINO, BUDDY HOLLY, JERRY LEE LEWIS, LITTLE RICHARD, ELVIS PRESLEY, IKE AND TINA TURNER, GENE VINCENT...
• UNITED STATES
• 1950S

The rock 'n' roll era officially began in 1955 when Bill Haley & His Comets topped the American chart with "Rock Around the Clock." It's the quintessential rock 'n' roll single: an insanely catchy three-chord song with a strong backbeat. Teenagers who went to see *Blackboard Jungle,* the movie in which the song was featured, got so excited that they rioted and tore up the seats. Rock 'n' roll was meant to have that aura of danger. The term, coined by DJ Alan "Moondog" Freed to refer to the music that drove his listeners crazy, was actually a euphemism for having sex. Black R&B artists had been "rocking" for years. Ike Turner, who would later become notorious as Tina's abusive husband, recorded "Rocket 88," arguably the first rock 'n' roll single, in 1951. It was supposedly about a car, but the jiving vocal left no one wondering what kind of fun they were having in the backseat. "Rocket 88" was recorded at Sun Studios, where Elvis Presley's mixed country and the blues to give rock its distinctive backbeat. His massive success in the mid-1950s inspired hordes of imitators. Jerry Lee Lewis may have been the greatest. The pianist sizzled like a Tennessee Williams stud on the souped-up boogie-woogie of "Great Balls of Fire" and "Whole Lotta Shakin' Goin' On." He lived his backwoods existence out loud, too. The discovery that he was married to his teenage cousin nearly derailed his career.

Controversy accompanied rock 'n' roll stars, and moral crusaders tried to stamp out the wildfire Presley ignited. Rock 'n' roll songs always communicated an allegiance to good times and distrust of authority, summed up in Eddie Cochran's "Summertime Blues." Others were simply a

Jerry Lee Lewis in the United States (c. 1950).

Left:
Cover of Rock and Roll, Vol. 1, released by Philips.

How was Buena Vista Social Club's Ibrahim Ferrer making a living before he was rediscovered?

threat because of their rock 'n' roll image. Little Richard was a bisexual black man in gold lamé and a six-inch pompadour who thumped a piano and howled songs like "You Keep a Knockin'" as if he was about to be committed to an asylum.
Gene Vincent wore *The Wild One*-style black leathers, limped around the stage, and oozed hair oil.
Like most rebellions, rock 'n' roll was quickly put down. Little Richard cut "Tutti Frutti," but it was white-bread entertainer Pat Boone who sent it into the charts. Buddy Holly was capable of straddling both worlds—writing and recording rock songs and ballads alike—but died in a plane crash during a stormy winter night. Cochran also died young. Elvis enlisted. Sanitized pin-ups like Fabian took over, but Pandora's box was opened. In Liverpool, four teenagers were listening, writing songs, and waiting to take over the world.

! He worked as a shoe shiner in Havana.

Highschool by Guy Peellaert (1974). From left to right: The Fleetwoods (Barbara Ellis, Gary Troxel, and Gretchen Christopher), Connie Francis, Dirk Clark, Brenda Lee, and The Teddy Bears (Annette Bard, Marshall Leib, and Phil Spector) in front of Buddy Knox; seated: Frankie Lymon, Pat Boone, Paul Anka, Frankie Avalon, Ricky Nelson, Fabian, and Tommy Sands.

Left:
Les Chaussettes Noires on stage at ABC in Paris. November 21, 1961.
Eddy Mitchell, Aldo Martinez, Tony d'Arpa, and Jean-Pierre Chichportich.

The Beach Boys

• *ALL SUMMER LONG* (1964), *SUMMER DAYS (AND SUMMER NIGHTS!!)* (1965), PET SOUNDS (1966), *WILD HONEY* (1967), *FRIENDS* (1968)...
• FORMED IN 1961 AND DISBANDED IN 1996
THE BEATLES, THE BIG THREE, THE BYRDS, DICK DALE, THE HALIFAX THREE, JAN AND DEAN, THE JOURNEYMEN, THE LOVIN' SPOONFUL, THE MAMAS AND THE PAPAS, THE MONKEES, R.E.M., SAINT ETIENNE, THE TURTLES

The Beach Boys were the nearest thing America had to the Beatles. While the Beatles wanted to hold your hand, this Californian vocal quintet imagined a California of sun, surf, and sweethearts. One of leader Brian Wilson's songs even promised "two girls for every boy" on this mythical shore. Wilson's competitive streak made him match the Beatles' achievement song for song, until, in 1966, he made the *Pet Sounds* album —an unsurpassable masterpiece—and retreated into a long fade of mental illness.

Wilson, his brothers Carl and Dennis, cousin Mike Love, and friend Al Jardine didn't invent surf music—in fact, Dennis was the only one who surfed. They were inspired to harmonize together by the success of vocal groups like the Four Freshmen. If Dick Dale's manic guitar instrumentals captured the excitement of hanging ten, their five voices seemed to ebb and flow like the ocean itself.
The ocean terrified Brian Wilson, but he was an unsurpassable pop craftsman who turned Love's lyrics about girls, cars, and girls in cars into

The Beach Boys by Guy Peellaert, 1974.

Right:
Cover of the DVD *The Beach Boys*, a collection of the group's classic hits from 1968 to 1969, including "California Girls."

national anthems. Wilson alternated staccato verses with soaring choruses on songs like "Fun, Fun, Fun," and opened the 1964 chart-topper "I Get Around" with a rousing a cappella fanfare. Churning out up to four albums a year, Wilson hit musical puberty quickly, and the songs developed an anxious undercurrent. "Surfer Girl" is a melancholy ode to an unattainable beach goddess, while "In My Room" forsook the beach entirely. As a stay-at-home producer, Wilson created an overdubbed tidal wave of sound while the brothers toured. He had only one real rival—the Beatles' "Tycoon of Teen" producer Phil Spector—and plenty of acclaim. Critics likened Wilson to Mozart, and on *Pet Sounds*—his retort to the Beatles' *Revolver*—he lived up to the comparison. Opening with the sound of plucked heartstrings, it was a thematically coherent and dizzyingly arranged album Wilson called "a teenage symphony to God." Listen closely and you can hear him shouting at the orchestra and choir in his quest for musical perfection.

Simultaneously, Wilson was putting together the greatest single ever made from ninety hours of tape. Pet Sounds unexpectedly flopped, but the disconnected movements, intricate harmonies, and eerie-sounding theremin of "Good Vibrations" sold a million copies. "Good Vibrations" was but part of Wilson's next anticipated masterpiece, *SMiLE*—an album that would blow the Beatles off the planet.

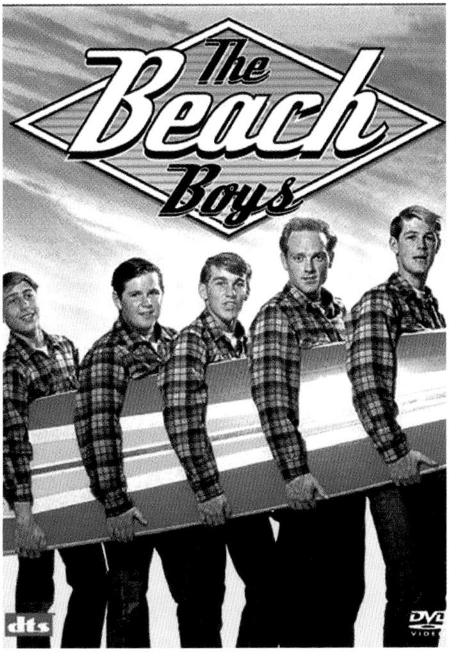

In 1967, he shelved *SMiLE* and, in the ensuing years, it became one of the most legendary unreleased albums of all time.

Drugs and psychosis led Wilson to take a hiatus from the music industry. While he slowly fell from public view, the Beach Boys continued to make music of free-spirited charm. Wilson's contributions to the group were few and far in between, and marred by his mental instability: one song contained directions to Wilson's home. Remarkably, he came 'round to a semblance of sanity. In 2004, *SMiLE* was finally released and, while far from perfect, it was the blissful sound of an America where girls outnumbered boys two to one.

?

Who was the first rap group to sign a commercial endorsement deal?

The Beatles

• *RUBBER SOUL* (1965), *REVOLVER* (1966), *SGT. PEPPER'S LONELY HEARTS CLUB BAND* (1967), *THE BEATLES* [WHITE ALBUM] (1968), *ABBEY ROAD* (1969)
• FORMED IN 1960 AND DISBANDED IN 1970
AIR SUPPLY, THE BEACH BOYS, BLU, THE BYRDS, THE CORAL, BOB DYLAN, FLEETWOOD MAC, DON HENLEY, OASIS, THE ROLLING STONES, THE WHO, THE ZUTONS

The Beatles are the indisputable masters of international popular music. On eleven albums produced over ten years of their existence, John Lennon (guitar, vocals), Paul McCartney (bass guitar and vocals), George Harrison (guitar), and Ringo Starr (drums), moved from being youth idols to being the most inventive musicians of their generation, turning London into the new Eldorado of Pop. The DJ Bob Wooler, followed by Brian Epstein, who became their manager, was the first to take interest in the group when it formed at the Cavern, a Liverpool club. In 1962, their vocal qualities and excellent musical technique put their song "Love Me Do" at the top of the charts. From that point on, Beatlemania raged, and the band became inextricably linked to all aspects of the momentous decade. The exuberant pop guitar of their first albums quickly evolved into foreign sounds and instruments. One song

! Run-D.M.C. Adidas paid the trio $2 million to be their spokesmen.

opened with a nostalgic melody, another introduced a string quartet, and a third called for an Indian sitar. *Revolver* (1966) made use of magnetic tape, while *Sgt. Pepper's Lonely Hearts Club Band* (1967) used the recording studio as its primary musical instrument, playing with unusual distortion and magnification of sounds. But their talent was not limited to music; it was also completely evident in the lyrics of McCartney and Lennon. The former excelled in performance ("Eleanor Rigby") and the expression of intimate emotion ("Yesterday"). Lennon's inspiration was notably more allegorical and anguished ("Lucy in the Sky with Diamonds" and "A Day in the Life").

The meeting between John Lennon, a cynical idealist, and Paul McCartney, an optimist overflowing with imagination, sometimes bears resemblance to a great and tumultuous love story. In the beginning, they equally divided the earnings from their work. But as time went on, a real competition developed between the two. This double-headed eagle, or more precisely, this two-way mirror, is seen explicitly in the singles produced with two Side As, offering, for example, "Strawberry Fields Forever" on one side, and "Penny Lane" on the other. The collage of experimental sounds of one song answers the tender reverie of the other. When Brian Epstein died, the group took refuge in an ashram at the foot of the Himalayas. This experience partly contributed to the group's disintegration. But there are many who believe that it was the enormous influence of Yoko Ono on Lennon which led directly to the breakup of the "Fab Four," despite the recording of a new album, *The Beatles* (1968), followed by *Abbey Road* in 1969. The Beatles' songs remain immortal; they are on the lips of children and are still the envy of their pale imitators around the world. These "little" songs reflect the heritage of jazz, country, soul, blues, and even concert hall classical music. The breakup of the group in 1970, and the assassination of John Lennon in 1980, doubly assured the group's legendary status. The Beatles' music is immortal.

Nothing Is Real by Guy Peellaert (1974). The artwork's title is taken from the refrain of the song "Strawberry Fields Forever."

Left: The police trying to control fans at Buckingham Palace when the Beatles were honored as Members of the British Empire in 1965. Four years later, John Lennon would return the title in protest of England's politics.

Top Models:

What do these models have in common?

Answer

Naomi Campbell, Linda Evangelista, Tatiana Patitz, Christie Turlington, and Cindy Crawford all appeared in George Michael's video for "Freedom 90," a single from his album *Listen without Prejudice, Vol. 1* (1990).

Dance Crazes

• BUNNY HOP, CHICKEN DANCE, ELECTRIC SLIDE, HITCHHIKE, HOKEY POKEY, HULLY GULLY, HUSTLE, JERK, LAMBADA, MACARENA, MADISON, MASHED POTATO, ROBOT, SHAKE, WATUSI, Y.M.C.A...
• INTERNATIONAL
• 1800S–

Personalities from the 1960s, including Jackie Kennedy and Jean Cocteau, dancing the Twist in a popular club. Illustration by Guy Peellaert. (*Twist*, c.1970).

Right:
Illustration depicting the basic steps for the Hustle.

People are constantly on the lookout for trend-setting dance moves, and just as fast as the newest dance craze hits the floor, it's usually replaced by a faster or sexier one. Every generation can claim its own craze—from the slow waltzes of the 1780s to the rockabilly Jitterbug of the 1930s to the Electric Slide of the 1970s. In its heyday during the 1920s and 1930s, swing dancing was dominated by the Charleston—a high-spirited dance in which the heels are kicked outward while the knees are bent—and the Lindy Hop, which danced out of Harlem ballrooms and into a scene in the Marx Brothers' *A Day at the Races* (1937). In the 1950s, movies and TV shows like *American Bandstand* taught kids the high-energy, full-contact jive dances of rock 'n' roll, and made parents hot under the collar.
By far, the biggest craze of the 1960s was the Twist, whose popularity was fed by a stream of hit singles. Chubby Checker's "Let's Twist Again" LP came with an explanation of how to do the dance: "Imagine you are stubbing out

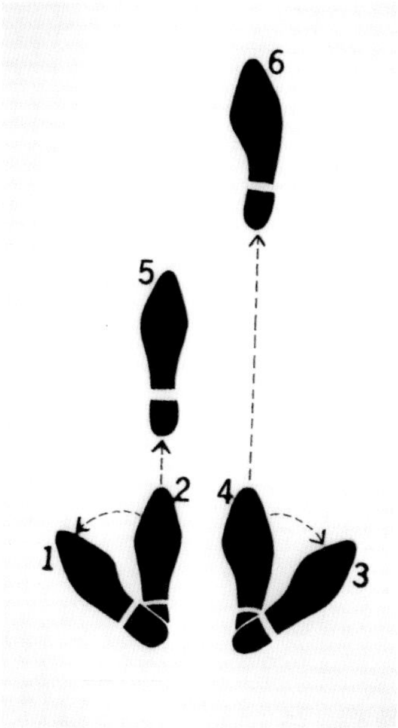

a cigarette with both feet whilst drying your back with a towel." The truly radical thing about the Twist was that both parties didn't have to touch. Mom and dad breathed a collective sigh of relief.

Everyone tried to capitalize on the Twist by inventing the craze that could top it. Heralded by a 45 that issued instructions, these dances were no more complicated than names like the Jerk, the Hitchhike, or the Shake implied. The Watusi almost rivaled the Twist in popularity. According to the Vibrations' "The Watusi," "You slide to the left, then to the right/ Take two steps up and keep it tight."

The disco explosion didn't revive the Watusi, but inspired its own fads. One of the earliest disco singles was called the "Hustle" and it inspired its own moves: the dancer stepped backwards or forwards for the first three beats, and then tapped their feet on the fourth. Discos also made formation line dancing popular. At the wilder dance parties in New York, break dancing combined a variety of sharp movements in a competitive style that became an important element of hip-hop.

Accompanied by hit novelty tunes, the Y.M.C.A and the Macarena achieved brief global popularity during the 1980s and 1990s, and always one to jump on a trend, Madonna's "Vogue" was a No. 1 song that encouraged dancers to "strike a pose." Break dancing fell out of favor, but was reborn as krumping, an energetic style of dance that originated in the African-American community of South Central Los Angeles. Performed in elaborate clown make-up that recalls tribal markings, krumping's freestyle dance moves offer an alternative to the street violence widespread in many of the areas where it is performed. Filmmaker David LaChapelle's documentary *Rize* (2005) offers an intimate portrayal of the clown dancing subculture. He says of the movement, "What Nirvana was to rock 'n' roll of the early 1990s is what these kids are to hip-hip," proving that the movers and shakers influence trends just as much as the musicians do.

Which American No. 1 song has the oldest set of lyrics?

Bob Dylan

• *BRINGING IT ALL BACK HOME* (1965), *HIGHWAY 61 REVISITED* (1965), *BLONDE ON BLONDE* (1966), *BLOOD ON THE TRACKS* (1975), *LOVE & THEFT* (2001)...
• 1941
THE ANIMALS, JOAN BAEZ, THE BAND, THE BEATLES, THE BYRDS, LEONARD COHEN, DIRE STRAITS, GRANT LEE BUFFALO, JIMI HENDRIX, MANFRED MANN, JONI MITCHELL, PAUL SIMON, BRUCE SPRINGSTEEN, TOM WAITS, NEIL YOUNG

! The Byrds' "Turn! Turn! Turn!" The lyrics come from the Book of Ecclesiastes.

Bruce Springsteen once said that "Like a Rolling Stone," a six-minute tempest of fairground organ and contempt "sounded like somebody had kicked open the door to your mind." Dylan's songs did that for anyone who heard them. He was the voice of a generation who changed music through sheer willfulness. He made songs longer. His stream-of-consciousness lyrics made songs stranger. And when the folk singer retired his acoustic guitar for an electric one to make the loudest rock music yet heard, he served notice that anything was possible.

Dylan was the greatest songwriter of his age. His early protest anthems refused to make obvious points about the Cold War, Vietnam, and Civil Rights. He drew on literature and drugs to invent surreal figures like Mr. Tambourine Man and the outcasts of Desolation Row. His songs motivated the Beatles to stop writing boy-meets-girl ditties and start writing about what they were feeling.

The Beatles in turn inspired him to "go electric." Dylan and his new rock band—soon to be called the Band—enraged folk purists in 1965, the summer of "Like a Rolling Stone." If that single kicked open doors, the three albums that followed—*Bringing It All Back Home* (1965), *Highway 61 Revisited* (1965), and *Blonde on Blonde* (1966)—restructured rock, country, and blues into a new kind of musical architecture.

Dylan played ramshackle noise as much to enrage the old followers who called him Judas as to win new converts. Artists still flocked to cover his daring material. Dylan's nasal vocals are an acquired taste, so harmony groups like the Byrds and Peter, Paul & Mary made his songs hits, and guitarist Jimi Hendrix's version of "All Along the Watchtower" was even more incendiary than the original.

Each Bob Dylan release was pored over and analyzed like the latest Harry Potter novel. To escape the scrutiny, Dylan dropped out of sight after a 1966 motorcycle accident. Going underground, he and the Band made the mysterious unreleased "basement tapes" that went on to become rock music's first bootleg.

Bob Dylan in 1968.

When he resurfaced in 1967, Dylan confounded again. He went back to his folk roots, then started playing country music on *Nashville Skyline* (1969) and committed commercial suicide with *Self Portrait* (1970). It was a form of disguise, but these records couldn't help but be massively influential. The Byrds started playing country rock, and the singer-songwriter movement cribbed from the naked honesty of *Blood on the Tracks* (1975).

He endures in his singular way. Like Louis Armstrong, Dylan never sings a song the same way twice. Even bad records provide clues to his enigma. In the 1980s, he began a never-ending tour that carries on to this day. The troubadour can't escape his mighty relevance. When his thirty-seventh album, *Love and Theft,* was released on September 11, 2001, no record made more sense at the terrible dawning of a new world.

Detail:
Who is this?

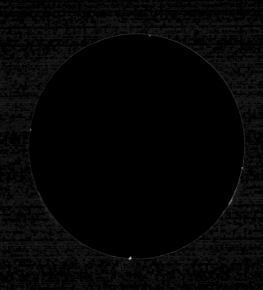

MARILYN MANSON.

Folk Songlines

• JOAN BAEZ, HARRY BELAFONTE, THE BYRDS, DONOVAN, BOB DYLAN, WOODY GUTHRIE, BURL IVES, THE KINGSTON TRIO, PHIL OCHS, PETE SEEGER, SIMON AND GARFUNKEL, BRUCE SPRINGSTEEN...
• UNITED STATES
• 1930S–

Nowhere do musical songlines run stronger than in folk music. Now a remnant of a vanished way of life, a folk song served several functions. It preserved old legends. It acted as both reportage and editorial. Most importantly, though, it was transmitted from one performer to another.

Guitarist Woody Guthrie, 1936.

America's greatest folk musician was Woody Guthrie. The troubadour from Oklahoma sang about what he knew—the victims of the Great Depression and the injustices of a nation still teething. His protest songs pointed the finger at the corrupt while lionizing the fugitive spirit of America embodied by John Steinbeck's *Grapes of Wrath* hero Tom Joad. During the Second World War, Guthrie proudly wrote on his guitar, "This machine kills fascists." His friend Pete Seeger once said, "Plagiarism is the basis of all culture." Guthrie's best-known song, "This Land Is Your Land," bore out that statement. Its stirring melody came courtesy of an old gospel number. A different hymn became Seeger's Civil Rights anthem, "We Shall Overcome." Their protégé Bob Dylan was an adept thief, too. His tribute "Song to Woody" borrowed its tune from

Guthrie's "1913 Massacre," which in turn was purloined from the song "One Morning in May." Guthrie was one of the few mentors Dylan acknowledged. The young iconoclast warned off imitators, as if to say the folk tradition came to a full stop with him. In the 1967 documentary *Don't Look Back,* Dylan swipes at his British rival Donovan by playing him "It's All Over Now, Baby Blue." Nevertheless, his astonishing impact inspired a search for the artist who would be his successor.

One of these "New Dylans" was Bruce Springsteen. His raucous music looked back to the New Jersey bar bands he grew up among. But his torrential poetry was straight from the Book of Bob. As he grew older, Springsteen embraced his fate. Like Dylan singing "Only a Pawn in Their Game" or Guthrie singing "Talking Dust Bowl Blues," he lamented the broken promised land, except "The Boss" offered rock music as a life-giving elixir for society's ills. In 1995, he released his folkiest album yet, the skeletal *The Ghost of Tom Joad,* whose title bore the specter of a song Woody Guthrie wrote fifty-five years earlier.

Bruce Springsteen on his *Born in the USA* tour, 1985. He plays here against an American flag in Los Angeles. October 7, 1985.

(upper right):
Donovan in 1967.

How did Eminem first come to the attention of Jimmy Iovine, his record label boss?

The Rolling Stones

• *AFTERMATH* (1966), *BETWEEN THE BUTTONS* (1967), *LET IT BLEED* (1969), *STICKY FINGERS* (1971), *EXILE ON MAIN STREET* (1972), *SOME GIRLS* (1978)...
• FORMED IN 1963
AEROSMITH, THE BLACK CROWES, FACES, GUNS N' ROSES, THE KINKS, NEW YORK DOLLS, OASIS, THE SMITHEREENS, ROD STEWART, THE WHO, THE YARDBIRDS

! Iovine saw him place second in the freestyle category at the 1997 Rap Olympics.

The name the Rolling Stones—originally taken from a song by Chicago bluesman Muddy Waters—embodies everything rock 'n' roll is about. In their forty-year career, this London gang has remained perennially popular by honoring blues roots while titillating audiences with their bravado. They justifiably call themselves the World's Greatest Rock and Roll Band.

The Stones were just another group of British blues enthusiasts who were turned into a national sensation by their ringmaster manager Andrew Loog Oldham. A former Beatles publicist, he established them as the bad boy ying to the Fab Four's clean-cut yang. "Would you let your daughter go with a Rolling Stone?" the papers cried, frowning at their surly look and outrageous stunts, like urinating in public. Oldham didn't stop there. He locked singer Mick Jagger and guitarist Keith Richards in a room together until they learned how to write their own songs.

The so-called "Glimmer Twins" turned out to be as formidable as

Lennon-McCartney. Richards's genius was for the raunchy rhythm guitar riff. Jagger, born with a voice that belonged on a Mississippi riverboat, wrote lyrics that updated the blues' sexual innuendo and baited society. In 1965, "(I Can't Get No) Satisfaction," with its fuzz-tone guitar hook and Jagger's malcontented air, made the band international stars.

The Stones knew how to press the Establishment's buttons. Jagger reflected the decadent mores of the Swinging Sixties on songs like "Let's Spend the Night Together." Drug busts and the death of founding guitarist Brian Jones—responsible for memorable musical flourishes, like the sitar on "Paint It Black"—were all part of the gig. They became victims of their own PR when, after declaring their "Sympathy for the Devil," a concertgoer was stabbed to death at the infamous Altamont free festival in California.

Richards's heroin addiction ravaged his body, but kept the Stones a potent musical force through the 1970s. He crafted their greatest album *Exile on Main Street* (1972), which crystallized their brand of sex 'n' sleaze. After a disastrous flirtation with psychedelia in the late 1960s, the Stones realized they should stick with what they knew best. Richards's distinctive riffs announced the song, Jagger's charisma cranked it up, and there were only brief detours into unknown musical territory.

The group inevitably grew into a corporation. Jagger embraced high society. Richards became an outlaw millionaire. When they head out on one of their blockbusting tours, though, audiences are still galvanized by the whiff of aged rebellion and the posturing Jagger learnt from James Brown and Tina Turner. They have made their name by living up to the hype.

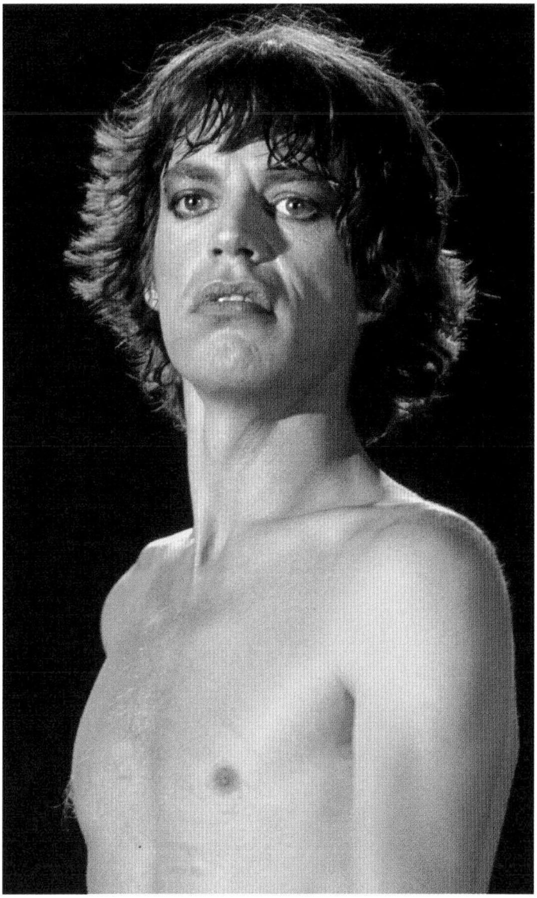

Mick Jagger during a concert in the United States, 1979.

Left:
The Rolling Stones. Clockwise from left: Bill Wyman, Charlie Watts, Keith Richards, Brian Jones, and Mick Jagger.

Instruments: *What are the names of these instruments?*

Answer

1. Kazoo, which was used on Ringo Starr's *You're Sixteen* (1973).
2. Didgeridoo, which was used on Jamiroquai's *Digital Vibrations* (1997).
3. Vibraphone, which was used on Ben E. King's *Spanish Harlem* (1961).
4. Swarmandal, which was used on the Beatles's *Strawberry Fields Forever* (1967).
5. Nyckelharpa, which was used on Väsen's *Kapten Kapsyl* (1997).
6. Melodica, which was used on Augustus Pablo's *East of the River Nile* (1978).
7. Marimba, which was used on Rolling Stone's *Aftermath* (1966).
8. Mandolin, which was used on Rod Stewart's *Maggie May* (1971).

1

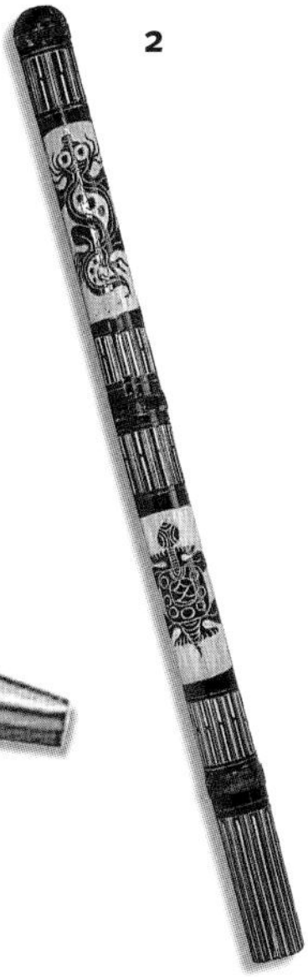
2

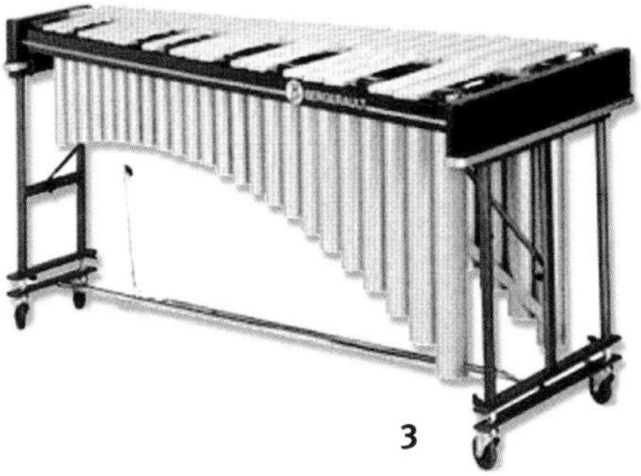
3

4

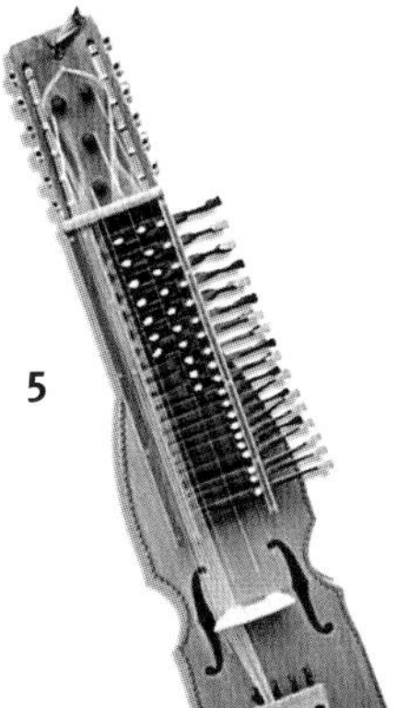
5

6

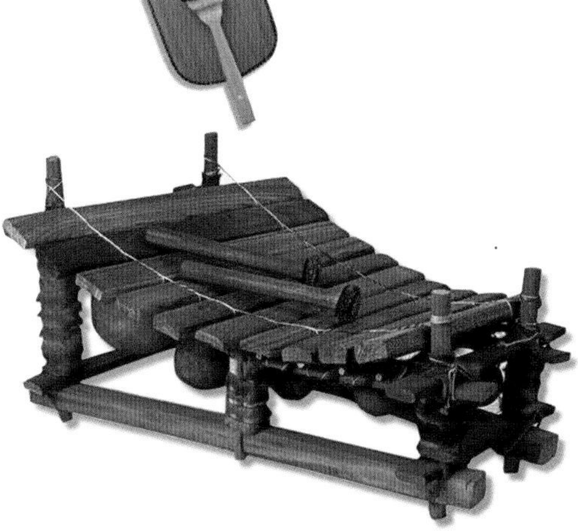
7

8

Johnny Hallyday

• *VIENS DANSER LE TWIST* (1961), *LA GÉNÉRATION PERDUE* (1966), *QUE JE T'AIME* (1969), *J'AI UN PROBLÈME* (1973), *SANG POUR SANG* (1999), *A LA VIE À LA MORT* (2002)...
• 1943
CLAUDE FRANÇOIS, ELVIS PRESLEY

It all began in the spring of 1960, when Line Renaud introduced a newcomer, Jean-Philippe Smet, during his TV variety program, *L' École des vedettes.* Blond and young, handsome and packed in black leather, he sang, "T'aimer follement" (the French version of Floyd Robinson's "Makin' Love"), accompanied by his electric guitar. Thousands of young French fans went wild. A star was born. His name was Johnny Hallyday. Since that day, this rock idol has been a living myth, a true French institution that continues to draw unbelievable crowds to each and every sold-out concert. At age eighteen, he collected James Dean photographs and was crazy about American rock 'n' roll, helping to bring it to France. Influenced by Elvis Presley, Gene Vincent, and Bill Haley, he recorded his first 45 at Vogue. After a wild concert at the Paris Alhambra, he performed at the Alcazar in Marseille. Since then, his albums have all gone gold, with each new record constituting a major event. Singing "Be Bop a Lula" and "Quelque chose Tennessee," "Retiens la nuit," and "Noir, c'est noir," Johnny is a performance king. The power of his voice, his legendary swagger, and his costumes and sets make his performances real extravaganzas. The singer's life has been as tumultuous as rock 'n' roll itself. His charged relationships always make headlines, from his 1965 marriage to Sylvie Vartan (another *yé-yé* generation star) to the relationship with his present-day wife, the young Laeticia. His son, David Hallyday, also a singer, wrote his father's album *Sang pour sang* (1999) and was raised in the United States. This big French rocker has also had noteworthy roles in films. They include *D' où viens-tu Johnny* (1963) by Noël Coward (with Sylvie Vartan), *Mischka* (2001) by Jean-François Stévenin, and three autobiographical movies: *L' Aventure, c' est l' aventure* (1971) by Claude Lelouch, *Love Me* (2000) by Laetitia Masson and *Jean-Philippe* (2006) by Laurent Tuel. Awarded the medal of knighthood by the Legion d'Honneur in 1997, Hallyday

now has more than nine hundred songs to his name, more than eighty million records sold, and thousands of die-hard fans.

Johnny Hallyday during a performance.

Left:
Johnny Hallyday greeting his fans in the 1960s.

?

Why was Jerry Lee Lewis arrested in front of Elvis Presley's Graceland mansion in 1976?

The Yé-Yé Generation

• ADAMO, RICHARD ANTHONY, ANTOINE, DANNY BOY, PETULA CLARK, CLAUDE FRANÇOIS, FRANCE GALL, DANYEL GÉRARD, CHANTAL GOYA, JOHNNY HALLYDAY, FRANÇOISE HARDY, FRANKIE JORDAN, EDDY MITCHELL, DICK RIVERS, SHEILA, SYLVIE VARTAN...
• FRANCE
• 1960S

With Johnny Hallyday, rock took hold of France as early as 1960, and it was at the Golf Drouot (a former miniature golf course turned into a club) where it all shook down. There, new idols—almost teenagers—formed the *yé-yé* (as in "yeah yeah") generation, and French music was never the same. Every night on the television station Europe 1, Franck Tenot and Daniel Filipacchi hosted *Salut les copains.* The show was a huge success and led them to start a magazine bearing the same name, of which more than a million copies were sold. At the same time, Albert Raisner launched *Age tendre, tête de bois,* a popular TV program that also showcased new talent. As early as 1961, Sylvie Vartan became a big star with her first 45, "Quand le film est triste." A young woman from a good family, she entered the world of music almost by chance. She first appeared on stage when someone dropped out of her brother's show. Her beautifully resonant, solid voice, along with her easy stage presence quickly made her the first *yé-yé* girl idol. Another popular idol of the time was Sheila. She took a huge leap from her parent's nest to overnight stardom when, in 1963, she sang Claude Carrère's hit "L'École est finie." But, perhaps the most popular and beloved of all the *yé-yé* girls was Françoise Hardy. Hardy was unique from the start of her career. A tall, young, and shy woman, she was raised in a convent and gave up her German studies to record her first album, *Tous les garcons et les filles* (1962), which was a huge success. Her stage presence was singular.

! A security guard alleged that Lewis was brandishing a gun and claimed he was going to kill Presley.

Keeping motionless onstage and wearing no make-up and simple, plain clothes, she mumbled her romantic melodies with a sad voice. Thousands of girls dreamed of becoming her. Besides Hardy, there was also France Gall, an adorable singer whose ingénue-like presence and fresh voice charmed an entire generation. In 1965, she won the Eurovision song contest with "Poupée de cire, poupée de son," a song written for her by Serge Gainsbourg. Her other big songs were "Attends ou va-t'en," "N'écoute pas les idoles," and "Sucettes à l'anis." But the *yé-yé* generation wasn't just for the girls. Claude François's career began with a bang with "Belles, Belles, Belles," a song based on an American hit. "Clo-Clo," as he was nicknamed, became a teenage idol in 1962. His hits include, "Marche tout droit," "Si j'avais un marteau," and "J'y pense et puis j'oublie." Eddy Mitchell, Dick Rivers, Danny Boy, Frankie Jordan, Richard Anthony, and Danyel Gérard were also among the idols adored by the new generation that danced the Twist and the Madison. The most original among them was Antoine who, with his flowered shirts and guitar in hand, incorporated both humor and insolence into his music. His turbulent tour in 1966 and especially his huge hit, "Les élucubrations," drove his fans wild.

Johnny Hallyday, Sheila, Sylvie Vartan, and Françoise Hardy on vacation in Saint-Raphaël. August 22, 1969.

Left:
(top)
Yé-Yé emblem as published in *Salut les copains,* 1960s.

(bottom)
Cover of Antoine album that went gold twice. Released by Vogue in 1970.

Recording Studios

• ABBEY ROAD, BLACK ARK, CHESS STUDIOS, THE HIT FACTORY, KLING KLANG POWER STATION, ROLLING STONES MOBILE STUDIO, SUN STUDIOS, TOERAG STUDIOS, TRIDENT STUDIOS...
• INTERNATIONAL
• 1910S–

A recording studio can be either someone's bedroom or a multimillion-dollar facility. It's where a musician puts his or her music on tape or computer. Basic studio equipment includes microphones, a multitrack recorder, and a mixing console that allows everything to be combined together onto one track. A proper recording studio will usually consist of two rooms. In the first, the artist plays the music. A producer and engineer monitor the recording in the control room, which is separated from the studio by soundproof glass. Any sound picked up by the microphones is called a signal. The control room's mixing console gives each signal its own channel. Sound can be compressed, equalized, and otherwise modified with effects.

Initially, recording studios were far more elementary. Sometimes there weren't even speakers, making it virtually impossible to listen to playback. Instead, musicians and singers were grouped around a single microphone and played into it. The introduction of multitrack recording in 1955 allowed vocals and instruments to be recorded separately. Mistakes could be corrected. Overdubs could be added. Separate channels also allowed DJs to remix songs by rearranging the diverse elements into an entirely new track.

In the 1970s, studios went from making analog recordings on magnetic tape to digital recording, which stored the music electronically so it could be manipulated with computer programs. Now the number

(top)
Michel Polnareff during a recording session. October 26, 1974 in Brussels.

(bottom)
The Memphis Sun Studio, Tennessee, 1997. Here, Sam Philips signed *Cry Cry Cry* (1955), the first album by Johnny Cash.

Right:
The Beatles, Abbey Road Studio, 1963.

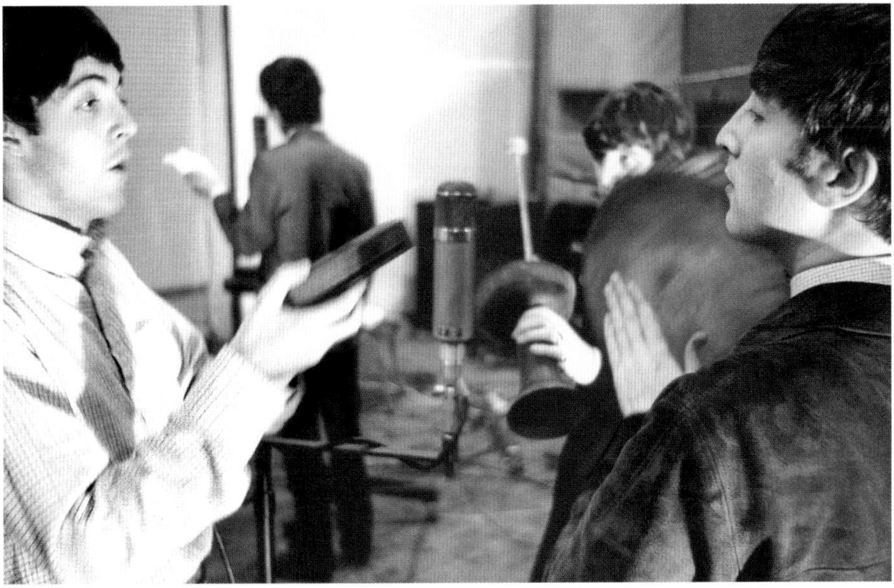

of tracks available for recording is only limited by a computer's memory, and software like ProTools can turn a computer into a recorder, mixing desk, and sampler all in one.

Studios are renowned for having their own ambience, and a skilled producer will factor it into a recording. A studio like Memphis's Sun Studios, where Elvis Presley first recorded, or London's Abbey Road, where the Beatles made their greatest records, has a mythic resonance. Smaller, cheaper studios with old-fashioned analog technology also have their advocates, such as the miniscule Toerag studios in London where the Detroit duo the White Stripes worked. Artists sometimes build their own home studios so they can record at their convenience. The Rolling Stones built a mobile studio, which they used to record *Exile on Main St.* (1972) while the band lived in tax exile in France. Modern-day equipment is now so portable that almost anywhere can become a studio. Nine Inch Nails made their album *The Downward Spiral* (1994) in the home where Sharon Tate was slain by the Manson Family, for instance.

All this convenience may make the studio go the way of the dodo. With the Beatles, producer George Martin realized the studio's potential as a musical train set for artists to play with. Now, he says, "With iPods, mini-recorders, and all the new technology, people can lie in their bath and make a rock record."

?

How did Ray Charles write his 1959 hit "What I'd Say"?

Music Magazines

- *ALTERNATIVE PRESS, BROADCAST, CREEM, DOWNBEAT, GRAMOPHONE, HIT PARADER, LES INROCKUPTIBLES, MAGNET, MOJO, NO DEPRESSION, REVOLVER, ROLLING STONE, SALUT LES COPAINS, SPIN, TECHNIKART, UNDER THE RADAR, VIBE...*
- EUROPE, UNITED STATES
- 1960s–

He improvised the song at a concert after his band ran out of material to play.

"Rock journalism is people who can't write, interviewing people who can't talk, for people who can't read," the American rock composer Frank Zappa once said. In spite of or perhaps because of this basic inarticulacy, entire forests have been pulped in the name of writing about rock. With their news, interviews, photos, and features, magazines give fans a way of understanding more about their favorite musical heroes, inarticulate or not.

It wasn't until the 1960s, with the advent of rock and pop, that music magazines became trendy, representing what was the then new teenage market. *Broadcast* (launched in 1962 to promote and popularize Greenwich Village folk songs) and *Disco Revue* (launched in 1961 by Jean-Claude Berthon) sold several thousand copies. But, *Rolling Stone* (launched in 1967) and *Salut les copains* (launched in 1962) revolutionized the music scene. Little by little, music audiences took more and more interest in the private lives of stars. *Rolling Stone* set the example, building its reputation by covering John Lennon and Jefferson Airplane's every move. When Daniel Filipacchi and Franck Tenot launched *Salut les copains* in France, they sold more than a million copies in a few short months. Setting trends and laying down the rules, music magazines quickly became true conduits of business, often despite themselves. With their success, the controversial and subversive origins of some publications were buried. Launched in 1969, *Creem* specialized in new rock and promoted punk, which was given life in its columns.

Today, music publications cover everything from specific musicians

or genres of music to mainstream pop culture to information on digital recording devices and editing technology. There are magazines created by musicians for musicians and magazines written for average music buffs and ones for true aficionados. It seems that there are just as many publications as there are genres of artists, proving that the printed word is music to the masses.

Rolling Stone cover of Gwen Stefani. January 27, 2005.

Left:
Salut les copains cover of Françoise Hardy. November 1966.

THE MUSIC PAGES

GOSSIP AND SCANDAL

Missed Opportunity

The Beatles, who had their start at the Cavern, signed their first contract with Parlophone and released their first single *Love Me Do* in 1963. The label Decca had previously refused to include the group in their catalog. (1962)

• **Rock in France**
The press was confounded by the hysteria over Johnny's concerts. In 1961, *France-Soir* stated, "They say he's a charming singer. I find it quite silly, but fitting for a concert hall."

• **Revelation**
In 1959, fans at the Newport Folk Festival, who had come to hear folk greats like Oscar Brand, Odetta, Earl Scruggs, and Jean Richie were introduced to an amazing newcomer. Joan Baez had her first concert before an audience of thirteen thousand people. A star was born. (*Horizon*, September 1962)

• **Change at the Helm**
The change of government in Cuba has forced director Carol Reed to rewrite the screenplay for *Our Man in Havana* thirty-nine times. He was hoping to shoot the spy film in the Cuban capital. He was also forced to change the hairdos and costumes of his actors. (1960)

• **Caption?**
Colonel Parker, Elvis Presley's manager, sent this telegram to a concert organizer who was offering $75,000 to produce the King in Europe: "OK for me. Stop. How much you offering Elvis?" (*Salut les copains*, number 25, 1977)

• **Corrections**
Charlie Parker was thirty-four when he died, not between fifty and sixty, as a coroner judged from an autopsy on his heroin-ravaged corpse. (1955)

• **Pioneer**
"(We're Gonna) Rock Around the Clock," by Bill Haley, produced by Milt Gabler, was a huge success worldwide and became the first hit in the history of rock 'n' roll. (1955)

• **Bad Frequency**
Scandal erupted in England in 1969, even though pirate radio was a huge success. The murder of Reg Calvert, head of Radio City, brought tensions between Radio Atlanta and Radio City to a head, forever leaving a sinister mark on free radio.

CURRENT EVENTS AND NEWS IN BRIEF

• Act of Faith

Six months after John Lennon made shocking statements about how Christianity was in decline and how the Beatles' notoriety was surpassing Christ's, the Emperor of the KKK, Bob Scoggin, set afire the group's albums in South Carolina.

• *It's a Wonder*

With the album *Little Stevie Wonder*, the Motown label launched a new artist who was barely thirteen years old. (1963)

• Paranoia

The Doors claimed to consume 170 grams of marijuana a day. Richard Nixon called Jim Morrison "the most dangerous man in America." (1967)

RECORD-SELLING SONGS IN 1962

		millions
"White Christmas"	BING CROSBY	25
"Rock Around the Clock"	BILL HALEY	15
"I Want to Hold Your Hand"	THE BEATLES	10
"It's Now or Never"	ELVIS PRESLEY	9
"Diana"	PAUL ANKA	9

The British Invasion

• THE ANIMALS, THE BEATLES, PETULA CLARK, THE DAVE CLARK FIVE, GERRY AND THE PACEMAKERS, HERMAN'S HERMITS, THE KINKS, MANFRED MANN, THE ROLLING STONES, THE WHO, THE ZOMBIES...
• UNITED STATES
• 1960s

The Kinks. From left to right: Mick Avory, brothers Ray and Dave Davies, and John Dalton (c. 1970).

Left:
Cover of the Who album *The Kids Are Alright* (1979).

It is said that the Beatles' first appearance on *The Ed Sullivan Show* in 1964 was watched by more people in America than any TV show in history. This seismic event had two knock-on effects. It inspired a wave of British bands to flood 1960s America in what became known as "the British invasion." In turn, American kids picked up guitars and tried to play rock 'n' roll themselves.
The British groups were a varied lot. Many bands from Liverpool shared the Beatles' sound (and manager). These so-called "Merseybeat" groups, like Gerry & the Pacemakers, sang upbeat chiming ditties seemingly torn from the Beatles songbook. Manchester's Herman's Hermits were also packaged as parent-friendly entertainers, down to their 1965 pop hit "Mrs. Brown, You've Got a Lovely Daughter."
Other bands were R&B enthusiasts with a more dangerous edge, like the Rolling Stones. The Animals' version of the folk song "The House of the Rising Son"—all swirling organ and howling vocals—topped the U.S. charts in 1964. The Kinks and the Who outgrew their R&B fixations and boasted a pair of sharp songwriters in Ray Davies and Pete Townshend. Their use of feedback-heavy riffs couldn't obscure a sharp dissection of hormonal mores on hits like "You Really Got Me" and "My Generation."
The British invasion bands looked to the Beatles for cues, so the psychedelic cavalcade of *Sgt. Pepper's Lonely Hearts Club Band* (1967) was like a lava lamp landing on their heads. Everyone felt they had to match the album's ambition. The Who's Townshend was best suited to the challenge, crafting an expansive, double-LP "rock opera" about a deaf, dumb, and blind "pinball wizard" called *Tommy* (1969), while the Kinks pursued more parochial concepts, delicately suffused with

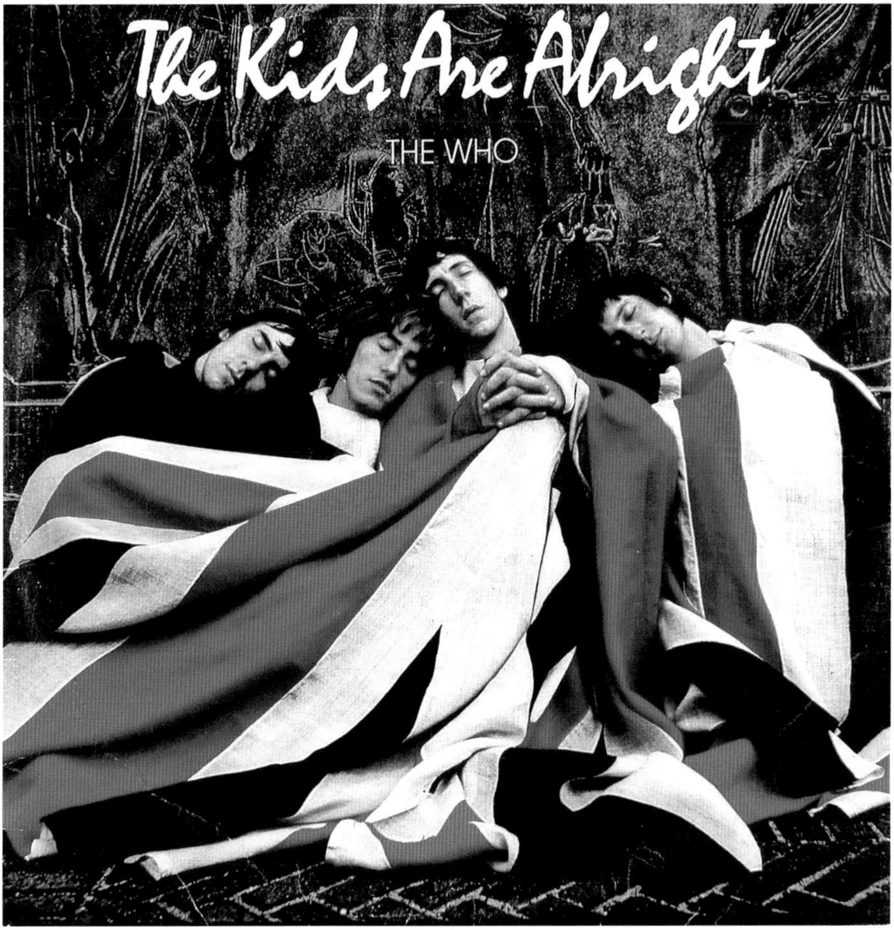

post-imperial wistfulness on *The Village Green Preservation Society* (1968).

The British invasion inspired countless American garage bands, so-called because their rudimentary sound was honed in their parents' carports. If *A Hard Day's Night* inspired them to buy Rickenbackers, *Sgt. Pepper's* inspired them to take drugs. Most of these bands became one-hit wonders, vanishing as soon as their bizarre singles blossomed in the charts' nether regions. In the 1970s, these lost groups, with their sound of adolescent frenzy, were reappraised as punk rock progenitors. Their idiosyncratic example was inspirational. In the 1990s, the country was overrun again—this time by hyperactive Swedish garage rockers. the Hives, proving that America was still vulnerable to a foreign musical assault.

?

What is the West African *kora*?

The Managers

• DON ARDEN, BRIAN EPSTEIN, PETER GRANT, DON KIRSHNER, KIT LAMBERT, LARRY PARNES, ROBERT STIGWOOD...
• EUROPE, UNITED STATES
• 1950S–

Behind every great star, there is a great manager. They do everything the star is incapable of: dealing with the tour promoters, bookers, publicists, and journalists, and acting as the liaison with the label that distributes their records. And at the same time, a manager is an advisor, guardian, friend, and the band's biggest fan. At least, that's how it's supposed to work.

With one eye on the big picture, a manager tries to make his clients more marketable. Larry Parnes turned a stable of good-looking singers into Britain's very own rock 'n' rollers by giving them exotic names like Billy Fury, Marty Wilde, and even Dickie Pride. Brian Epstein, a closeted gay man, fell in love with the Beatles from the moment he first saw them perform. But he realized their leathers would never make the hit parade, and ordered them to wear sharp-looking suits and distinctive mop-tops haircuts.

Other managers might have an influence on a band's artistic direction. The Rolling Stones' manager made the band start writing their own songs. Kit Lambert was an aspiring filmmaker who was determined to turn the Who into the flagship band of Britain's "mod" movement. He inspired Pete Townshend to write about the lives of his style-conscious fan-base and, when the band needed a breakthrough, encouraged them to make the rock opera *Tommy* (1969).

Other managers became legendary for their strong-armed tactics. Ex-wrestler Peter Grant collected Led Zeppelin's ticket receipts himself, and roughed up anyone caught bootlegging their live shows, even tangling with one promoter's teenage son. When Robert Stigwood tried to add the English mod band the Small Faces to his client roster, their manager, Don Arden, had him

! The *kora* is a harp-lute with twenty-one strings. The body is made from a bisected calabash covered with cow skin.

The Small Faces, the popular English group from the 1960s, photographed here with Bill Corbett.

Left:
Executives walking on CDs, 1995.

dangled out of a fourth-story window. For this reason, many impresarios will look to other schemes to make their fortune. Don Kirshner realized at the beginning of the rock era that there was a dearth of quality songs, so he started a songwriting factory in New York's Brill Building. The walls of each office were thin enough that the songwriters who worked there, like Neil Diamond, could hear what the others were doing. The competitive spirit inspired some of the 1960's greatest songs, like "Will You Still Love Me Tomorrow" and "Save the Last Dance for Me." Kirshner also wasn't above conjuring bands out of thin air. He formed the TV group the Monkees from auditions.

Robert Stigwood recovered from his brush with death to become a movie producer who used his acts to create soundtracks. When the Bee Gees supplied the songs for the disco film *Saturday Night Fever* (1977), he made a fortune. After all, a manager rarely does all that stuff for free.

Logos:

What singer or group does each logo represent?

Answer

1. Marilyn Manson.
2. Led Zeppelin.
3. Grateful Dead.
4. Prince.
5. Nine Inch Nails.
6. Rolling Stones.

2

1

3

4

6

5

The Sacred and the Secular

- ALEX BRADFORD, JAMES BROWN, SOLOMON BURKE, RAY CHARLES, SAM COOKE, THOMAS A. DORSEY, ARETHA FRANKLIN, CLYDE MCPHATTER, WILSON PICKETT, SISTER ROSETTA THARPE...
- UNITED STATES
- 1930S–

God can be found in music where He's least expected. Take *qawwali*. It's a beautiful type of Sufi devotional music, the only kind that can be played during religious ceremonies. The *ghazal* form of qawwali, however, seems at first to be very secular indeed. As the *tabla* and *dholak* drum play, the ghazal singer vocalizes about the pleasure of drinking, or the pain felt when one's beloved is gone. It's all a matter of interpretation. *Ghazal* is tolerated because the intoxication described is the feeling that comes from loving Allah. Similarly, the pain comes from being far from God, not a lover. A similar effect occurs in a gospel hymn when the words "Jesus" are changed to "baby." With this minor word change, a hymn can become soul music. That switch is exactly what happened when, in 1953, Ray Charles took an old gospel tune and turned it into "I Got a Woman."

God is heard moving across the face of every form of popular music. Thomas A. Dorsey, the songwriting genius called the "The Father of Gospel," was also a bluesman known as "Georgia Tom" who used the tricks he picked up in barrooms to create a new musical sound. Jazz began as a funeral march and was used by John Coltrane to scale transcendent heights on masterpieces like *A Love Supreme* (1964). Many of Tin Pan Alley's Jewish songwriters incorporated *hazzanut*, the songful prayer of the synagogue, into their music. One of them—George Gershwin—applied his knowledge of gospel to his "folk opera" *Porgy and Bess* (1935). For many immigrants new to America, religious music was as necessary as pop. Jewish cantors and African-American preachers became recording stars, and old-time and blues musicians had to have spiritual songs in their crowd-pleasing repertoire.

This traffic between the secular and sacred was scarcely encouraged. When Sam Cooke deserted his gospel quartet to make soul music, he was ostracized by the very

Right:
Alex Bradford and the Bradford Family, one of the best known gospel groups of the United States, around 1970.

congregations that once swooned at his sexy testifying. The choir was still a great training ground for singers. Tempted away from the church by record contracts, the prodigal Aretha Franklin returned home with a gospel album in 1972. This dichotomy meant that the struggle between the Lord and the flesh constantly played itself out in soul music. After all, change the words "baby" to "Jesus" and the song is suddenly a gospel hymn. In rock, the war is less between sin and salvation than between belief and doubt. As songwriters adopted a more personal tone in the 1970s, they attacked religious hypocrisy and asked listeners to imagine there was no heaven. Christian, Jewish, and Islamic imagery has been appropriated in music videos, both exalting spirituality and attacking it, and Satan has become a convenient boogeyman for heavy metal bands and others to associate with. But as the world finds a greater need for some kind of faith, bands like U2 and even hip-hopper Kanye West have put forward spiritual messages. The contemporary Christian music scene even makes rock to pray to. Proof, as if any was needed, that God moves in mysterious ways.

?

What sound effect did the Sex Pistols add to the beginning of "Holidays in the Sun"?

Motown

- THE FOUR TOPS, MARVIN GAYE, GLADYS KNIGHT AND THE PIPS, JACKSON 5, RICK JAMES, MABEL JOHN, LIONEL RICHIE AND THE COMMODORES, THE MARVELETTES, THE MIRACLES, BARRETT STRONG, THE SUPREMES, THE TEMPTATIONS, MARY WELLS, STEVIE WONDER...
- UNITED STATES
- 1960S–1980S

Motown was the name ex-boxer Berry Gordy gave his fledgling record label in 1959. It was short for "The Motor City," the nickname of his Detroit hometown and America's car manufacturing capital. Motown was also a kind of factory. Instead of Fords, the company built a sleek line of effervescent pop-soul records and teen-friendly acts. Over the next decade, Motown produced nearly one hundred Top 10 hits, created a roster of superstars, and could boast of introducing a generation of white fans to black music.

Gordy ran Motown like a production line. His youthful stars came straight off the Detroit streets and were instructed by an in-house charm school to look, act, and dance like superstars. Competing songwriting teams penned and produced the songs. A house band provided Motown's trademark sound. The hyperactive rhythm section bounced around like a fidgety rabbit, but was made tame for radio play through sweetening strings and smooth harmonies. Gordy had the last say on everything, and held weekly meetings where he would personally approve singles for release. Everyone was eager to please the boss.

The songwriting teams each had an instantly recognizable style. Holland-Dozier-Holland fashioned upbeat arias with clever hooks like "Stop! In the Name of Love." A Motown song was inevitably about the joy or pain of young love. This was Smokey Robinson's forte. The

The sound of marching Nazi jackboots.

The Primettes in concert, 1960. In 1961, the Primettes became the Supremes, led by Diana Ross.

Left: Stevie Wonder, September 1, 1980.

songwriter-performer with the Miracles wrote metaphysical odes like "The Tracks of My Tears" that led Bob Dylan to dub him America's greatest poet. In the late 1960s, Norman Whitfield kept Motown current by penning songs for the Temptations about deadbeat dads and social upheaval, which he gave groovy psychedelic trappings.

Motown stars went from being factory-produced acts to being true artists. The label's initial hits came from vocal groups with names like the Supremes and the Vandellas. Their animated performances matched the upbeat sound, although Robinson's brokenhearted falsetto and Levi Stubbs of the Four Tops' desperate rasp stood out from the pack.

In the 1970s, Marvin Gaye and Stevie Wonder took control of their careers and began writing and producing their own albums, experimenting with the sounds of soul and tackling personal issues of sex and salvation with "songs in the key of life."

The youthful Jackson 5 kept the innocent Motown spirit going in the early 1970s with bubblegum hits like "ABC," but Gordy's fold was maturing. Motown became a label for solo stars. In the 1980s, balladeer Lionel Richie and funk super freak Rick James were wholly responsible for their own material. In the late 1980s, Gordy sold the label he started with an $800 loan for millions.

His job was done.

Bossa Nova

• PIERRE BAROUH, CHARLIE BYRD, STAN GETZ, GILBERTO GIL, ASTRUD GILBERTO, JOÃO GILBERTO, ANTONIO CARLOS JOBIM, NARA LEAO, CARLOS LYRA, VINICIUS DE MORAES, SILVIA TELES...
• BRAZIL
• 1950S–1960S

Who doesn't know the girl from Ipanema with her eye-popping figure and tan skin? In 1964, she became the world's "new fiancée." The composers Antonio Carlos Jobim and Vinicius de Moraes, as well as singer-guitarist João Gilberto, regulars at the Veloso Bar in Ipanema, were, as was everyone, captivated by the charming and shapely Brazilian woman. They were also at the heart of the carioca energy, which they drew on for their sublime work. Bossa nova style was originated by João Gilberto together with Antonio Carlos Jobim. Gilberto combined his unique vibratoless vocal style with Jobim's musical compositions and arrangements. This new rhythm became known as bossa nova, which literally means "the new way." Jobim, who died in 1995, became the most famous and internationally acclaimed Brazilian songwriter of all time. A living legend, João Gilberto is known as the Pope of Bossa Nova or "O Papa da Bossa Nova", in Portuguese. Bossa nova was introduced in Brazil in 1958 with the release of João Gilberto's song "Chega de Saudade," a composition by Antonio Carlos Jobim and Vinicius de Moraes. The hit single had an enormous impact on Brazilian music as it was the first time that the new rhythm—created by Gilberto and combined with the compositions and arrangements by

Cover of Astrud Gilberto's *The Girl from Ipanema* (1962).

Left: João Gilberto (left) and Antonio Carlos Jobim.

Jobim—was heard. The success of this single was followed by the release of an LP, featuring Gilberto (but not Jobim), which was also titled *Chega de Saudade* (1958). This album became a bestseller in Brazil and solidified the success of the bossa nova style. Jazz musicians went crazy for bossa nova, adding it to their repertoires. The American guitarist Charlie Byrd discovered the new rhythm during a tour in Brazil and hastened to share it with his friend, the jazz saxophone player Stan Getz.
The 1962 album Jazz Samba was the result. Bossa nova gained international fame in 1964 with the success of "The Girl From Ipanema" and the best-selling album Getz/Gilberto (1963). This album contained Astrud Gilberto's very first vocal recording of "The Girl From Ipanema," together with her then-husband João Gilberto's; it simultaneously marked the first recording of any kind by Astrud Gilberto. The single of this song, which garnered international popularity, was a shorter, edited version that contained a vocal by Astrud Gilberto only. Over the years, bossa nova has gone in and out of style, depending on the dominant musical fashions and tastes of the day. Its ardent followers, however, are die-hard and vocal. Among them is musician Pierre Barouh, who ceaselessly promotes the music he writes. Beyond Barouh, bossa nova has influenced countless other musicians and, in the process, has ensured Antonio Carlos Jobim, João Gilberto, and Astrud Gilberto's entry into the pantheon of twentieth-century musical greats.

What was Elvis Presley's occupation before he recorded "That's All Right, Mama"?

Tropicália

- GAL COSTA, GILBERTO GIL, OS MUTANTES, CAETANO VELOSO, TOM ZÉ...
- BRAZIL
- 1960S

Tropicália was nothing less than a full-scale artistic revolution held on the stages of Brazil in the late 1960s. Equal parts bossa nova, architecture, American rock, theater, samba, art, Beatles, *cinema nova,* poetry, native folk, blues, the bomb, and Bardot, Tropicália had a lasting impact on musical thought.

Its two main ideologists were Caetano Veloso and Gilberto Gil, both from the northeastern state of Bahia. Inspired by the poet Oswald de Andrade's *Cannibal Manifesto* (1927), which described the Brazilian tendency to make imported culture its own, they chose to confront the country's dictatorship with music that nibbled on everything they could think of. Veloso would later claim Tropicália's aim "was to sort out the tension between Brazil the Parallel Universe and Brazil the country peripheral to the American Empire." Traditionalists bristled at the new compositions they unveiled at the 1967 Festival of Brazilian Pop Music song competition. Tropicália sucked the marrow out of bossa nova and turned up the volume. Veloso was booed for his use of electric guitars on the joyous "Alegria, Alegria." Besotted with the Beatles' "Day in the Life," Gil described his impetuous song "Domingo no Parque" as "Bahia meets George Martin."

Named after an art installation, Tropicália reveled in surreal lyrics and juxtapositions, many of them courtesy of Dadaist arranger Rogério Duprat. On "Panis et Circensis," the group Os Mutantes mixed Strauss waltzes with girl group choruses and smashing glass. The inventive Tropicálistas went beyond traditional rock instruments. Os Mutantes

! He was a truck driver.

inverted their guitar's wah-wah pedal to make a wooh-wooh pedal, and the classically trained Tom Zé's orchestrations used everything from blenders, typewriters, and floor polish to create sound.

Their anarchic sensibility was collectively displayed on 1967's *Tropicália* compilation, but the following year, the government cracked down, censoring song lyrics and persecuting any performer who was opening critical of Brazil's military dictatorship. Gil and Veloso spent two months in jails for "antigovernment activity" and another four months under house arrest before they were forced into exile in London. Tropicália went underground and became *musica popular Brasileira* or MPB. In the following decades, Gil and Veloso would become global superstars, still using music to explore their national identity. Gil came to enjoy the ultimate irony: the one-time enemy of the state is now Brazil's minister of culture.

Cover of the self-titled *Caetano Veloso* album (1968).

Left:
Gilberto Gil with the members of the group Os Mutantes (Rita Lee, Arnaldo Baptista, and Sérgio Dias) (c. 1968).

Who Doesn't Fit In?

Who never sang a duo with Elton John?

Answer

The odd one out is Cat Stevens.
B.B. King sang with Elton John for „Rock This House" in 2005.
Eric Clapton sang with Elton John for „Runaway Train" in 1992.
France Gall sang with Elton John for „Donner pour donner" in 1980.
k.d. lang sang with Elton John for „Teardrops" in 1993.

B.B. King

Eric Clapton

France Gall

Cat Stevens

k.d. lang

The Electric Guitar

• FENDER MODELS: BRONCO, DUOSONIC, JAGUAR, JAZZMASTER, MUSTANG, STRATOCASTER, TELECASTER; GIBSON MODELS: FLYING V, GIBSON ES-150, GIBSON ES-335, GIBSON L5, LES PAUL; KRAMER (ALSO OWNED BY GIBSON); OVATION; RICKENBACKER; STEINBERGER (ALSO OWNED BY GIBSON)...
• INTERNATIONAL
• 1923–

Although the saxophone runs it a close second, the electric guitar is the most important instrument of the twentieth century. Without it, blues might have stayed a minority interest, rock 'n' roll is unimaginable, and Jimi Hendrix would have stayed in the army. It's had an incredible impact on almost every popular genre, become a design classic to rank with the Coke bottle, and makes anyone who picks one up look cool.

The electric guitar was created in order to make the instrument as loud as the other musicians in the big bands of the 1920s and 1930s. In 1923, Lloyd Loar made the first prototype of guitar with a proper microphone. Steel strings helped, but more was needed. In 1931, George Beauchamp tried adding electromagnetic pickups to his guitar to amplify the strings' vibration. However, the sound bounced around the guitar's body, creating feedback. Innovative jazz guitarist Les Paul solved the problem in 1940 by attaching the strings and pickups made from telephone parts to a plank. Gluing the halves of a regular guitar body to either side of "The Log" made it more aesthetically acceptable. In 1943, radio repairman Leo Fender made a cheaper model with pickups and tone controls, and soon the electric guitar was in mass production.

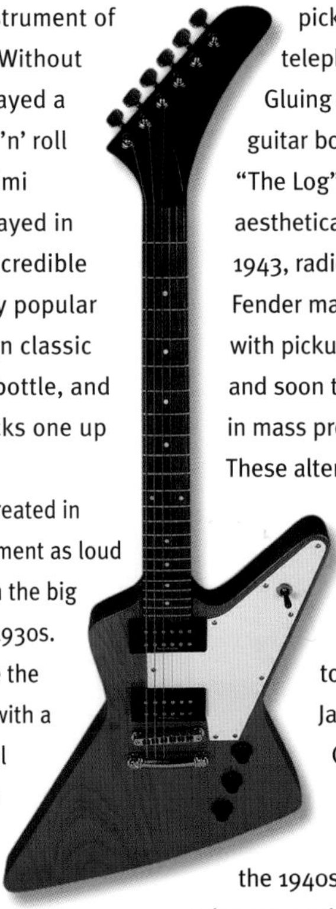

The Gibson Explorer model from 1958.

Right:
Illustration of different models of electric guitars on a Nashville bus, 1988.

These alterations made the guitar sound different. Musicians could distort and sustain notes, or bend them to change their pitch. Jazz guitarist Charlie Christian began to play his Gibson ES-150 in a single-note style in the 1940s. The ability to play solos meant the guitarist was now one of the most versatile members of a band. Rock 'n' roller Chuck Berry could both play rhythm and improvise solos, too. The electric guitar became a must-have

accessory for any aspiring rocker. The Fender company responded to demand by making several different versions of the guitar and marketing them in a variety of stylish colors. The Fender Stratocaster resembled the finned cars coming off the Detroit production lines. Its futuristic design was copied by Gibson, whose Flying V was made popular by Jimi Hendrix.

New models offered increased potential. The Fender Stratocaster included a vibrato system that let the players control the pitch of the guitar strings. A tremolo arm of "whammy bar" could change the pitch by lifting the guitar's bridge. The Rickenbacker twelve-string sounded like two guitars chiming at once, and the distinctive jangle was heard on the Byrds' "Mr. Tambourine Man" and early Beatles' records. The Ovation guitar, which was launched as the "Balladeer" in 1967, was particularly attractive to live acoustic musicians who constantly battled feedback problems—its synthetic bowl and early use of pre-amps, onboard EQ, and piezo pickups helped deliver high volume without unwanted distortion.

An array of accessories offered even more options. Turning up the volume of a second "pre-" amplifier distorted the tone. Effects boxes also offered a range of tonal options. Notes could echo with reverb or be given a fuzzy or wah-wah tone. With the help of the MIDI (Musical Instrument Data Interface), musicians are able to control multiple instruments from a single keyboard—a phenomenon that contributed to the "wall of synthesizers" sound popular in the 1970s and 1980s. As technology advances, so does the range of sounds musicians are able to produce and control. Today, the possibilities, like rock music itself, are endless.

? Who shot the Tejano singer Selena to death in 1995?

Rock Guitar Gods

• ERIC CLAPTON, JIMI HENDRIX, JOHNNY MARR, HANK MARVIN, BRIAN MAY, JIMMY PAGE, JOHNNY RAMONE, KEITH RICHARDS...
• EUROPE, UNITED STATES
• 1960S–

When guitars became amplified, they offered its players the freedom to push their art to the very edge. Tuning the strings, controlling feedback from the amplifiers and a range of effects pedals allowed players to cultivate individual voices on their instrument. Although the electric guitar gave rock its heavy beat, soon the solos were as exciting—and personal—as they were in bebop jazz.

Though the first electric guitar went on the market in 1931, the phrase "guitar god" didn't come into parlance until graffiti appeared in mid-1960s London and proclaimed that Eric Clapton "is God." The English guitarist understood the instrument's history. He was obsessed with the strange picking of the Mississippi bluesmen, and established his reputation as a fiery soloist with R&B enthusiasts the Yardbirds and John Mayall's Bluesbreakers. As the 1960s went on, his deft instrumental excursions got lengthier and more emotional. Clapton made the solo the test of a guitarist's skill. Jimi Hendrix's arrival in London set a new standard of excellence. The American had an intimate relationship with his Telecaster guitar. (In fact, rumors circulated that he slept with the instrument.) He played it behind his head and with his teeth, ground his hips against it like he was making love, and even set it on fire. In his hands, the guitar wailed and talked. Hendrix used feedback and amplification effects to broaden his instrument's vocabulary. Hendrix didn't recognize musical boundaries either, and could play blues, R&B, and jazz as well as rock.The true guitar gods were more than just soloists. Listen to the way Keith Richards or Jimmy Page construct a riff, using silence and tone to create a dynamic hook. These are guitarists inspired to pick up instruments by unfussy musicians like the Shadows' Hank Marvin, whose guitar carried the melody of 1950s instrumentals, like "Apache." Others set out to reinvent the instrument. Joni Mitchell retuned her guitar to shape unusual-sounding chords. Queen's Brian May used his guitar to replicate instruments in an orchestra,

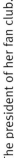

! The president of her fan club.

Jimi Hendrix, 1970.

playing each part with a coin for a pick. Progressive rock and heavy metal had their own guitar heroes, but punk rock placed aggression, like Johnny Ramone's drag racer roar, over technique. The guitar greats of the 1980s were the ones who could create a distinctive tone—not dazzle with fusillades of bent notes. Post-punk bands like the Smiths created emotional texture with layers of jangling Rickenbackers, and My Bloody Valentine's symphonies were so reliant on effects pedals set on the floor that their music became

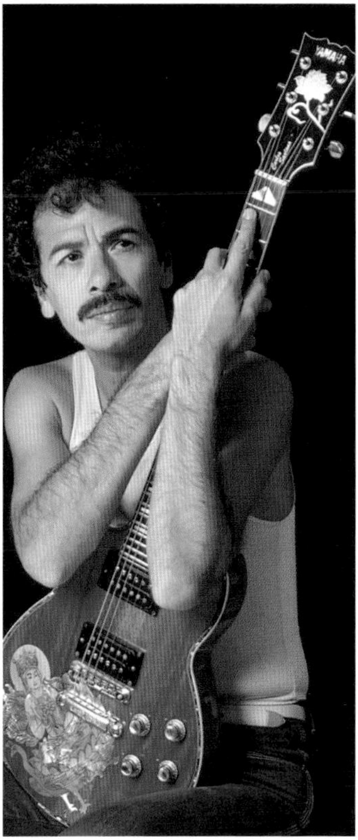

Carlos Santana in San Francisco, February 4, 1981.

Left:
Eric Clapton (c. 1970).

known as "shoe-gazing." The cult of personality that led to the creation of the guitar god has vanished in the reaction against rock pomposity. The solo became the province of jazz or blues musicians, not rock, although Clapton can still draw an audience with his dryly tasteful playing style. Contemporary heroes like Radiohead's Johnny Greenwood are as likely to spend an entire concert behind a keyboard as indulging in guitar skronk, but the instrument nevertheless remains as potent as ever. Nothing combines noise and beauty quite so well.

What are the only three colors the two members of the White Stripes wear?

Music on TV

- *AMERICAN BANDSTAND, AMERICAN IDOL, THE DAVID LETTERMAN SHOW, DON KIRSHNER'S ROCK CONCERT, THE ED SULLIVAN SHOW, THE JAY LENO SHOW, MAD, OLD GREY WHISTLE TEST, POP IDOL, READY SET GO, SALUT LES COPAINS, SATURDAY NIGHT LIVE, SOUL TRAIN, TOTAL REQUEST LIVE, THE OSBOURNES...*
- INTERNATIONAL
- 1960S–

The first music video played on MTV in 1981 was "Video Killed the Radio Star" by the Buggles. The British synth duo's claim came true some time after the fact. Television had long been an essential outlet for rock music, a genre that was as much about how performers looked as how they sounded.

When rock 'n' roll was born, however, the idea of a channel playing music videos twenty-four hours a day was ridiculous. The only place you could see Elvis Presley was on variety shows hosted by comedians like Steve Allen (who famously made the King perform "Hound Dog" to a basset in a tux). On *The Ed Sullivan Show*, singers appeared in-between ventriloquists and plate-spinners. The stone-faced host was nevertheless a keen talent spotter, and when Sullivan heard about a British chart-topping band called the Beatles, he put them on his show in February 1964. Their five songs were watched by an unprecedented seventy-three million people and after years of dippy teen idols, made rock music exciting again.

By then, pop music had a TV home at *American Bandstand,* hosted by Dick Clark since 1956. Clark's format of Top 40 acts playing for a dancing audience was imitated both on Britain's modish *Ready Set Go* and France's *Salut les copains.* Most of the bands lip-synched their hits, but here was a chance to see

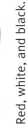

Red, white, and black.

The Beatles on *The Ed Sullivan Show*. This was one of their first televised appearances. February 9, 1964.

Left:
(top)
The MTV logo.

(bottom)
The host of the British TV show, *Pop Star*.

the men and women whose music sounded so exciting. Four musicians were even turned into a band called the Monkees, who had their own immensely popular sitcom and a string of hits during the mid-1960s.

As rock got hairier and scarier, bands became sideshows again. The late-night satirical program *Saturday Night Live* began featuring regular musical guests, and the nocturnal Don Kirshner's *Rock Concert* aired live performances. *Soul Train,* an R&B-oriented showcase of performances that premiered in 1970, became a barometer for the latest urban fashions and dances, and helped break acts like Prince and Run-D.M.C.

When MTV began airing videos nonstop, it changed the TV landscape. Having established its brand, MTV diversified into channels dedicated to country, Latin, and Indian music. It has even brought American pop to China. Other countries have followed suit, with France starting its own music channel: MCM. Television is now so essential to an artist's success that many artists market their music to use in advertisements just to get them heard, and a rash of talent shows like *American Idol* and *Pop Idol* has launched a slew of middle-of-the-road balladeers into stardom. Having transformed music consumption, though, MTV seems tired of it. Its biggest show has turned out to be *The Osbournes,* where cameras eavesdrop on scenes from metal god Ozzy Osbourne's mundane home life. Will reality kill the video star?

Legends: *Which artist is associated with what object?*

Answer

1. Maurice Chevalier and his boater hat.
2. Dizzy Gillespie and his trumpet.
3. Billie Holiday and her gardenia.
4. Elton John and his glasses.
5. Michael Jackson and his glove.

1

2

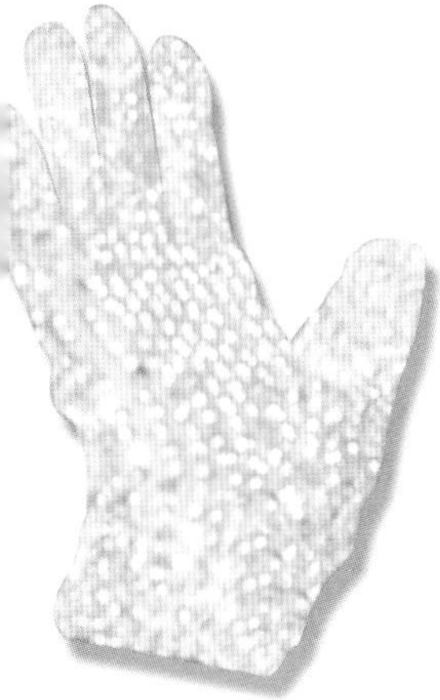

5

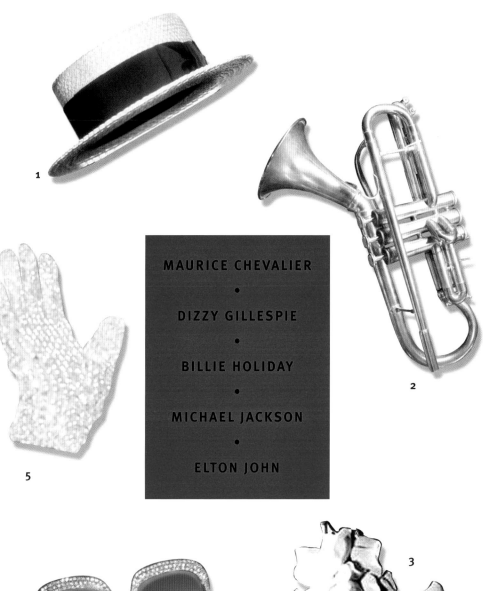

MAURICE CHEVALIER

•

DIZZY GILLESPIE

•

BILLIE HOLIDAY

•

MICHAEL JACKSON

•

ELTON JOHN

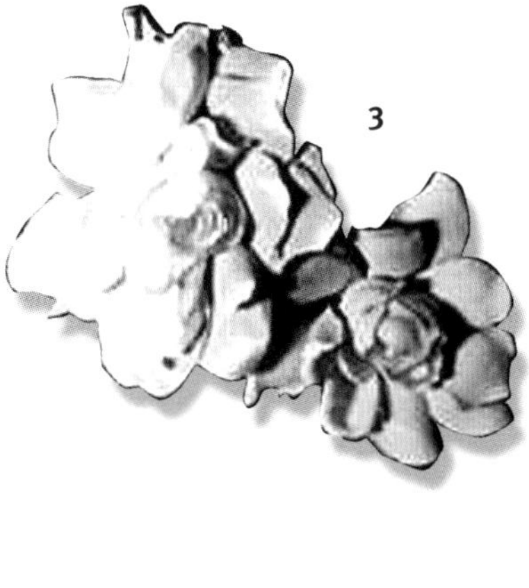

3

4

Funk

• BOOTSY'S RUBBER BAND, JAMES BROWN, EARTH, WIND AND FIRE, FUNKADELIC, THE HEADHUNTERS, THE ISLEY BROTHERS, RICK JAMES, KOOL AND THE GANG, THE METERS, THE OHIO PLAYERS, PARLIAMENT, PRINCE, SLY AND THE FAMILY STONE, WAR...
• UNITED STATES
• 1960S–

Sly and the Family Stone, fronted by Sylvester Stone (c. 1965).

Right: George Clinton in 1980.

In 1965, when James Brown announced "Papa's Got a Brand New Bag," everyone wanted to know what it was. The Top 10 single presented R&B in its rawest form, with the groove dictating what every instrument did. The bass played the riff. Guitars punctuated the rhythm. Horns urged the beat along. Brown's voice practically pushed the listener onto the dance floor. The brand new bag was funk.

Funk was uncompromising in its lack of structure. Some of Brown's jams were so long they took up both sides of a 45-rpm single. All the music had to do was keep people moving, so it became easy to incorporate other genres. When San Francisco DJ Sylvester Stone started his multiracial Family Stone in 1967, the music was as colorful as his band line-up. R&B, pop, and psychedelic rock were mixed up like a delirious radio show, with Stone's dry raps and Larry Graham's slapped bass holding it down.

Former hairdresser George Clinton saw even grander possibilities. His bands Parliament and Funkadelic became a freaky refuge for many of James Brown's musicians, and soloists like guitarist Eddie Hazel and keyboardist Bernie Worrell wigged out over loose grooves. Their sonic adventurousness and Clinton's Barnum-esque flair for onstage excess drew fans of all racial stripes. "Free Your Ass and Your Mind Will Follow," went one song, and if getting butts to shake was the chief goal, it wasn't the only one. Sly Stone celebrated "Everyday People" but the late 1960s social upheaval inspired his terrifying album *There's a Riot Goin' On* (1971). Clinton preferred to satirize Nixon's America with cartoon-like personas like Dr. Funkenstein and the alien Starchild.

Through the early 1970s, funk was in the vanguard. Sly Stone and Miles Davis jammed together. Jazz pianist Herbie Hancock started his own funk

group, the Headhunters. New Orleans incorporated percussive keyboards into its unique funk, and the music even inspired Fela Kuti's Nigerian Afrobeat. But disco took that respect for the beat, smothered it in strings and melodrama, and soon overtook funk in popularity.

In the 1980s, bass-playing journeyman Rick James inaugurated a new funk reign by using computers to create a cocaine-dusted synthesized sound. Where Sly Stone blurred race, he perverted gender with floor-fillers like "Super Freak," a trick his protégé Prince was only happy to take to even further extremes.

Hip-hop rose to prominence on the back of funk, excessively sampling Brown and Clinton, and rock bands like the Red Hot Chili Peppers started worshipping at the temple of the groove, too, even as the religion waned in popularity. But don't count it out. After all, people will always want to get up on the down stroke.

What did Janis Joplin leave $2,500 aside for in her will?

Psychedelia

- 13TH FLOOR ELEVATORS, THE BEACH BOYS, THE BEATLES, BUBBLE PUPPY, DONOVAN, THE DOORS, THE GRATEFUL DEAD, JEFFERSON AIRPLANE, THE JIMI HENDRIX EXPERIENCE, LOVE, PINK FLOYD, THE UNITED STATES OF AMERICA...
- GREAT BRITAIN, UNITED STATES
- 1960S

! To fund a party held in her honor. The invitations were to read "Drinks are on Pearl."

Take drugs, add music, and hey, presto! You've got psychedelia. During the late 1960s, as marijuana and LSD became recreational pursuits for musicians, they began to make music that replicated their state of expanded consciousness. They distorted the sound of their instruments, used sound effects, and gravitated toward the "heavy" sound of India and free jazz. The result? Far out, man.

The Beatles called the trippy tune with their increasingly bizarre singles, where tapes played backwards and lyrics surreally mixed Liverpudlian wordplay with *Alice in Wonderland*-like whimsy. *Sgt. Pepper's Lonely Hearts Club Band* (1967) made psychedelia legit. It began with an orchestra

tuning up and ended with a sound only dogs could hear. In between there were farmyard noises, sitars, music hall pastiches, and a psychedelic song called "Lucy in the Sky with Diamonds."

Sgt. Pepper's inspired others to attempt something just as ambitious, but there was definitely something in the air. At the same time and in the same Abbey Road studio, Pink Floyd, led by Syd Barrett, crafted *The Piper at the Gates of Dawn* (1967), a debut whose musical experiments were as absurd as the lyrics, which were about bikes and cross-dressers. In San Francisco, a group called the Grateful Dead performed wild jams at author

Ken Kesey's "acid tests," where LSD was downed with Kool-Aid. Where the British delighted in nonsense, the Americans relished in distortion. Live, psychedelic bands like the Doors and Cream blew minds with their cosmic jamming. In the studio, they did so with unique effects. Music traveled from one speaker to another, as in *Jimi Hendrix's Electric Ladyland* (1968). Unusual instruments like the whining theremin and electric harpsichord were used and albums could incorporate the sound of a crazed circus, like the United States of America's self-titled opus. The Who's *Tommy* (1969) inspired other bands to try their own concept albums. Pink Floyd played with psychedelia on the soundtrack to Barbet Schroeder's *More* (1969), one of the great psychedelic cinematic masterpieces of all time and a cult classic in France. No matter how you looked at it, this was music to turn on, roll a joint to, and ponder life's sheer expansiveness.

Jefferson Airplane, the Grateful Dead, Country Joe and the Fish, by Guy Peellaert, 1974.

Left:
(top)
Pink Floyd in concert, 1994. RFK Stadium in Washington.

(bottom)
Jim Morrison of the Doors, in the 1960s.

Woodstock

• JOAN BAEZ, THE BAND, JOE COCKER, THE GRATEFUL DEAD, ARLO GUTHRIE, RICHIE HAVENS, JIMI HENDRIX, INCREDIBLE STRING BAND, JEFFERSON AIRPLANE, JANIS JOPLIN, SANTANA, RAVI SHANKAR, SLY AND THE FAMILY STONE, TAJ MAHAL, THE WHO...
• BETHEL, NEW YORK
• AUGUST 15–17, 1969

Woodstock is the most famous rock festival of all time. Its name is synonymous with the baby boomer generation who thought they could change the world with free love and positive vibes. It is one of the 1960s musical high points—nearly every band on the three-day bill was able to build a career from their appearance. And it didn't even take place in the upstate New York arts community for which it's named.

The original plan was to hold the festival in Woodstock where, in 1969, Bob Dylan was recuperating from a motorcycle crash. Protests from the locals forced the organizers to relocate fifty miles away at a Bethel dairy farm. Although Dylan stayed at home, the line-up boasted some of the decade's biggest names, including Jimi Hendrix, Jefferson Airplane, and Joan Baez.

Organizers expected a crowd of around two hundred thousand when the doors opened on August 15. However, ticketless fans soon tore down the flimsy fences that surrounded the sixty-acre site. The promoters gave up and announced Woodstock had become a free festival. Thousands more headed for Bethel during the weekend, leading to food shortages and eight-mile-long traffic jams.

As captured in the Michael Wadleig's *Woodstock* (1970) documentary, the half-a-million citizens of the Woodstock nation got high, splashed naked in the mud, and witnessed epochal performances. The unknowns Joe Cocker and Santana impressed with their wild stage presence and lyrical jamming respectively. When "yippie" activist Abbie Hoffman interrupted a performance of *Tommy,* the Who kicked him offstage. And on early Monday morning, Jimi Hendrix deconstructed "The Star Spangled Banner" for a dwindling crowd of fifty thousand, his guitar sounding like exploding napalm.

Woodstock's three days of peace and music were eulogized in song by Joni Mitchell (who wasn't there), and represented a mythical utopia where hippies escaped the

Peace and love: the hippie generation at its peak during the historic Woodstock gathering.

Left:
Poster for Woodstock, 1969.

realities of Nixon and Vietnam. The people power on display renewed the enthusiasm of war protestors and environmental activists, and restored the optimism shaken by 1968's days of rage. Although the Rolling Stones' own attempt at a "free festival" in Altamont, California, ended in murder, Woodstock inspired copycat events which thrive to this day, like Britain's celebrated Glastonbury get-together. Woodstock remains a moment when music changed the world.

What composer once described one of his works as "seventeen minutes of orchestra without any music"?

The 27 Club

- KURT COBAIN, JIMI HENDRIX, BRIAN JONES, JANIS JOPLIN, JIM MORRISON
- UNITED STATES
- 1970S–

When Nirvana's front man Kurt Cobain committed suicide at age twenty-seven, he quoted the lyrics from Neil Young's song, "My, My, Hey, Hey" in his suicide note: "It's better to burn out than fade away." Certainly, the untimely deaths, during the 1970s, of four of rock's greatest legends echo that sentiment. Strangely, like Cobain, each of these musicians was twenty-seven years old when they passed away, lending a kind of mythical, albeit macabre, status to the age.

Brian Jones, rhythm guitarist of the Rolling Stones, was found dead in his swimming pool on July 3, 1969. The Doors' Jim Morrison died in his bath two years to the day later, while Janis Joplin and Jimi Hendrix both overdosed in 1970. Jones was a burnt-out drug casualty and Morrison, during *The Very Best of the Doors* (1973) days, was bloated beyond recognition from alcohol and drug experimentation, but Joplin and Hendrix were two of rock's great "might-have-beens."

Joplin was a powerhouse vocalist who put every ounce of hurt she had experienced as an unloved Texan into each bluesy note. Hendrix had established himself as a guitarist of cosmic capabilities on three tremendous albums. Joplin's solo disc *Pearl* (1971), which was released six months after she died, only hinted at what she could do with decent musicians and material. Hendrix's legacy suffered when producers decided to overdub unreleased outtakes with studio musicians. Fans eagerly purchased these posthumous albums in an effort to fill in the missing pieces to Hendrix's musical puzzle.

Morrison remained un-mourned until the Doors' psychedelic music appeared in Francis Ford Coppola's *Apocalypse Now* (1979) and Oliver Stone's reverent biopic *The Doors* (1991) elevated him to titanic status. Tell-all memoirs, live releases, and a revived version of the Doors with a rotating cast of rock singers only added to the legend. Morrison's flower- and graffiti-festooned Père Lachaise headstone is a tribute to his undying appeal.

Sadly, the rock 'n'roll ethos of partying hard and maintaining

Maurice Ravel, talking about his *Bolero*.

a larger-than-life image has its consequences. Wrought with alcoholism, substance abuse, and a general chaotic existence, these members of the 27 Club burned out before audiences could see the full depths of their talent. What would Jimi Hendrix have done had he lived just a little longer? What audacious music could Janis Joplin have created? Or what new musician would have been inspired by Kurt Cobain's maturing lyricism? The world will never know.

The Greatest Show on Earth by Guy Peellaert, 1973. Representation of the tragic and premature deaths of four music greats (all dead at age twenty-seven). From left to right: Jim Morrison, Brian Jones, Janis Joplin, and Jimi Hendrix.

Left:
The blues singer Janis Joplin in concert, 1969.

Serge Gainsbourg: *Who performed what Gainsbourg tune?*

Answer

1. Isabelle Adjani, “Pull marine” in 1983.
2. Catherine Deneuve, “Dieu est un fumeur de havane” in 1980.
3. France Gall, “Les Sucettes” in 1965.
4. Brigitte Bardot, “Harley Davidson” in 1968.
5. Charlotte Gainsbourg, “Lemon Incest” in 1984.
6. Vanessa Paradis, “Tandem” in 1987.

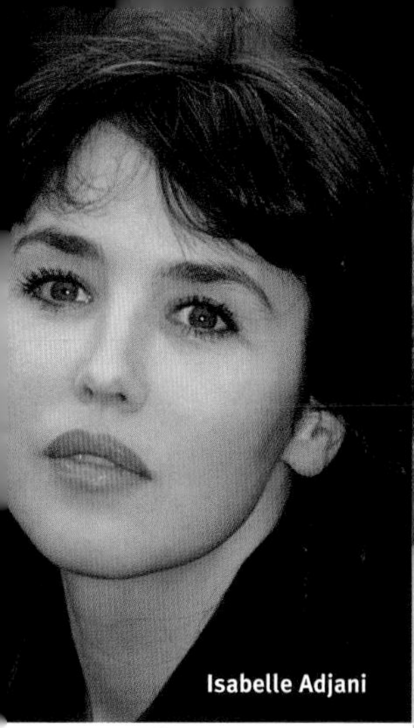

Isabelle Adjani

Catherine Deneuve

France Gall

1 2 3

"DIEU EST UN FUMEUR DE HAVANE"

•

"HARLEY DAVIDSON"

•

"LEMON INCEST"

•

"PULL MARINE"

•

"LES SUCETTES"

•

"TANDEM"

4 5 6

Brigitte Bardot

Charlotte Gainsbourg

Vanessa Paradis

Reggae

• HORACE ANDY, BUJU BANTON, BURNING SPEAR, JOHNNY CLARKE, JIMMY CLIFF, THE CONGOS, COXSONE DODD, I-ROY, KING TUBBY, BARRINGTON LEVY, BOB MARLEY, LEE "SCRATCH" PERRY, PRINCE BUSTER, THE SKATALITES, U-ROY...
• JAMAICA
• 1950S–

You can't mistake reggae music for anything else. While rock is built on a boom-boom-chk beat, reggae prefers to accent the third beat in the measure, with both the bass drum and the rhythm guitarist playing the distinctive chk-chk-BOOM! "riddem." It's an island sound that introduced Jamaica to the world, bringing with it a gospel based on freedom, marijuana, and the Rastafarian religion, not necessarily in that order.

In the 1950s, Jamaica didn't really have a music to call its own. The traveling discos known as "sound systems" got their hottest floor-fillers from the United States.

(top)
Jimmy Cliff at the Antibes Juan-les-Pins Jazz Festival, in 2004.

(bottom)
Cover of Jimmy Cliff's album *The Harder They Come* (1972).

Right:
Burning Spears.

Sound system owners would travel to America to scour record stores, or head down to the Kingston docks to buy the latest hit from sailors. Then they would remove the labels to make sure the competition couldn't spy on what they were playing.

The dancers loved the R&B and jump blues that drifted island-ward on the airwaves of radio stations based in New Orleans and Tennessee. As rock 'n' roll became popular, the sound systems were faced with a sudden shortage.

So they began to record the hits themselves. Top-notch local dance bands and soulful singers provided a talent pool. They added the off-beat of Jamaica's folk music mento, and ska was born.

Sound-system owner Prince Buster made ska truly Jamaican when, in 1960, he featured Rastafarian drummers on his hit 45 "Oh Carolina." Inspired by the Afrocentric teachings of Marcus Garvey, the Rastafarians believed Ethiopian Emperor Haile Selassie was God incarnate, or "Jah." Exiled in "Babylon," the Rasta's dreadlocks and ganja-enhanced "reasonings" expressed their faith, and its philosophy gave reggae its central lexicon.

Reggae was born during the summer of 1966, when it became too hot to dance to ska's upbeat "skank." Reggae was ska performed at a snail's pace;

its slow, easy-going rhythm made it very adaptable. American hits were cut in a reggae style, and world music artists took up its sunny beat. Meanwhile, producers like Lee "Scratch" Perry and King Tubby took instrumental "versions" of reggae tunes and literally remixed them to form bass and echo-heavy "dub" plates.

Reggae and ska caught on among Britain's punk youth and West Coast teenagers. As ska revivals hit Britain and the U.S. in the 1980s, reggae was overtaken on its home turf by dancehall music—in which DJs spoke/sung obscene or incendiary rants over dub plates. Soon the elementary rhythms of Casio keyboards heard on tracks like "Under Mi Sleng Teng" took over, and the new wave of "ragga" DJs modeled themselves on American rappers, teasing listeners with their sexy lyrics.

The carefree sound of reggae is still Jamaica's glory. The only industries to rival it are tourism and coffin-building.

In which movie did tango legends Carlos Gardel and Astor Piazzolla appear together?

Bob Marley

• *BURNIN'* (1973), *CATCH A FIRE* (1973), *NATTY DREAD* (1974), *EXODUS* (1977), *BABYLON BY BUS* (1978)...
• 1945–1981
BUJU BANTON, BLACK UHURU, DENNIS BROWN, ERIC CLAPTON, JIMMY CLIFF, THE SKATALITES, STEEL PULSE, PETER TOSH, UB40, STEVIE WONDER

The twelve-year-old Piazzolla played a street urchin in Gardel's *El Dia que Me Quieras* in 1933.

Bob Marley is the intimidating spirit behind every Jamaican rude boy who wants to be a reggae star. He spread Jamaican music around the world through his intense charisma and an enduring series of songs. With his enduring creed of love and independence,

Cover of Bob Marley & the Wailers' *Uprising* (1980).

Left:
Bob Marley, the king of Jamaican reggae, at home in Kingston, Jamaica, March 1980.

the singer/guitarist/songwriter Robert Nesta Marley is a messianic symbol, second only to the revolutionary Che Guevara in his posthumous ubiquity. When Marley's mother first moved to Kingston with her son in the 1950s, they lived in the government tenant yard he immortalized in "No Woman, No Cry." Marley ran with the Rude Boys street gang, but the one they called "Tuff Gong" was no mere thug. In 1961, his debut single warned "Judge Not (Before You Judge Yourself)." Marley's songs always engaged with the problems of Jamaica's poor. After he formed the Wailers with the towering guitarist Peter Tosh and boyhood friend Bunny Livingston, they topped the Jamaican charts in 1964 with "Simmer Down," a plea to stop ongoing gang violence. Conviction and Rastafarianism fired his art. "Get Up, Stand Up" demanded listeners to think for themselves. He was a masterful seducer, too. "Waiting in Vain" was a tender ballad, and "One Love" hugged the entire world. Marley became both a global superstar and a potent force for change in Jamaica. He survived an assassination attempt in 1976, and two years later, united the country's political rivals at the One Love Peace Concert.

Marley was also an incredible live performer: his eyes would roll back into his head in ecstasy and his dreadlocks would fly as his band would lock into another chugging groove. This shamanic figure created an instant bond with his audience, inspiring them to chant back "No Woman, No Cry's" soothing refrain, "Everything's gonna be alright." He had fans like Eric Clapton, who covered "I Shot the Sheriff" in 1974, and Stevie Wonder, who wrote "Master Blaster" in tribute.

In 1981, Marley was struck down with cancer. He left as his last testament the acoustic "Redemption Song," from his last album *Uprising* (1980). It asked, "Won't you help to sing these songs of freedom?" A worldwide chorus has taken up the challenge. Marley lives on in the voices of his fans and, like Guevara, as the face on a million of their T-shirts.

Serge Gainsbourg

• *GAINSBOURG PERCUSSIONS* (1964), *HISTOIRE DE MELODY NELSON* (1971), *ROCK AROUND THE BUNKER* (1975), *L'HOMME À TÊTE DE CHOU* (1976), *AUX ARMES ET CAETERA* (1979), *MAUVAISES NOUVELLES DES ÉTOILES* (1981), *LOVE ON THE BEAT* (1984), *YOU'RE UNDER ARREST* (1987)...
• 1928–1991
BRIGITTE BARDOT, ALAIN BASHUNG, JANE BIRKIN, ALAIN CHAMFORT, JACQUES DUTRONC, FRANCE GALL, JULIETTE GRÉCO, ANNA KARINA

Pygmalion, composer, songwriter, singer. Serge Gainsbourg left a major body of work, making him an unsurpassable figure in French popular music. When he was young, this son of a Russian immigrant wanted to be a painter, but became a bar pianist, like his father. His start in French chanson, in 1957, was in the tradition of the café scene on Saint-Germain-des Prés Boulevard. Although his nasal voice, angular face, and protruding ears didn't match the time's tastes, his songwriting was brilliant and he often penned songs for other

Jane Birkin and Serge Gainsbourg singing "Elisa" and "Ne dis rien (Say No More)" for *Mid Mad Mod,* a TV show hosted by Peter Knapp and Gérard Pirès. February 26, 1969.

Serge Gainsbourg in the 1980s.

musicians. He wrote "La Javanaise" for Juliette Gréco, for example, and it became a classic.

Gainsbourg rivaled Burt Bacharach with his entourage of French female singers (Anna Karina, France Gall, Françoise Hardy, Petula Clark, among others). Even Brigitte Bardot, the ultimate sex symbol, succumbed to his melodies and charms during a relationship that was as passionate as it was short-lived. He found solace in the arms of Jane Birkin, who agreed to re-record Bardot's heavy-breathing "Je t'aime . . . moi non plus" in 1969 (Bardot had refused to release her recording of the song). Birkin's faked orgasm was heard around the world and boosted Gainsbourg's reputation.

In the 1970s, the artist devoted himself to his solo career and produced two masterpieces *Histoire de Melody Nelson* (1971), with arrangements that are still mesmerizing, and *L'Homme à tête de chou* (1976), a spiteful album, on which the erotic metaphor is perfectly incorporated. His 1979 reggae version of "La Marseillaise" finally attracted young and ardent fans and unleashed the outrage of a more conservative portion of the population. It was during this period that "Gainsbarre," his alcoholic and derelict double, came to the fore and provided France with a handful of memorable media scandals. His last albums, *Love on the Beat* (1984) and *You're Under Arrest* (1987), drew on rap influences, which attracted an even larger audience.

An exceptional songwriter, a great wordsmith, Gainsbourg excelled at playing with alliteration and puns. His unique style was filled with self-mockery and provocation, which hid his immense sensitivity. Musically, he combined diverse styles (jazz, funk, bossa nova, reggae) and bridged French chanson and Anglo-Saxon pop, bringing the continents together. Everyone from Etienne Daho to Air, from The Divine Comedy to Franz Ferdinand—the list grow longer every days—has taken a page from his book.

What did Björk use to make her 2004 album *Medulla* after deciding "instruments are so over"?

The Velvet Underground

• *THE VELVET UNDERGROUND & NICO* (1967), *WHITE LIGHT/WHITE HEAT* (1967), *THE VELVET UNDERGROUND* (1969), *LOADED* (1970)
• FORMED IN 1964 AND DISBANDED IN 1973
BAUHAUS, DAVID BOWIE, ECHO & THE BUNNYMEN, BRIAN ENO, GALAXIE 500, IGGY POP, JOY DIVISION, MC5, THE MODERN LOVERS, MORRISSEY, THE NEW YORK DOLLS, R.E.M., PATTI SMITH, SONIC YOUTH, THE STOOGES, THE STROKES, TELEVISION

! She made it entirely from vocal samples and *a cappella* singing.

It's been said of the Velvet Underground that while only a few people bought their albums, every one of them started a band. Led by Lou Reed and John Cale, this New York quartet was the rock era's first and greatest cult act. Playing an uncompromising mixture of guitar feedback and songs about sex and drugs, the "VU" were as menacing as a dark alleyway and dazzling as all tomorrow's parties.

Reed and Cale met at Pickwick Records, where Reed was a staff songwriter churning out novelty tunes. They were an odd pair. Reed was a doo-wop fan from Long Island who studied poetry with Delmore Schwartz. John Cale was a Welsh composer who played with the avant-garde luminaries LaMonte Young and John Cage. Theirs would not be any ordinary rock band. Andy Warhol discovered them playing in a New York club, introduced a glassy-eyed German model as a second singer alongside Reed, and put his name and a banana on the cover of *The Velvet Underground & Nico* (1967).

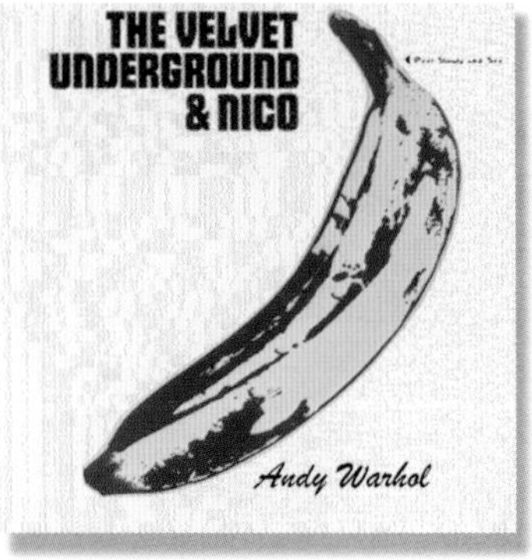

Released when the Monkees were No. 1, the album found Reed singing about S&M sex on the droning "Venus in Furs" and proclaiming on "Heroin," "It's my wife and it's my life" over Maureen Tucker's pounding drums. This stark reportage from the Gotham streets was set to innovative music that ranged from pretty lullabies to freak-outs that sounded like free jazz saxophonist Ornette Coleman playing a chainsaw.

Noise was at the core of *White Light/White Heat*, with Reed and Sterling Morrison's guitars howling over the roughest song forms. The 1967 album was dominated

The Velvet Underground in Cambridge, Massachusetts, 1969.

Left: Andy Warhol's cover for *The Velvet Underground & Nico* (1967).

by "Sister Ray," an inimitable seventeen-minute opus that related a Brechtian orgy beneath an unholy racket of sound.

With nowhere to go from there, VU changed course. Their self-titled third album was so quiet Reed joked it was mixed in a closet. "Candy Says" and "Pale Blue Eyes" were two of his most intimate songs, their mood of disappointment perhaps inspired by Cale's departure in 1968. Reed was discovering that the heart could be just as treacherous as a desperate junkie or as fabulous as Warhol's arty superstars.

Loaded followed in 1970. So-called because their record label wanted it loaded with hits, it was, but no one heard them. The band split, and their legend began. "Sweet Jane" became a rock standard—in part because of Reed's makeover into a glam rock star by fan David Bowie—and "Rock and Roll" was a lasting testimony to four people whose lives were changed by their years in musical obscurity, and who would go on to change many more.

Puzzle:
Which rock groups are represented by these images?

Answer

1. Black Flag (United States).
2. The White Stripes (United States).
3. Green Day (United States).
4. Téléphone (France).
5. Pink Floyd (Great Britain).
6. Whitesnake (Great Britain).
7. Red Hot Chili Peppers (United States).
8. The Black Crowes (United States).

1

2

3

4

5

6

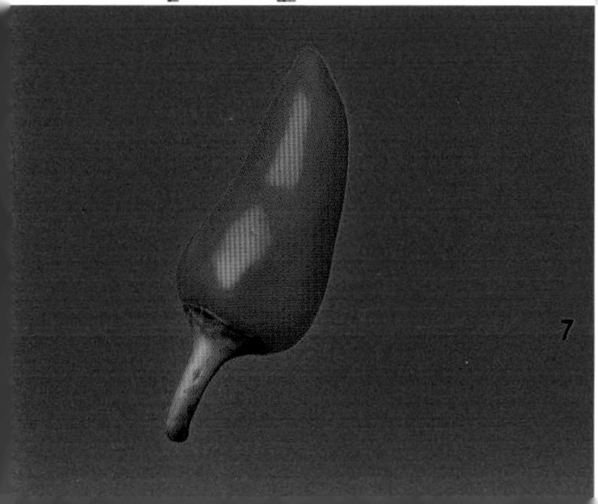

7

8

Led Zeppelin

• *LED ZEPPELIN* (1969), *LED ZEPPELIN II* (1969), *LED ZEPPELIN III* (1970), *LED ZEPPELIN IV* (1971), *PHYSICAL GRAFFITI* (1975)...
• FORMED IN 1968 AND DISBANDED IN 1980
AC/DC, AEROSMITH, TORI AMOS, THE BLACK CROWES, BLACK SABBATH, BON JOVI, BOSTON, CREAM, THE DARKNESS, DEF LEPPARD, IRON MAIDEN, KISS, NAZARETH, T. REX, VAN HALEN, THE WHITE STRIPES, WHITESNAKE

Led Zeppelin helped define heavy metal, and became for the 1970s what the Beatles were to the previous decade. Instead of making a career out of hit singles, the English band only released albums—often without titles. With Jimmy Page playing bludgeoning guitar riffs and shredding solos over a rampaging blues rhythm, they wielded their influences into everything great about rock 'n' roll —sex, abandon, and noise.

The band was a strange mixture of individuals. Jimmy Page was Swinging London's most in-demand session guitarist. The shy musician had perfected a proficient but anonymous style on hits by the Who and the Kinks.

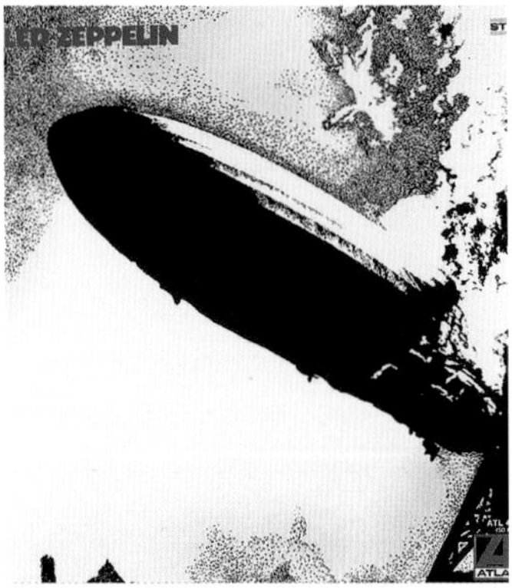

He met the classically trained bassist/arranger John Paul Jones while making Donovan's "Hurdy Gurdy Man," and drafted Robert Plant and John Bonham from a Midlands pub band to form the "New Yardbirds" in 1968. Keith Moon joked it would go down like a "lead zeppelin," hence the band's name.

Lengthy tours made them enormously popular—Led Zeppelin could blow any band offstage. They often played for hours, spinning their originals and blues favorites into epic jams. The hard-living Bonham played drums like thunder. Fey Page would use a violin bow to coax strange new noises from his guitar. Plant sang in an androgynous scream, usually bemoaning a cold-hearted vixen or spinning a *Lord of the Rings*-derived tale. They were just as exciting on record, where Page incorporated elements like Indian orchestras and embraced gentle English folk on *Led Zeppelin III* (1970). They soaked up musical influences at a ferocious rate, and even approved of the very punks who dismissed them as dinosaurs. As had happened to their blues heroes

The lead singer of Led Zeppelin, Robert Plant, in concert (c. 1970).

Left: Cover of *Led Zeppelin* (1969).

(who they often blatantly plagiarized for hits like "Whole Lotta Love"), Zeppelin's tremendous success led many to suspect they had done a deal with the devil. Their interest in the sorcerer Aleister Crowley and on-tour antics, which included an unprintable story involving a groupie and a shark, gave them a dark image. The devil demanded his due and in the second half of the 1970s, the band was beset with accidents and addiction. Bonham's death in 1979 effectively ended Zeppelin, but plenty of bands were there to take up where they left off.

?

What did Liverpool Airport change its name to in 2001?

Singer-Songwriters

• JACKSON BROWNE, JOHNNY CASH, NICK CAVE, LEONARD COHEN, BOB DYLAN, LÉO FERRÉ, CAROLE KING, JONI MITCHELL, GRAHAM NASH, RANDY NEWMAN, PAUL SIMON, BRUCE SPRINGSTEEN, JAMES TAYLOR, TOM WAITS, NEIL YOUNG...
• UNITED STATES
• 1960S–

Singer and songwriter used to be two entirely separate occupations. Since the dawn of recording, the music industry had been set up where vocalists interpreted songs written by other people. When Bob Dylan and the Beatles began scoring hits with self-penned material, though, the song became a vehicle for personal expression. Their followers were known as singer-songwriters. Shying away from psychedelia's sonic convolutions, these songwriters of the late 1960s and 1970s presented their songs in a plain style. They sang in untutored voices that were full of character, accompanied by just an acoustic guitar or small combos of bass, drums, perhaps a piano, and conga. The emphasis was on the melody and, especially, the words. Singer-songwriters prided themselves on memorable tunes, but fans listened because of what they said about their intimate lives and concerns.
Individual voices emerged and their songs might seem like pages torn from their diaries.
Joni Mitchell was a painter with a Cubist's approach to melody and lyrics, who saw life from "Both Sides Now." She sang in several

! Liverpool John Lennon Airport.

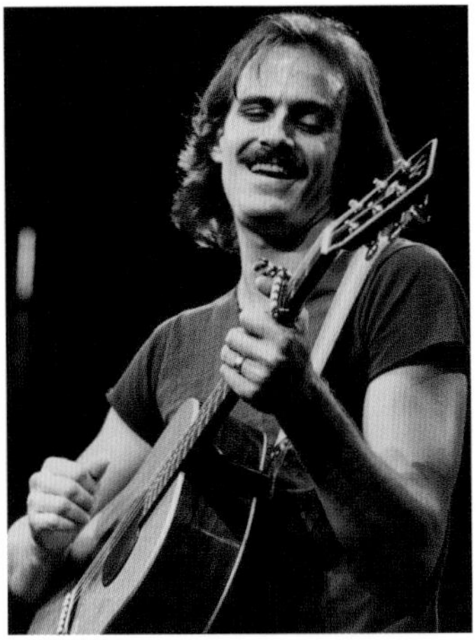

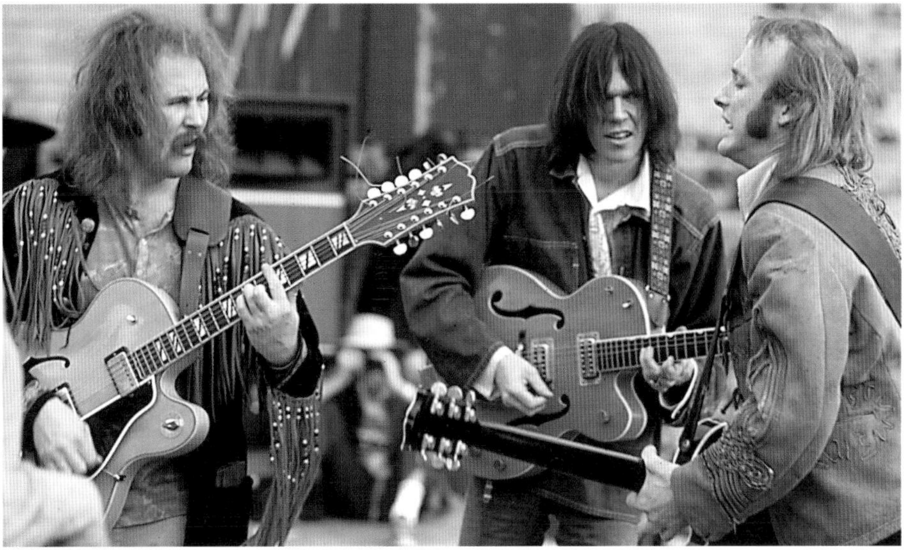

different voices, alternating between a weary tone and childish falsetto. But Mitchell was no kid. Her muse led her to explore world rhythms and the music of jazz great Charles Mingus.

Not everyone was quite so adventurous. Her Canadian compatriot Leonard Cohen was a novelist who brought his literary credibility to songwriting. James Taylor had survived two spells in a mental hospital to sing reassuring songs that papered over the cracks in his personal relationships. Jackson Browne chronicled his own romantic woes in minute detail and Biblical metaphor. Randy Newman preferred the rolling pianos of New Orleans R&B, and brought an unsparing irony to songs about racism and his peers' pretensions. At times, the singer-songwriters could seem narcissistic and even incestuous. Super-group Crosby Stills & Nash's Graham Nash dedicated "Our House" to Mitchell, who wrote the title track of her melancholy masterpiece *Blue* (1971) about Taylor. Taylor married Carly Simon, whose song "You're So Vain" might have been about him, Mick Jagger, or the actor Warren Beatty.

Today's most successful artists have mastered the art of the pen, writing their own material and setting it to impassioned music. Beneath Bruce Springsteen's rock bluster, Tom Waits's avant-garde clatter, or Nick Cave's tremble is the legacy of storytelling and character sketches. Human drama has never sounded so good.

The musicians David Crosby, Neil Young, and Stephen Stills playing in San Diego. December, 1969.

Left:
(far left)
Detail from the cover of Joni Mitchell's *Both Sides Now* (2000).

(right)
James Taylor playing at Madison Square Garden during the No Nukes Concert in 1980. Sponsored by Warner Brothers.

The Cantautori

• FABRIZIO DE ANDRE, CLAUDE BAGLIONI, FRANCO BATTIATO, LUCIO BATTISTI, ANGELO BRANDUARDI, PAOLO CONTE, LUCIO DALLA, FRANCESCO GUCCINI, JOVANOTTI, EROS RAMAZZOTTI, LUIGI TENCO, ZUCCHERO...
• ITALY
• 1960S–

One of the most significant events in Italian pop music history occurred in 1967 during the *San Remo Song Festival.* The televised contest was one of Italy's most prestigious events. When Luigi Tenco's "Ciao Amore" was eliminated from the competition, the young singer from Cassine committed suicide. He could not believe the nation was not ready for his art.

Tenco was the first of a generation of performers known as the *cantautori.* Like Tenco, these singers were influenced by jazz music and the literate songwriting of Bob Dylan and Leonard Cohen. Their pungent lyrics attacked society's conventions and celebrated love in explicit terms. San Remo wouldn't recognize them, but the extreme student unrest of 1968 made Italy take notice.That year, Fabrizio De André released his first album. This son of a Maquis fighter sang about prostitutes, protested the death penalty, and translated songs by Dylan and chansonnier Georges Brassens.

His angry street sensibilities fit perfectly with the post-1968 days of rage.

But throughout the 1970s, he was a controversial figure. Like many cantautori, De André made concept albums. He satirized the Ten Commandments in *La buona novella* (1970), a musical retelling of the life of Christ. When De André was kidnapped in Sardinia in 1979, he absolved his captors and wrote an LP about the island's people.

The cantautori reacted against derivative Italian pop in different ways. Some, like De André, based their music on regional styles. Reporter-turned-songwriter Francesco Guccini even compiled a dictionary of his Apennine hometown's local dialect, as well as recording scathing denouncements of contemporary Italian life. Others, like the frizzy-haired Angelo Branduardi, arranged their songs in a Baroque style or experimented with electronics.

The cantautori suffered the fate of every reactionary movement. They were swallowed up by the mainstream.

In 1977, the students took to the streets again—this time to protest high ticket prices. The cantautori survived as institutions. Lucio Battisti's soulful psychedelic songs became hits in the U.S. and U.K., and were even translated by David Bowie. De André's Mediterranean tribute *Creuza de Ma* (1984) was hailed as one of the best Italian albums of the decade and praised by Talking Heads' David Byrne. The Sicilian singer Franco Battiato went

Portrait of Paolo Conte, January 1993.

from working with VCS-3 synthesizers on obscure albums like *Fetus* (1971) to becoming one of the 1980s' biggest pop stars. It's as if Frank Zappa turned into Elton John.

The prickliest of the cantautori, however, is also the most renowned. Since his debut in 1974, Paolo Conte has maintained a steady allegiance to jazz and the salty vocabulary of his native Asti. The grizzled singer's dissolute songs have gained him an international following. Perennially dressed in black, stroking hopeless melodies from his piano with his nicotine-stained fingers, croaking odes of regret, Conte is like a ghost of missed chances.

Other notable cantautori include Lucio Dalla, whose music has enjoyed four decades of success; Claudio Baglioni, who, besides his music career, also maintained a separate acting career, appearing in several films by Franco Zeffirelli; Eros Ramazzotti, who was especially popular in Germany, Mexico, and Argentina during the 1990s; Zucchero, who founded the band Le Nuove Luci as a teenager and went on to become one of the best-selling artists in Italy and a favorite all over Europe in the early 1990s; and Jovanotti (born Lorenzo Cherubini), who made his name in the music business first as a DJ for a radio station, then as a television host for *DJ TV* and *1,2,3 Casino.* His hit recording of "Cancella Il Debito" in 2000 cemented his position among fellow musical greats. Luigi Tenco would approve of this newest generation of cantautori stars.

What word did Prince print on his face during the 1990s?

Fela Kuti

• *CONFUSION* (1975), *SHUFFERING AND SHMILING* (1977), *ZOMBIE* (1977), *COFFIN FOR HEAD OF STATE* (1981)...
• 1938–1997
DAVID BYRNE, COMMON, D'ANGELO, JANE'S ADDICTION, YOUSSOU N'DOUR, RED HOT CHILI PEPPERS, SADE, TALKING HEADS

An iconoclast who bowed to no one, Fela Kuti is one of the African continent's greatest stars.
He invented Afrobeat, a so-called "music of many colors," which incorporated James Brown's funk, American jazz, West African dance music, and the supernaturally syncopated rhythms of drummer Tony Allen. From a nightclub in his native Lagos, Nigeria, the multitalented musician and dancer continually threatened the military authorities with his music until his untimely death from AIDS in 1997.
Afrobeat was wholly at the mercy of its creator's whims. Based around an endless groove and punctuated with the upbeat horn fanfares and bubbly guitars of West African highlife, songs went on for as long as Kuti wanted them to. He often warmed up the audience with an infectious beat before delivering a rant in pidgin English—the accepted common language of Africa—about whatever was on his mind. Meanwhile, his immense ensemble would try to out-dance the throbbing crowd.
Lagos's Empire Club became Kuti's pulpit. While touring America in the late 1960s, he was introduced to black radicalism; his awakened consciousness inspired him to write inflammatory material like "Gentleman," a song that criticized Africans for wearing Western-styled clothing. He attacked organized religion on "Shuffering and Shmiling." His indictment of the military rulers of Nigeria on 1977's "Zombie" led to an attack on his commune by over a thousand soldiers. Kuti was left with a broken collarbone. His mother was killed. Kuti delivered her body to the army barracks, then in 1981, wrote "Coffin for Head of State."
Nigeria's underclass loved Kuti for his provocations, and mimicked his robotic dance moves at demonstrations. But he was resolutely unlovable and erratic. He recorded misogynist material like "Mattress," married twenty-seven of his dancers at a single ceremony, and dismissed AIDS as "a white man's disease" and condoms as "un-African." His music brought Paul McCartney to tears. Kuti denounced the Beatle from the stage and accused him of

! "Slave." He was protesting his record deal.

Fela Kuti on stage, 1992.

"stealing black man's music." Since his death, when a million people clogged the streets of Lagos, Kuti's influence has spread well beyond the walls of the Empire Club. His music is now sampled by rappers and praised by the likes of Talking Heads and Blur. But most importantly, he set an example for African musicians like Youssou N'Dour and Salif Keita to follow: sing loudly and the world will hear you.

The Cuban Sound

• RAY BARRETTO, RUBÉN BLADES, BUENA VISTA SOCIAL CLUB, WILLIE COLÓN, CELIA CRUZ, OSCAR D'LEON, BENY MORÉ, EDDIE PALMIERI, TITO PUENTE, ARSENIO RODRÍGUEZ...
• COLOMBIA, CUBA, DOMINICAN REPUBLIC, PUERTO RICO, UNITED STATES, VENEZUELA
• 1930s–

In 1996, Ry Cooder snuck into Cuba. The American guitarist's mission was to track down members of the Buena Vista Social Club, a 1940s gathering place for an elite group of vocalists, pianists, and players of a seven-stringed *armonico* guitar. He uncovered some of the elderly fraternity in unlikely places. But the club's reunion album became one of the year's biggest commercial successes.

Many discovered Cuban music through that album, but there are those for whom it has always been a way of life. Music is Cuba's biggest export; its rhythms are a memory of when Spanish colonists and their West African slaves settled there in the sixteenth century and traded musical ideas. The Caribbean island's music grew out of the slaves' Santeria superstition, which assigned each of its deities a particular rhythm that became, in turn, a secret kind of language. Those rhythms became the dialect of many styles, all of them associated with dancing—the sedate *danzon* performed by plantation owners, the lewd moves of the forbidden *rumba,* and the *son* of Cuba's eastern provinces. *Son* was a flexible alliance of Spanish instruments and African beats. To the distinctive toc-toc sound of the *clave,* musicians like the blind guitarist Arsenio Rodríguez added an army of horns,

Street scene in Cuba, 1991. The group is playing *samba*, a very popular style of Latin dance and music. The improvised choreography centers around Laura de Vison, Rio de Janeiro's most famous transvestite.

Left: Scene from Wim Wenders's *Buena Vista Social Club* (1999), starring singer Ibrahim Ferrer, pictured here.

a piano, and conga drum.
He formed the most influential orchestra of the 1940s, whose improvised solos drove audiences wild. Other pioneers like singer Beny Moré freely mixed *son* with *guajiro* folk music. With his rousing vocals, the self-styled "Barbarian of Rhythm" became a national hero.
The 1959 revolution forced Cuban music abroad—Rodríguez was one of those who fled; Moré stayed. In America's melting pot, *son* was exposed to new flavors like jazz, the big band sound, and Puerto Rican folk songs popular in the urban barrios of New York. This unique recipe became *salsa.* The word means "sauce," and was cried out to applaud a particularly scorching solo, although others swear it comes from "Echale Salsita," a *son* about a street vendor whose chorus exuberantly cried, "Salsaaaaaa!"
Salsa spread like wildfire. Visitors to the sugar town of Cali in Colombia are told they're in "the *salsa* capital of the world" —a long way away from "Nu Yorica." There is *salsa romantica, salsa erotica,* the *salsa pop* of Gloria Estefan and Marc Anthony, and various local variants created when salsa arrived in Venezuela and the Dominican Republic. Whether played by Havana retirees or young *salseros,* Cuban music is a club open to everyone.

What did drug dealers take from trumpeter Chet Baker in 1966 when he couldn't pay them?

Krautrock

- CAN, CLUSTER, AMON DÜÜL, FAUST, KRAFTWERK, NEU!, TANGERINE DREAM...
- GERMANY
- 1960S–1970S

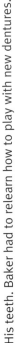

Krautrock was an attempt by West German musicians in the late 1960s and early 1970s to make a style of music they could call their own. Impressed by Karlheinz Stockhausen's electronic experiments and thrilled by the possibilities of free jazz, a series of groups made propulsive, intellectual, and sometimes truly weird music that reflected Germany's industrial rebirth, and that influenced much of modern rock to come.

At the time, West Germany was at a historical crossroads. Europe had been shaken by the upheavals of 1968. The Cold War was being slugged out between America and the Soviet Union while Vietnam raged far away. Post-war Germany was experiencing an "economic miracle," and both Stockhausen and Joseph Beuys were making people take German art seriously. Students could either retreat from the world into a commune or confront it, as did the Baader-Meinhof Gang, with force.

Krautrock found itself in the middle. Bands like Can and Neu! —named after the most common term in German advertising—were like jazz bands in the sense that their music was the product of improvisation. They jammed until they hit a rhythmic stride that was as raw and intense as James Brown in jackboots. Neu!'s Klaus Dinger called his precise beats "motorik." Both bands used the studio as its own instrument, editing away impurities or treating their instruments with effects for a more cosmic sound.

Krautrockers eagerly embraced the noise of the future in order to free their listeners from society or to comment on it. Edgar Froese formed Tangerine Dream after meeting Salvador Dalí, and used synthesizers to make spacey and sprawling music intended for "psychedelic meditation." By the 1980s, Tangerine Dream was making Hollywood soundtracks, the most famous being the cult classic, *Risky Business*. Kraftwerk went one further. The quartet's landmark 1974 album *Autobahn* was made of distorted samples taken from rides around Germany's endless motorways.

! His teeth. Baker had to relearn how to play with new dentures.

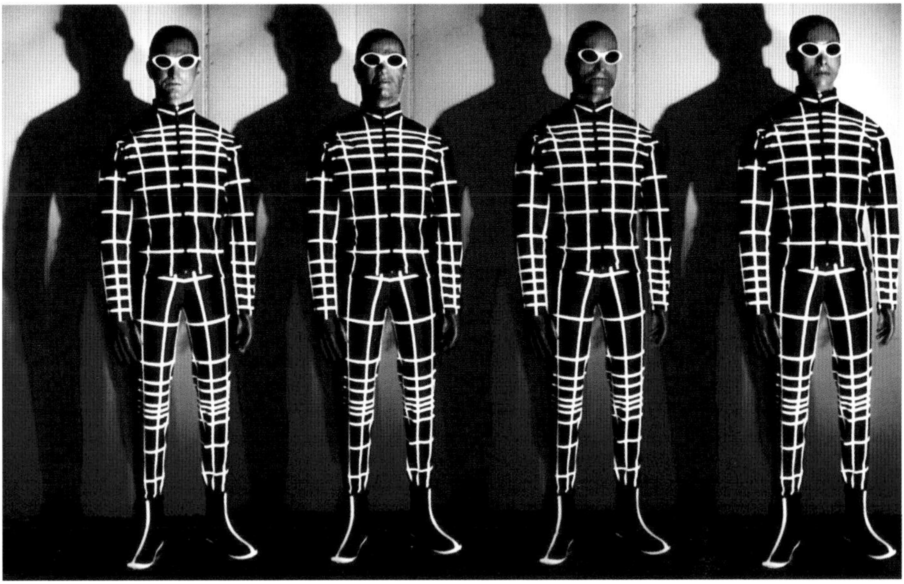

Kraftwerk, 1988.

Kraftwerk's music sounded like it was made by computers in their Kling Klang studio. The group even tried to replace themselves with robots. But there was a sense of human futility to the music, too. Their future was one whose dehumanized perfection was an unrealizable utopia.
This strange union of futurism and primitivism made for timeless music. David Bowie, U2, and Radiohead all found inspiration in the sound of Berlin and Cologne. In New York, Kraftwerk's coldness was recognized as the sound of the urban jungle.
Hip-hop DJs sampled their synthesized tones to create a sound called electro. The synthesizer soon became the instrument of choice for 1980s pop, while fledgling techno experimenters made their own all-electronic dance music and soundscapes, continuing to chart the still negotiable space between man and machine.

Lyrics and music
Who said what?

Plato

Woody Allen

Billy Idol

Bono

Maria Callas

Joe Cocker

Aretha Franklin

Avril Lavigne

Courtney Love

Carlos Santana

DJs

• PAUL VAN DYK, FATBOY SLIM, ALAN FREED, GRANDMASTER FLASH, MURRAY "THE K" KAUFMAN, KOOL DJ HERC, PAUL OAKENFOLD, JOHN PEEL, WOLFMAN JACK...
• GREAT BRITAIN, UNITED STATES
• 1950S–

When the American singer Beck sang, "I've got two turntables and a microphone" in his 1996 hit "Where It's At," the humble record player entered a musical pantheon that includes Johnny B. Goode's guitar and James Brown's funky drummer. Along with an audio mixer and a crate of vinyl records, those turntables are the stock in trade of the DJ.

"DJ" is short for "disc jockey" and first referred to a radio personality who talked in-between the records as he cued them up. The term now covers a variety of performers, ranging from the DJs who play records for thousands of clubbers to hip-hop DJs who provide beats for rappers. In Jamaica, a DJ is someone who talks or "chats" over the top of instrumental versions of hits played by a "selector" at a sound system dance. These "deejays"—a combination of cheerleader, newscaster, and storyteller—anticipated today's hip-hop MCs.

Radio DJs have played an important role in the history of rock music. Although their prominence is threatened by the popularity of MP3s, DJs are usually on the front line of the latest musical trend. Cleveland DJ Alan Freed gave rock 'n' roll its name, and ran package tours that helped popularize the music. The late BBC DJ John Peel was revered for championing misunderstood genres and oddball groups like the Fall—although he often played the records at the wrong speed.

But the dance floor is now the true territory of DJs. Filling it is their ultimate goal. In the mid-1970s, Jamaican-American DJ Kool Herc got New York crowds going by repeating the breaks from their favorite funk records. The sound system vet

—who sometimes rhymed over these instrumental passages—prolonged the break by switching between two copies of the same record with his audio mixer. Herc's jumping between the two records gave the hip-hop genre its name. Grandmaster Flash broadened the DJ vocabulary by cutting between two tracks right on the beat to create a segue, using his hands to "rewind" a record and replay a passage, and changing the turntable speed for effect. His 1981 single "The Adventures of Grandmaster Flash on the Wheels of Steel" established the DJ as a star. Hip-hop DJs also now scratch records back and forth to improvise new pieces of music from prerecorded tracks. Most club DJs prefer to manipulate the mass euphoria of raving dancers through their record selection. Some are so skilled at maintaining a crowd's chemically-enhanced excitement levels that they command outrageous salaries for a night's work. Superstar DJs like Paul van Dyk and Fatboy Slim have gone on to remix others' music to suit the clubs and make their own records to spin. Like a revolving twelve-inch disc, the DJ has come full circle.

Above:
A DJ at his turntable.

Left:
Fat Boy Slim, aka Norman Cook, during a rehearsal for the MTV Video Music Awards at New York's Metropolitan Opera House. September 4, 2001.

?

How did Jimi Hendrix avoid being drafted into the army during the Vietnam War?

Heavy Metal

• ANTHRAX, BLACK SABBATH, THE DARKNESS, DEEP PURPLE, DEF LEPPARD, GUNS N' ROSES, IRON MAIDEN, JUDAS PRIEST, KISS, LED ZEPPELIN, MEGADEATH, METALLICA, MÖTLEY CRÜE, NAPALM DEATH, POISON, RATT, RUSH, SLAYER...
• GREAT BRITAIN, UNITED STATES
• 1970S–

When the American beat writer William S. Burroughs coined the term "heavy metal" in his 1962 novel *Naked Lunch,* he couldn't have guessed what it would eventually mean. Launched by the British bands Led Zeppelin and Black Sabbath in the 1970s, heavy metal became a thunderous music of screaming rock guitars playing simple riffs underneath theatrical singing. Heavy metal enjoyed great popularity in the 1980s and 1990s despite controversy over its offensive lyrics and its stars' outrageous appearances.

Heavy metal grew out of bands seeking to imitate Jimi Hendrix and Cream's hard rock sound by turning up their guitar amps and replacing their blues swing with a steady four-on-the-floor plod. Led Zeppelin are thought of as metal godfathers, but it was the less-proficient Black Sabbath who popularized the genre. Guitarist Tony Iommi, who lost his fingertips in a factory accident, down-tuned his guitar for a grimier sound. Singer Ozzy Osbourne gave their songs a truly creepy demeanor. The more capable Sabbath became, the less effective they were, but their first four albums found plenty of followers.

The new wave of British heavy metal was equally inspired by punk. Bands like Iron Maiden wore leather and toughened their sound by speeding up Sabbath's swampy tempo and showcasing frequent duels between their two lead guitarists. Their erudite lyrics drew as much on Thucydides as on comic books.

Other groups looked to the outlandish image and vaunting ambition of 1970s arena rockers

! By pretending he was gay.

like Kiss. Hair metal embraced the androgyny and riffs of glam rock. Following the No. 1 success of Def Leppard's *Pyromania* in 1983, a wave of opportunists, with a beautician's worth of mousse and makeup, supplied the fledgling MTV with a readymade cast of threats to society. Loaded with misogynist double entendres and flaunting satanic props for shock value, the likes of Mötley Crüe made their teenage fans shout at the devil. Alternating party anthems with sappy ballads, hair metal dominated the 1980s while an underground scene developed in reaction. Head-banging thrash bands competed to see who was faster—the shortest track on Napalm Death's *Scum* (1987) lasted four seconds. Metal's aggression inspired other anti-social offshoots. Death metal was a bass-heavy grind with lyrics that read like autopsy reports. Nirvana shamed metal's excesses, although their punk revolution was ironically predicated on Sabbath's grotty grind. The most successful 1990s metallers—Metallica, Nine Inch Nails, and Red Hot Chili Peppers—survived because of their ability to absorb outside elements like funk and programmed beats, while tapping into the same introspective self-pity as Kurt Cobain. Other bands have added hip-hop elements.

Metal looks likely to survive for as long as there are parents to complain about the noise.

Mötley Crüe during the Monsters of Rock Festival in Hasselt, Belgium. August 1991.

Left:
Black Sabbath in concert in Copenhagen, January 1974.

Glam Rock

• DAVID BOWIE, ALICE COOPER, GARY GLITTER, NINA HAGEN, JOBRIATH, KISS, NEW YORK DOLLS, SUZI QUATRO, QUEEN, SLADE, SWEET, T. REX, ROXY MUSIC . . .
• GREAT BRITAIN, UNITED STATES
• 1970S

Six months after the Beatles split up in April 1970, T. Rex's electric warrior Marc Bolan reported for duty. His first U.K. Top 3 hit, "Ride a White Swan," was a return to pop music's innocence. Its crisp guitar lines played over a handclapped beat. T. Rex gave their bubblegum sound added sweetness by swathing it in strings. This was the sound of glam rock. If the 1960s had Beatlemania, the 1970s had T. Rexctasy.
Bolan was a former teenage model and folk singer inspired by the simplicity of early rock 'n' roll. Compared to psychedelia's baroque density, glam rock barely needed more than three chords. Glam rockers played insanely catchy pop songs that went all the way back to the Beatles in their "Please Please Me" phase. As other bands capitalized on T. Rex's sound, repetitive lyrics like "Bang a Gong" and "Skweeze Me Pleeze Me" were the order of the day. Only the chameleon-like David Bowie —a folkie gone glam—and Roxy Music were clever enough to put their pop in quotation marks.
Roxy Music's Bryan Ferry filled his songs with imagery taken from cigarette ads and old movie posters, as bandmate Brian Eno processed their sound through strange effects generators.
Glam declared its extraordinariness through its theatrical fashion sense.

New York Dolls in Dallas, February 10, 1974. From left to right: Arthur Kane, Sy Sylvain, David Johansen, Jerry Nolan, and Johnny Thunders.

Left: Glam rocker Marc Bolan.

What did singer Cat Stevens do after nearly being swept out to sea?

Inspired by Elvis Presley's sequined jumpsuits, glam rockers like Slade and Sweet looked like they beamed down from another planet, a conceit that Bowie embraced on his concept album *The Rise and Fall of Ziggy Stardust and the Spiders from Mars* (1972). Bolan daubed glitter around his eyes while Bowie wore a thunderbolt across his face on the cover of *Aladdin Sane* (1973). Roxy Music even wore leopard skins. Americans thought glam rock was too fey, with two notable exceptions: trash rockers the New York Dolls and the hard rock band Kiss, who adopted the spangled outfits and make-up for cartoonish shock value. When the hit machine dried up and Bolan's pixie looks started to get puffy, glam became yesterday's glitter. It was hard not to laugh at the ridiculousness of it all, but glam proved less throwaway than anyone could have imagined. Bowie survived the end through a series of musical transformations, and at the other end of the 1970s, punk rockers, heavy metallers, and even post-punkers reached for hairspray. Glam expressed to them a basic truth: a little glitter can make anyone look like a star.

David Bowie

• *THE MAN WHO SOLD THE WORLD* (1970), *HUNKY DORY* (1971), *SPACE ODDITY* (1972), *ZIGGY STARDUST* (1972), *ALADDIN SANE* (1973), *DIAMOND DOGS* (1974), *YOUNG AMERICANS* (1975), *LOW* (1977), *HEROES* (1977), *LET'S DANCE* (1983) . . .
• 1947
JOHN CALE, JULIAN COPE, CULTURE CLUB, DURAN DURAN, BRIAN ENO, INXS, QUEEN, LOU REED, ROXY MUSIC, THE SMITHS, SUEDE, RUFUS WAINWRIGHT

The man who sold the world. Aladdin Sane. The thin white duke. Will the real David Bowie ever stand up? No modern performer has proved himself such a cracked actor, and few artists his age seem to sustain their vitality. The former David Jones has been the greatest exponent of the pop star as a chameleon. It's resulted in strange shifts in musical styles and kept him young with the wondrous possibility of re-invention. Although songs like "The Laughing Gnome" displayed a quaint appreciation of the music hall psychedelia of Swinging Sixties London, Bowie became a star with the star-spangled sound of glam rock. His record company was ready to give up on the former mime when he released *The Rise and Fall of Ziggy Stardust and the Spiders from Mars* (1972). With guitarist Mick Ronson as his musical director, David Bowie eclipsed his friend Marc Bolan as glam's leading figure, and brought mentors like Lou Reed along for the glitter. Bowie internalized Stardust's apocalyptic fantasies into *Aladdin Sane* (1973), adopting the album's title as the namesake of his alter ego, a character not unlike his real-life mentally ill brother, Terry Jones. Then he changed again. In 1974, he released *Diamond Dogs* and, while on the American tour of the new album, shocked audiences with pleated pants, frosted hair, and his face bleached whiter than cocaine. With his next album, *Young Americans* (1975), Bowie invented plastic soul. If backing singer Luther Vandross helped Bowie negotiate R&B, his next collaborator was even more crucial. Brian Eno was the famed member of Roxy Music who couldn't play an instrument. He just provided ideas. In Berlin, Bowie teamed with Eno to create a musical trilogy

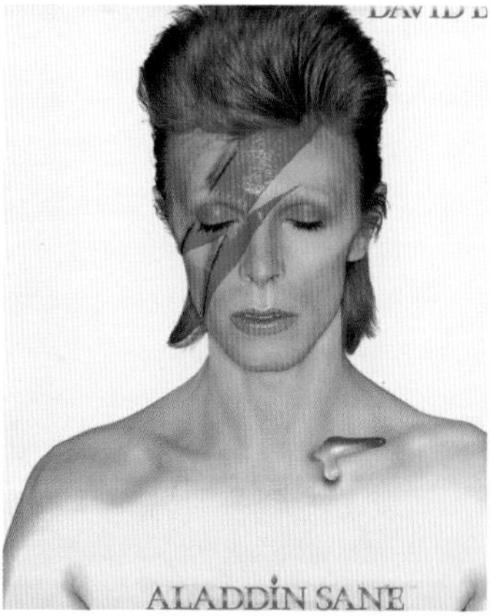

! He converted to Islam.

Portrait of
David Bowie.
Brussels, 1996.

Left:
Cover of David Bowie's
Aladdin Sane (1973).

influenced by Kraftwerk's computerized alienation and William S. Burroughs's choppy writing style: *Low* and *Heroes* (both 1977) forged a sound that wouldn't be truly appreciated until the New Romantics took it up in the 1980s; *Lodger* (1979) went further by getting the players to trade instruments—making lead guitarist Carlos Alomar play drums, for example. The result was a bold, otherworldly sound. Bowie bought into the 1980s materialistic dream with a vengeance, surprising everyone with the success of "Let's Dance." Now a bona fide pop star, Bowie was scrutinized harder than ever before by the media, and his subsequent albums were found wanting. Chastened, Bowie vanished back into the laboratory with Eno for *Outside* (1995). This album skewed pop-art-rock and was his strongest collection of songs in years. The jungle loops of 1997's *Earthling* and the soft rock he's begun to play in the twenty-first century would have sounded farcical in another's hands, but Bowie's been laughing from the sidelines for almost forty years now.

David Bowie: *Arrange these photos in chronological order.*

Answer

1. 1986: David Bowie in Jim Henson's movie *Labyrinth.*
2. 1980: David Bowie in his video "Ashes to Ashes," directed by David Mallet.
3. 1995: David Bowie on tour after the release of his album *Outside.*
4. 1972: David Bowie as Ziggy Stardust after the release of his album *Ziggy Stardust.*
5. 1983: David Bowie on his U.S. *Moonlight* tour.

1

2

3

4

5

Positively Shocking

• G. G. ALLIN, ALICE COOPER, GUNS N' ROSES, NINA HAGEN, MADONNA, MARILYN MANSON, JIM MORRISON, OZZY OSBOURNE, IGGY POP, ELVIS PRESLEY, PRINCE, LOU REED, AXEL ROSE...
• INTERNATIONAL
• 1950S–

Throughout musical history, performers have teased their audiences, courting scandal and outrageous behavior for the sake of shock value.

Some musicians' exploits can even be aggressive, if it means winning over a crowd. Elvis's suggestive hip swaying, considered shocking to parents and a danger to youth in the 1950s, gave birth to a generation of rockers ecstatic by volume and their newfound freedom. In the 1960s, singers like Jim Morrison and Iggy Pop pushed the envelope even further with their own brand of sexual suggestiveness; their offensive behavior landed them both in court. In the 1970s, Lou Reed shocked audiences with his outlandish make-up, as did his androgynous-looking friend David Bowie. During the same period, Alice Cooper, wanting to embody the mutant child of American society, presented himself as equally macabre, androgynous, and sexually deviant; sometime he would lasciviously pet a boa constrictor on stage. And no one will ever forget the first televised appearance of the Austrian Nina Hagen in 1978, when she demonstrated proper masturbation techniques to the general public. In 1991, Axel Rose of Guns N' Roses went so far as to leap from the stage to attack an audience

member, which triggered a fight in the theater. G.G. Allin invited female fans to perform fellatio on him. He even threw his excrement into the audience, after relieving himself in public. Marilyn Manson is known for a whole array of equally surprising taunts and attacks. In *Antichrist Superstar* (1996), he became even more blasphemous, criticizing American society in the stranglehold of political correctness. For some, shock represents sure success. Madonna probably can't count how many times she has offended. In 1984, Italian religious authorities, outraged by her behavior with her dancers, even called for the censorship of the *Like a Virgin* tour in their country. Some have, however, developed a sense of boundaries. Ozzy Osbourne, who once ripped off bat heads with his teeth, now stars in a reality show on television. Prince, who used to watch his girlfriend masturbate on stage, has withdrawn from the world and presently distributes Bibles with the Jehovah Witnesses, and the aforementioned Madonna has cooled in recent years by writing children's books. Perhaps the inundation of uncensored images has made audiences numb. At this point, normalcy is the most shocking act of all.

Alice Cooper on stage during a U.S. concert, 1975.

Left:
Marilyn Manson at the Fields of Rock Festival in Nijmegen, The Netherlands. June 2003.

What was the motto of '60s label Immediate?

Queen

• *SHEER HEART ATTACK* (1974), *A NIGHT AT THE OPERA* (1975), *A DAY AT THE RACES* (1976), *JAZZ* (1978), *THE GAME* (1980)...
• FORMED IN 1971 AND DISBANDED IN 1995
BEN FOLDS FIVE, DAVID BOWIE, JEFF BUCKLEY, THE CARS, THE CULT, THE DARKNESS, FOREIGNER, FRANKIE GOES TO HOLLYWOOD, JELLYFISH, RADIOHEAD, SCISSOR SISTERS, THIN LIZZY, ROBBIE WILLIAMS

With their crested insignia, Queen was one of the last vestiges of the "Rule Britannia" ethos. Although America slipped from their grip once the pop duo Wham! came along, the operatic rockers stayed huge everywhere else. It is impossible to imagine singer Freddie Mercury apart from his beloved stadiums, leading South Americans, Africans, and Japanese in note-perfect renditions of the cult classic "We Are the Champions." The band never apologized for their ambition. It was the reward of both sweat and Freddie Mercury's strange collaboration with guitarist Brian May. Mercury was a Gilbert and Sullivan enthusiast who grew up in post-Raj India before moving to the prosaic English suburbs. May was good with his hands —building his first guitar from the remains of an old fireplace— and always kept one eye on the stars, abandoning a college

! "Happy to Be Part of the Industry of Human Happiness."

dissertation on space dust to form Queen. The duo combined innovation and imperialism in equal measure. They refused to play live until they were signed. They intended "Bohemian Rhapsody" as a monolith: a six-minute opus so grandiloquent that the backing vocal tape was rendered virtually transparent in the studio, so un-performable Queen filmed a video to promote it, and so dramatic that its final gong crash still raises neck hairs. Bassist John Deacon and drummer Roger Taylor came into their own as songwriters after the band turned their backs on epics like "Somebody to Love" for three-minute pop songs. The American No. 1 "Another One Bites the Dust" saw Deacon co-opting a Chic bass line to introduce Queen to disco. Taylor's art was more suited to Thatcher's parochial Britain. In the 1980s, his "Radio Ga Ga" lamented the loss of old values in a video age, unashamedly accompanied by a recreation of Fritz Lang's *Metropolis* (1927) in one of the most lavish clips ever made. When they played the charity concert Live Aid in 1985, an awe-struck Bob Geldof noted, "It was the perfect stage for Freddie: the whole world." After Mercury was diagnosed with AIDS, the whiff of mortality only inspired the flamboyant performer to loftier heights. "Innuendo" and its accompanying album set new heights of ostentation—gypsy guitar solos, songs to Freddie's cats, Noël Coward tributes—but it was hard to hear May's tribute "The Show Must Go On" and not feel the neck hairs tingle again.

Freddie Mercury in concert in Paris, 1980.

Left: Queen in concert (c.1976–1979): Roger Taylor (drums), Freddie Mercury (vocals), Brian May (guitar), and John Deacon (bass).

N.Y. Punk

• BLONDIE, JOHNNY THUNDERS AND THE HEARTBREAKERS, NEW YORK DOLLS, THE RAMONES, RICHARD HELL AND THE VOIDOIDS, PATTI SMITH, SUICIDE, TALKING HEADS, TELEVISION...
• NEW YORK
• 1970S–

While 1976, the year of America's bicentennial and the Ramones' debut album, is punk rock's year zero, the word "punk"—an epithet for a male hustler—has an even longer history. Critic Dave Marsh first used the phrase "punk rock" to describe a 1960s garage band. Like those marginal groups with their homemade rock oddities, the New York punk of the 1970s was about making and doing things exactly the way you wanted to. In a decade where bands like Jethro Tull and Yes performed hopelessly complex symphonic fantasies, punk had to be something anybody could do. Songs were terse and the chords were simple enough for anyone to learn. Inspired by misfits like the Stooges and the Velvet Underground, punk was loud and meant to get up your nose. Bands cut away the chaff of presentation to directly connect with their disenchanted audience. Punk rock couldn't be ignored. British punk rock bands gave the music its notoriety, but the sound was born in New York City. Outsider groups and artists coalesced around the nightclub CBGB—short for Country Bluegrass and Blues—after Television's Tom Verlaine convinced the owner to put on rock bands. At CBGB, British fashion huckster Malcolm McLaren saw the ragged Heartbreakers and got

The Ramones in the 1970s.

Right:
Blondie, 1981. From left to right: Nigel Harrison (bass), Chris Stein (guitar), Debbie Harry (vocals), Clem Burke (drums), Frank Infante (guitar), and Jimmy Destri (keyboard).

the idea to start the Sex Pistols. The Ramones were punk *non plus ultra,* the ultimate in no frills thrills. From faraway Forest Hills, they dressed like an inner-city gang, all torn jeans and black leather jackets. The fourteen songs on their self-titled debut went by in a half-hour-long blur. There were no solos. The lyrics were comic strip minimal, tackling topics torn from the tabloids: sordid tales of glue-sniffing and child abuse followed sappy love songs.

There was more to New York punk than sheer aggression. Television absorbed John Coltrane and played long and lyrical guitar solos. Talking Heads' David Byrne once said he wanted to play his guitar like an African musician. Blondie went through stylish pastiches quicker than singer Debbie Harry did bottles of hair dye. Synth duo Suicide didn't even use guitars. Patti Smith and Richard Hell were poets who upped the lyrical ante. Hell's "Blank Generation" described the fans who mimicked his distraught fashion sense, while the buttoned-down Byrne took on the nervy persona of "Psycho Killer" among the Valium-addicted Me Generation.

Unlike their U.K. counterparts, these bands were more influential than successful. The Ramones spent the next two decades grousing about their inability to score a hit. But punk fostered underground scenes all over America. It has refused to die —when Nirvana finally brought the independent teen spirit to the Top 10 in 1991, plenty of identikit pop-punk bands like Green Day and Rancid whined in their wake.

Who shot soul singer Marvin Gaye to death on April 1, 1984?

U.K. Punk

• BUZZCOCKS, THE CLASH, THE JAM, JOY DIVISION, THE SEX PISTOLS, SIOUXSIE AND THE BANSHEES, WIRE, X-RAY SPEX...
• UNITED KINGDOM
• 1970S

The U.K. punk band the Sex Pistols only released one album during their brief lifetime, yet it was one of the most influential in rock history. With its wall of metallic guitars and singer Johnny Rotten's desperate scream, *Never Mind the Bollocks Here's the Sex Pistols* (1977) might be the only album to sound like it could bring down a government. The British punk scene was influenced by America—the Ramones' 1976 London Roundhouse concert was attended by Johnny Rotten (who was terrified of them) and members of the Clash. But it existed in a society where more was at stake. The punks went after the cows British society held sacred: the work ethic, post-war austerity, light entertainment, sexual repression, racism, the Queen's English. In the year of the Queen's Silver Jubilee, punk and Rotten's cry of "No Future" felt like the only legitimate response, accompanied by anti-social fashion—safety pin jewelry and rubber trousers—and violent battles with non-believers. Fashionista Malcolm McLaren formed the Sex Pistols from the lads who hung around Sex, his Kings Road boutique. Impressed by New York's punk scene, he intended them to be a Situationist détournement of the staid rock scene. The Pistols couldn't play their instruments or play the proper media games. They outraged the nation by swearing on television. But Rotten took McLaren's stunt further than he could have dreamed. His rants about abortion ("Bodies") and his generation ("Pretty Vacant") still draw blood today. Their brief flame-up (the Pistols split in 1978) inspired

! Marvin Gaye, Sr. killed his son during an argument.

many. Their nearest London rivals were the Clash. As the so-called "Only Band That Matters," the Clash demonstrated a true political nous in pogo-friendly punk like "White Riot." They played any kind of music that was an expression of the dispossessed—from reggae to early rap to music set to Allen Ginsburg's beat poetry. Other groups like X-Ray Spex and Siouxsie and the Banshees brought a female perspective, subverting sex roles with songs like "Oh Bondage, Up Yours."
In Manchester, Joy Division's punk made the alienated feel even more alienated—thanks to a pioneering use of echo chamber effects combined with Ian Curtis's permanently haunted croon on songs like "Isolation." Pete Shelley and Howard Devoto, who put on the Sex Pistols' 1976 concert in the city, formed the Buzzcocks, which made it safe for punks to write love songs that thumped like the heart of a wallflower being asked to dance.
A U.K. punk fanzine once printed three guitar chords, and said, "This is a chord, this is another, this is a third. Now form a band." The Sex Pistols opened a world of possibility like no one since the Beatles, and the punk movement could include retro groups like the Jam and the futuristic Wire. It swiftly splintered into post-punk, hardcore, and New Wave. Even if punk has lost some of its potency, its alternative ethos will always endure.

The Clash during their first American tour, February 1979. From left to right: Joe Strummer, Topper Headon, Paul Simonon, and Mick Jones.

Left:
Paul Cook from the Sex Pistols. London 1978.

Fashion: *Who's wearing what?*

Answer

1. Azzedine Alaïa for Grace Jones.
2. Dolce & Gabbana for Kylie Minogue.
3. Jean-Paul Gaultier for Madonna.
4. Bob Mackie for Cher.

1

2

DOLCE & GABBANA

•

AZZEDINE ALAÏA

•

BOB MACKIE

•

JEAN-PAUL GAULTIER

3

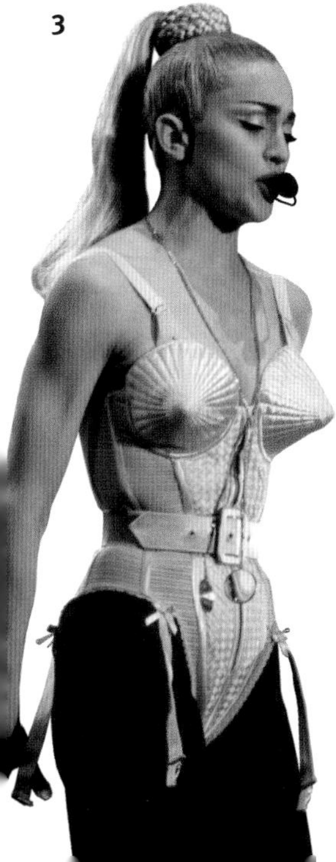

4

Disco

• ABBA, THE BEE GEES, BONEY M., CHIC, CLAUDE FRANÇOIS, GLORIA GAYNOR, PATRICK JUVET, VAN MCCOY, DIANA ROSS, SISTER SLEDGE, DONNA SUMMER, VILLAGE PEOPLE...
• INTERNATIONAL
• 1970S–LATE 1980S

Evolving out of soul and funk (with a hint of pop), disco emerged in the 1970s. James Brown, the self-named father of funk, was able to claim a kind of paternity over disco—after all, disco, like funk, worshipped bass lines and the beat. What funk lacked—lush sounds and suavity—disco claimed as its own. Its reliance on a steady rhythm combined with its fast beats and energy made it a crowd and club favorite. The beatbox, created by the German producer Giorgio Moroder, maintained disco's basic rhythms, and DJs played an important role in establishing the genre, giving lively energy to smooth-singing disco divas. As early as 1975, disco exploded with hits like "The Hustle" by Van McCoy and Donna Summer's "Love to Love You Baby." That same year, Dalida sang "J'attendrai," which quickly climbed the charts in France and Canada, and in the following year, Japan. France jumped into disco with Claude François and his "Cette année-là" and with Cerrone's now cult album *Love in C Minor* (1976). In 1977, disco was recognized worldwide after the success of the movie *Saturday Night Fever,* which featured an original soundtrack by the Bee Gees. Two years later, the French chic-styled disco queen Sheila and her group B. Devotion made waves with their song "Spacer." Patrick Hernandez found fame with "Born to Be Alive."

This Page:
(left)
The Bee Gees: Barry, Maurice, and Robin Gibb.

(right)
ABBA during a U.S. concert, 1979.

Right:
The Village People, 1979. From left to right: Randy Jones (cowboy), David Hodo (worker), Felipe Rose (Indian), Victor Willis (policeman), Glenn Hughes (biker), and Alexander Briley (soldier).

Hits came from all around the world: Sweden's Abba enjoyed great success with "Dancing Queen"; Holland's Boney M garnered fame for "Daddy Cool"; the Swiss Patrick Juvet's "I Love America" broke new ground. In America, The Village People, Chic, Diana Ross, and Sister Sledge encouraged people to get up and shake their groove thing. The famous musical film *Flashdance* (1983), with the song "What a Feeling," performed by Irene Cara, perfectly represented the vibe of an entire "dance" music generation. Disco clubs became just as famous as the music itself, with some, like New York's Studio 54 and Paris's Palace, serving as mythical venues, high-fashion homes to countless unforgettable parties full of fabulous people. Disco became such a force that even groups like the Rolling Stones and New Order made it part of their repertoires. But it had its enemies; "Disco sucks" became a popular (if inane) catchphrase. The backlash culminated in a 1979 rally where disco records were destroyed by a Chicago DJ with a bulldozer. But as "I Will Survive" singer Gloria Gaynor remarked, the music didn't die. It merely changed its name to "dance pop." From Madonna's earliest records to Michael Jackson's floor-filling *Thriller,* dance pop was the order of the day throughout the 1980s and 1990s, and in some discos still is.

?

Who moved to Berlin with David Bowie in 1976?

Bollywood

• AMITABH BACHCHAN, ASHA BHOLSE, R. D. BURMAN, AAMIR KHAN, KISHORE KUMAR, LATA MANGESHKAR, MOHAMMED RAFI, A. R. RAHMAN...
• INDIA
• 1930S–

Nearly every film made in Mumbai—or Bollywood—is a musical, and the music is a genre in its own right, often referred to by the Hindi word "filmi." Filmi is ubiquitous in India. You can hear it blaring from taxicabs, street vendors' stalls, election rallies, and TV programs. In a Bollywood film, the musical number functions like an opera aria. It can tell part of the story, let a character confide his or her innermost thoughts, or serenade two characters falling in love. The song sequence is an emotional high point and is usually accompanied by a lavish dance routine. Because the stars are not vocalists themselves, playback singers record the song and the actors lip-synch. Bollywood song lyrics are inevitably about love, related in exalted Hindi or Urdu with occasional lyrics in Arabic and Persian for added poetic effect. The melody is played by a masala of Indian tablas and sitars alongside Western instruments, like guitars and synthesizers. Songs were at first based on Indian classical music, but R.D. Burman became one of the first music directors to use Western elements in the funky soundtrack for 1966's *Teesri Manzil.* The iconoclastic Tamil composer A.R. Rahman scandalized purists by mixing pop, rock, reggae, and classical music in 1992's hit Hindu/Muslim romance *Roja.* Plagiarism is rife. Music directors often liberally adapt current Western hits and even other Bollywood numbers. Playback singers are stars in their own right and a senior citizen can still sing the role of a teenager. Lata Mangeshkar became so popular that she successfully lobbied in 1949 to be included in the credits. Her skyscraping soprano became a much-imitated modern standard. Mangeshkar is certified as the most recorded artist in the world, with over thirty thousand titles to her credit. She is seconded only by Mohammad Rafi—who has sung around twenty-six thousand songs—and rivaled by her sister, the versatile Asha Bholse. Playback singers can stamp their

! Iggy Pop. Bowie produced his albums *The Idiot* and *Lust for Life.*

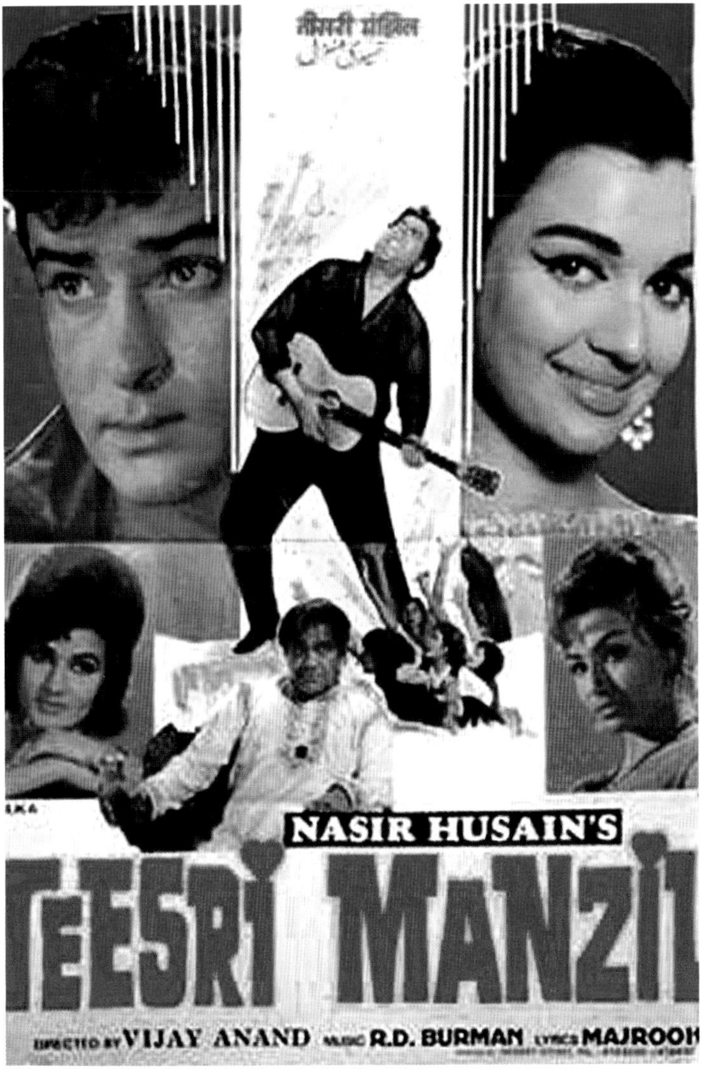

Poster for Vijay Anand's *Teesri Manzil* (1966), famous for its music composed by the great Indian composer, R.D. Burman.

own character on a song, and the eccentric Kishore Kumar became famous for his distinctive yodel.

Bollywood music has gradually attained global popularity. Young dance and hip-hop artists offer the South Asian diaspora remixed versions of old Bollywood hits. A.R. Rahman wrote the hit musical *Bombay Dreams* (2002), and songs like "Chamma Chamma" and Rafi's "Jaan Pehechaan Ho" have turned up in the Hollywood films *Moulin Rouge!* (2001) and *Ghost World* (2000). Bollywood isn't just for Mumbai cab drivers anymore.

Soft Rock and Adult Contemporary

• ERIC CLAPTON, PHIL COLLINS, DIRE STRAITS, GLORIA ESTEFAN, BRYAN FERRY, FLEETWOOD MAC, HALL AND OATES, ELTON JOHN, PAUL MCCARTNEY, GEORGE MICHAEL, BONNIE RAITT, SIMPLY RED, STING, WINGS...
• GREAT BRITAIN, UNITED STATES
• 1970S–

The 1960s' musical ferment changed pop's formula. So much for clean-cut singers fronting orchestras and big bands. Now the simple songs that delighted kids and charmed adults came with drums and electric guitars. Pop got a backbeat and became pop/rock; and it attracted both aspiring singer-songwriters and rock legends who found their long hair beginning to gray.
A pop/rock artist like Elton John rarely bothered playing solos on his piano or indulging in the musical tomfoolery practiced

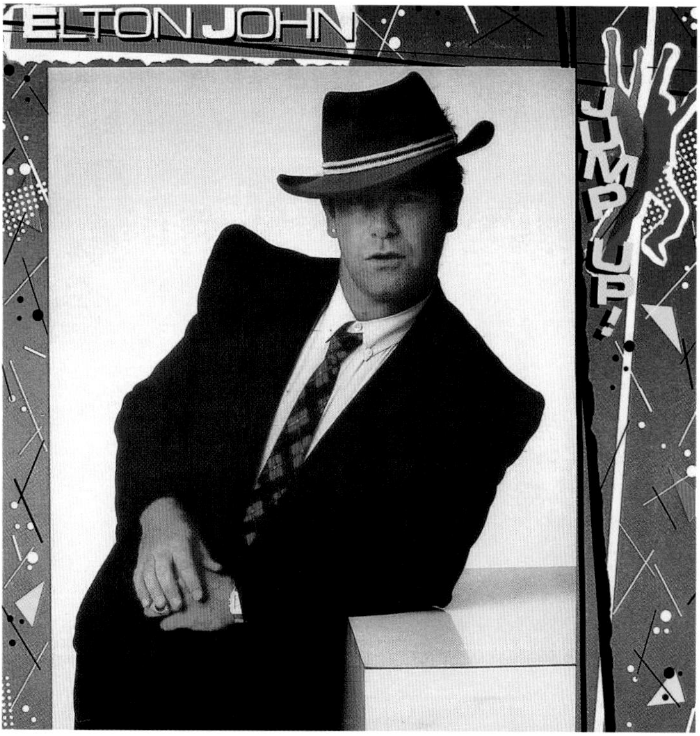

Cover of Elton John's *Jump Up!* (1982).

Right:
(left)
Bryan Ferry in Paris, 1955.

(top right)
Cover of the Genesis' *Invisible Touch* (1986).

(bottom right)
Cover of Murray Head's *Voices* (1981).

by 1970s progressive rockers (although he was fond of a wild costume). John held his listeners with a catchy melody and accessible romantic sentiments like "Your Song." Besotted with Motown, his tightly constructed songs shared similar production values. Likeminded artists Fleetwood Mac and Wings also became great favorites of conservative AM radio playlists. It was telling that Fleetwood Mac was a former 1960s blues band and Wings were led by ex-Beatle Paul McCartney. As pop/rock artists sought out synthesizers for an even more polite sound, acts that once represented rock's radical fringe turned into successful soft rockers.

Away from his art-rock group Roxy Music, Bryan Ferry cultivated the image of a modern crooner, while Phil Collins of Genesis wrote love songs whose coziness made them beloved of *American Psycho's* killer yuppie Patrick Bateman.

State-of-the-art synths and drum machines created an adult contemporary sound perfect for the CD era of the 1980s, just as aging baby boomers sought out a soundtrack for their brave new world of mortgages and divorce papers. Songwriters looked to the past for inspiration, crafting slick pastiches of soul (Simply Red and Hall & Oates), early rock 'n' roll (George Michael and Dire Straits), blues (Eric Clapton and Bonnie Raitt), Latin music (Gloria Estefan), and jazz (Sting). Elton John even imitated himself.

Today, adult contemporary songs serenade slow dancers at weddings and delight crowds at revival concerts. But time insures that there will always be new blood, as artists and audiences alike soften and mature. Everyone has to grow up sometime.

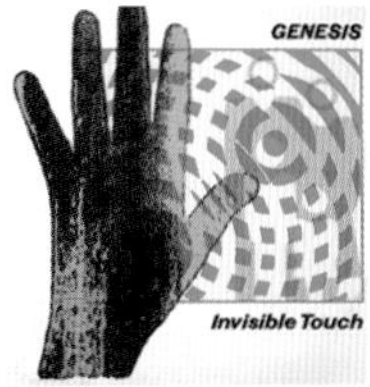

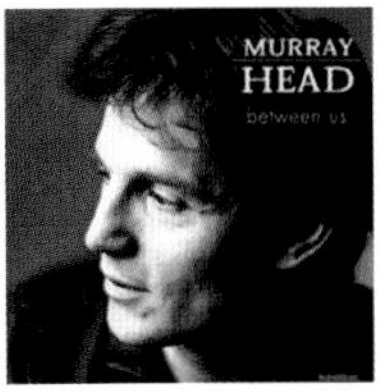

What do Prince, Bryan Adams, U2's Adam Clayton, and John Lennon have in common?

New Wave

- ADAM ANT, DAVID BOWIE, ELVIS COSTELLO, CULTURE CLUB, DEPECHE MODE, DURAN DURAN, THE ENGLISH BEAT, ERASURE, EURYTHMICS, A FLOCK OF SEAGULLS, HUMAN LEAGUE, KAJAGOOGOO, PET SHOP BOYS, THE POLICE, R.E.M. . . .
- GREAT BRITIAN
- 1980s

New Wave was the more acceptable face of punk music. The hair was still spiky and the lyrics still conscientious, but the safety pins were taken out and its performers weren't so bloody hard to like. British New Wave bands took punk's back-to-basics approach and, with new musical toys like the synthesizer, turned it into accessible pop music.

! They have all appeared nude on their album covers.

The Police and Elvis Costello weren't really punks at heart. They were smart and ambitious songwriters on the make. The Police played a light reggae skank they jokingly called "Regatta de Blanc" on one album, and lead singer Sting wrote tuneful melodies about prostitutes and Nabokov novels. During the early 1980s, Costello released likeminded singles that spoke out against Prime Minister Margaret Thatcher's conservative policies. The synthesizer's ability to sample any sound and play it back made it seem like the instrument of the future. Depeche Mode used theirs for alienating effect,accompanying songs about S&M with industrial sounds. The idea that an orchestra could be stored in a hard drive inspired songwriters to become synth poppers. Duos like Pet Shop Boys and Erasure applied Kraftwerk's glacial sounds to up-tempo disco tunes that satirized the 1980s and imparted coded celebrations of homosexuality. David Bowie was also a protean figure of fascination to the New

Wavers. His latest image as the clown Pierrot in 1980's "Ashes to Ashes" video made makeup and costumes a key part of the New Wave look. Singing fashion disasters like ex-punk Adam "Prince Charming" Ant became known as New Romantics. Some groups would take decades to live down their haircuts, but the vivid imagery of Culture Club's cross-dressing Boy George and Duran Duran's wild boy exoticism made them instant stars on MTV. The music these image-conscious bands made was mostly indebted to black styles. Duran Duran called their synth-heavy disco music "punk-funk," and part of Culture Club's appeal was Boy George's soulful take on Motown numbers. The Eurythmics' androgynous singer Annie Lennox could even go toe-to-toe with Aretha Franklin on their anthem "Sisters Are Doin' It for Themselves." Their surface slickness eventually caved beneath pop metal and guitars, but New Wave tried to give modernism a heart. As one band's name said, these disparate followers were the Human League.

This Page:
(top)
The Police: Sting, Andy Summers, and Stewart Copeland.

(middle)
Duran Duran.

(bottom)
Depeche Mode.

Left:
Boy George, 1983.

Detail:
Who is this?

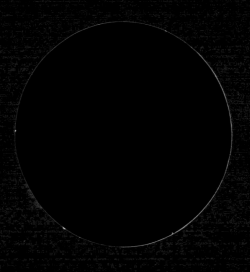

TOMMY LEE,
drummer and guitarist for Mötley Crüe.

Music Videos

• DIRECTORS: STEVE BARON, LAURENT BOUTONNAT, R. D. BURMAN, CHRIS CUNNINGHAM, BOB GIRALDI, JONATHAN GLAZER, MICHEL GONDRY, JEAN-PAUL GOUDE, SPIKE JONZE, DAVID LACHAPELLE, JEAN-BAPTISTE MONDINO, STÉPHANE SEDNAOUI...
• EUROPE, UNITED STATES
• 1980S–

Busby Berkeley's extravagant ballets and the experimental films of Maya Deren and Kenneth Anger are among the music video's antecedents. Hit parade performers often performed their hits in quickie two-reelers, which might illustrate the music with dramatic sequences. In the 1940s, short "soundies" were played on a visual jukebox known as a Panoram, an idea that was revived in the 1960s with the Scopitone. Inspired by the Scopitone's example, the Beatles filmed songs for foreign television. Soon, straightforward performances eventually became avant-garde foolery. Soon acts were making shorts to screen when the artists weren't available to sing their hits on TV shows like *Top of the Pops* or if—as in the case of Queen's groundbreaking "Bohemian Rhapsody" promo—the song was too radical to even to pretend to perform live.
In France, as early as the 1980s, several directors were set on having videos be considered art. These included Jean-Baptiste Mondino ("Un Autre Monde" by Téléphone and "Tandem" by Vanessa Paradis, to name a couple), Laurent Boutonnat

(for Mylène Farmer), Jean-Paul Goude (for Grace Jones), Stéphane Sednaoui ("Nouveau Western" by MC Solaar). Today, some even work outside of France. For one, there's the prolific Michel Goundry, who has worked with Björk, the Rolling Stones, the Chemical Brothers, Radiohead, Kylie Minogue, and the White Stripes. Today, with MTV (and MCM in Europe) airing these clips day and night, the video became a creative playground for artists and directors. There are several different types of video.
The performance video might dynamically present the band romping through their single

—sometimes in an incongruous setting reminiscent of the Scopitones. Many center on exuberant dance performances, edited into unique kaleidoscopes of movement. Some, like a-ha's "Take On Me" or Peter Gabriel's "Sledgehammer," take advantage of animation. Videos have also been used to promote movies with interpolated clips and as advertisements to both promote the song it accompanies and

Two stills from Jamiroquai's video "Virtual Insanity," directed by Jonathan Glazer in 1996.

package the act performing it. Videos of hip-hoppers with their budget-busting fleets of Bentleys and oceans of champagne, for example, endorse an entire consumptive lifestyle.
Videos can also be conceptual in nature, drawing on original ideas, like the so-called "visual palindrome" of Cibo Matto's "Sugar Water" or recycling already existing imagery. Videos still take inspiration from the iconography of Technicolor musicals, glamour photography, and horror films. The greatest video auteurs surrender themselves to this postmodern process, whether it's Madonna becoming the object of titillating fantasies, or her Icelandic counterpart Björk making herself a guinea pig for avant-garde scenarios. An integral part of the pop process, the music video has become as important an artistic statement as the music itself.

How did crooner Johnny Ace die in 1964?

Rap

• ALTO Y BAJO, BLACK MBOLO, KURTIS BLOW, ERIC B. AND RAKIM, GRANDMASTER FLASH AND THE FURIOUS FIVE, GRINJOLLY, DJ JAZZY JEFF AND THE FRESH PRINCE, LL COOL J, MC SHAN, POSITIVE BLACK SOUL, PUBLIC ENEMY, RUN-D.M.C. SLICK RICK, THE SUGARHILL GANG...
• INTERNATIONAL
• 1950S–

! He was fatally shot with a .22 revolver during a game of Russian roulette.

In 1985, a fight broke out over where hip-hop began between two New York rappers. MC Shan's "The Bridge" dared to claim it started in their borough of Queensbridge. KRS-One of Boogie Down Productions retorted with "South Bronx," recalling when "beat boys ran to the latest jam" at the parties across the Bronx River. MC Shan grumbled that KRS-One's name sounded "like a wack radio station," but the BDP rapper was right: hip-hop began in the Bronx. There, street DJs learned they could move a crowd by repeatedly playing drum breaks from funk and Latin records. As they spun discs by James Brown or Tito Puente, MCs boasted over-the-top rhyming styles derived from Jamaican dancehall comedians.

Hip-hop's rise coincided with the death of disco at the end of the 1970s, and soon the sound was coming from school gyms, parks, and clubs. Hip-hop culture traveled downtown, too, in the form of graffiti, which coated New York subways and break-dancers who popped robotic moves near Forty-second Street's Times Square.

In 1979, the style finally appeared on record with the Sugarhill Gang's "Rapper's Delight," the Rosetta Stone of the old-school style. The recycled disco beat is simple, the rhymes are humorous and innocent. The rappers tell stories about their shenanigans and blurt nonsense.

Hip-hop grew up in drug-ravaged neighborhoods, but social commentary only entered the music in 1982 with Grandmaster Flash and the Furious Five's "The Message," which showed an anxious side to inner city life. "It's like a jungle sometimes," went the rap. "It makes me wonder/ How I keep from going under."

The arrival of Run-D.M.C. refuted charges that hip-hop was merely a novelty. The Brooklyn trio looked like street toughs—hip and menacing—and they aggressively rhymed over rock breaks. Rap's "golden age" dates from 1986,

Public Enemy, 2004.

Left:
Missy Elliott during the premiere concert of the Verizon Ladies First Tour. Florida, 2004.

the year their *Raising Hell* (1986) became the first rap album to enter the U.S. top ten and their hit cover of Aerosmith's "Walk This Way" introduced MTV to hip-hop. Run-D.M.C's success opened the field. The Queens duo Eric B. and Rakim electrified audiences with their flow, using internal rhymes and wordplay in a way no one had heard before. Public Enemy took "The Message's" protest and set it to beats that sounded like war—all air-raid sirens, nonstop drums, chopped sound-bites, and teakettle whistles. Chuck D's stentorian raps were laced with Flava Flav's clowning cries of "Yeah, boyee." Heartthrob LL Cool J—whose name stood for Ladies Love Cool James—gave hip-hop a sensitive side with the mellow "I Need Love." The music from the Bronx grew into a multimillion dollar industry. "One week we're in station wagons," marveled one artist to historian David Toop. "The next week we're on Lear jets." If hip-hop had its start in New York, the golden age was about to end—as Los Angeles prepared to have its say. In America, they call it hip-hop. Far beyond Brooklyn, though, it's called hip-hop tuga, Pinoy rap, Bongo Flava, and j-rap. The music that began with MCs rhyming over break-beats in New York has become a universal means of expression. When even Fidel Castro

Rap

busts a rhyme with Cuba's Double Filo, you know rap has become a truly international phenomenon. Although Communist Cuba took their time before starting the Cuban Rap Agency in 2002, hip-hop got its first passport back in the day. In Tokyo's Yoyogi Park, Japanese kids started break-dancing and rapping as soon as they saw the urban movie *Wild Style* in 1983. B-boying was already big in New Zealand, where 1979's *The Warriors* introduced hip-hop style, and the Maori population used rap songs to express their demand for equal rights. Hip-hop could even be a perfect fit with indigenous folk sounds like Azerbaijan's *meykhana,* an a capella music whose singing groups would improvise lyrics. There was still a range of issues to deal with. For instance, were international rappers supposed to embrace the trappings of American hip-hop—the bling-bling jewelry, high-fashion lifestyles, and tough guy attitude—or were they duty-bound to celebrate and emphasize their own nationalities? Gokh-Bi System combined both worlds, wearing Nike sneakers when performing in Senegal, but donning their traditional *boubou* robes while touring in America. As if to claim their cultural backgrounds, many international rappers started rapping in their native tongues, even when they lacked English's hard consonants, which helped give rap its distinctive hard-edged sound. Today, rap is seemingly found in every language: French, German, Japanese, Wolof, Twi, Ga, and Hausa, for example. But what do international

(top)
MC Solaar in Paris, promoting his album *Prose Combat* (1994).

(bottom)
Puff Daddy.

Right:
Run-D.M.C. in Harlem, November 1987.

rappers write about? Many international scenes resemble hip-hop's golden age, making politics their subject. In Senegal, rap is credited with inspiring the turnout of young voters who swept a new president to power in 2000. Sene-rap MCs even slammed the country's *mbalax* music for avoiding political content. In the Ukraine, Grinjolly's "Together We Are Many" became the unofficial anthem of the Orange Revolution, while the Israeli-Palestinian conflict spilled onto wax with the lyrical battles of Subliminal and Tamer Nafer.

These global MCs also "keep it real" by incorporating local influences. Fascinating hybrids have been created in Ghana—where percolating guitars have been added to the hip-hop—and in Tanzania—where hip-hop's ingredients include Indian *filmi* music and Islamic *taarab*. In India, American hits are crossed with Indian pop hooks and Hindi or Punjabi lyrics. Guinean hip-hoppers incorporate native instruments like the *tam-tam* drum and *kora*. Crossover success, however, is elusive, in part due to the lack of innovative international producers. Some stars have prevailed against America's slickness however, like the sophisticated French wordplay of MC Solaar and the well-observed vignettes of the U.K.'s the Streets. France, in particular, may become the leader of the world revolution, having the second largest rap market outside of the U.S. IAM, a French hip-hop band from Marseille, attained international acclaim with their 1997 album *L' école du micro d' argent*, which took two days to become a gold record in France.

?

Who appeared with Madonna in her erotic 1992 book *Sex?*

Post-Punk

• THE BIRTHDAY PARTY, CABARET VOLTAIRE, CRASS, DEAD CAN DANCE, DEAD MILKMEN, ECHO AND THE BUNNYMEN, EINSTÜRZENDE NEUBAUTEN, THE FALL, GANG OF FOUR, THE JESUS AND MARY CHAIN, JOY DIVISION, LEGENDARY PINK DOTS, MISSION OF BURMA, MODERN ENGLISH, NEW ORDER, PSYCHEDELIC FURS, THE STRANGLERS, TALKING HEADS, THE THE, U2, WIRE...
• EUROPE, UNITED STATES
• 1980S

It didn't take long for punk rock to become the very thing the Sex Pistols and the Clash were rebelling against. They were opposed to conformity, but suddenly England was littered

with bands who looked, sounded, and talked like them. Not everyone was willing to get in line. Taking their inspiration from 1977's independent spirit, the leading lights of post-punk did everything they could to avoid the norm and the mainstream. Post-punk exploded the pop-music conceit. Gang of Four deconstructed their attempts to play funk with a guitar that sounded like it was at war with the rest of their instruments. This tension between the constituent parts of a band would be a post-punk hallmark. The Fall, a Manchester band made songs out of minimal riffs and their lead singer's rants made no concession to verses or choruses. One of their early songs expressed their modus operandi the best: "This is the three Rs: Repetition, Repetition, Repetition." Groups explored the potential of their tools. U2's The Edge and Echo & the Bunnymen's Will Sargent refused to play blues licks, and used so many effects on their guitars that the original sound was unrecognizable. The Jesus and Mary Chain went in the other direction. Their mid-1980s singles buried the surf pop of songs like "Taste of Honey" beneath slabs of feedback. While the New Wavers relied on the pre-packaged sound of synthesizers, post-punk musicians

! Models Isabella Rossellini and Naomi Campbell, and rappers Big Daddy Kane and Vanilla Ice.

pursued dub effects and experimented with tape loops. Like Gang of Four, Cabaret Voltaire made dance music, but unsettled the listener with creepy samples and sudden *musique concrète* juxtapositions. Their 1979 debut album said it all: *Mix-Up*. Some of punk's originators also became post-punk by the virtue of refusing to stand still. Talking Heads outgrew the CBGB scene by experimenting with world rhythms and Brian Eno became a kind of post-punk godfather thanks to the eerie 1970s albums he made with David Bowie. After Joy Division's singer Ian Curtis committed suicide, the surviving members became New Order, giving up their dark guitars for electronics and an urban club sound. "Blue Monday," a seven-minute track written to try out their new drum machine, became a leftfield club classic. The post-punks found welcoming homes at tiny independent labels like Factory, Rough Trade, and Creation but, with the exception of U2 and the Fall, none lasted beyond the 1980s. In 2004, however, a score of young bands, like Franz Ferdinand, for example, appeared that boasted a post-punk sound with New Wave ambitions. Their crucial misunderstanding was obvious—they all sounded the same.

Cover of Cabaret Voltaire's album *Mix-Up* (1979).

Left:
Jim and William Reid, members of The Jesus and Mary Chain (c. 1987).

Singers:

Can you name the lead singer for these groups?

Answer

Maurice White: Earth, Wind & Fire.
Bryan Ferry: Roxy Music.
Chrissie Hynde: The Pretenders.
Mark Knopfler: Dire Straits.

EARTH, WIND & FIRE

ROXY MUSIC

MARK KNOPFLER

•

CHRISSIE HYNDE

•

BRYAN FERRY

•

MAURICE WHITE

THE PRETENDERS

DIRE STRAITS

Michael Jackson

• *OFF THE WALL* (1979), *THRILLER* (1982), *BAD* (1987), *DANGEROUS* (1992), *HISTORY: PAST, PRESENT, AND FUTURE, BOOK I, INVINCIBLE* (1995)...
• 1958
BOBBY BROWN, JANET JACKSON, R. KELLY, GEORGE MICHAEL, PRINCE, JUSTIN TIMBERLAKE, USHER

Michael Jackson was the biggest musical star of the 1980s and one of the most popular artists of all time. Having grown up as a member of the Jackson 5, his second solo album *Thriller* (1982) became a phenomenon—a crossover recording that appealed to young and old, black and white, male and female, and sold forty million copies around the world. If the Beatles once joked that they were bigger than Jesus, Jackson was, for a brief moment, bigger than Jesus, Mickey Mouse, and David Beckham combined. Jackson did it by turning himself into all things for all people. *Thriller* still sounds like a master plan for world domination. The high-pitched, hiccupping voice might belong to a boy or girl. He snarls with a rock god's conviction on "Beat It" and mews with mushy vulnerability on "Human Nature." Producer Quincy Jones used his understanding of rhythm and soundtracks to create a seamless whole of heavy metal guitars, state-of-the-art disco, and middle-of-the-road balladry. There was something for everybody. The Jackson 5's years during the 1970s as America's greatest teen group taught Jackson about showmanship. His steelworker father religiously drilled the five siblings every morning before he went to work. A gifted mimic, Jackson studied James Brown's quick-footed dancing. At the time of *Thriller's* release, he dazzled audiences and even impressed Fred Astaire with his moonwalk. *Thriller* and its successor *Bad* (1987) demanded spectacular tours, but amid the special effects, Jackson worked the crowd like he was still fronting a Motown revue.
Jackson masterfully manipulated the media. He cannily used music

Michael Jackson on the TV program *Solid Gold*, 1975.

Right:
Michael Jackson in concert, 1998.

videos to showcase an image that owed more to cinema than the concert stage—turning himself into a trademark in penny loafers and a single white glove. His videos became ever more lengthy and lavish, featuring stars like Eddie Murphy and Marlon Brando and directed by the likes of legend Martin Scorsese. "The King of Pop" refused to give interviews, and titillated tabloids with stories of his eccentric plans to buy the Elephant Man's skeleton and sleep in a hyperbaric chamber to stay young. But plastic surgery and a gradual lightening of his skin coincided with his decline in popularity as new musical trends, like rap, escaped him. His fondness for children would become his undoing, as several kids accused him of molesting them. Jackson may have beat the rap, but one thing is for certain: the Peter Pan of pop has outgrown Neverland.

How did Marilyn Manson get his stage name?

Charity Rock

• THE 1971 CONCERT FOR BANGLADESH, THE 1979 NO NUKES CONCERT, BAND AID, LIVEAID, LIVE 8, NETAID, LES RESTOS DU COEUR, SPORT AID, USA FOR ARFICA...
• EUROPE, UNITED STATES
• 1960S

! Each member of the band combined the name of a dead actress with a serial killer.

Charity and contemporary popular music do not make easy bedfellows. Rock 'n' roll is meant to be an anti-authoritarian sound made by the disenchanted. Both rock and rap music are more about glorifying the individual than good intentions. During the 1960s, however, folk singers and hippie protesters saw music as a weapon for altruistic change, and musicians have often united to try to make a difference.

The three-day Woodstock festival showed that live concerts could be events in their own right. In 1971, George Harrison organized one of the earliest charity benefits for the newly independent Bangladesh. With a cast of performers that included Bob Dylan and Eric Clapton, it established the all-star show as an acceptable method of raising funds and awareness. At Madison Square Garden's 1979 No Nukes Concert, artists like Jackson Browne and Bruce Springsteen pled for disarmament.

The 1980s were charity rock's golden era, highlighted by the 1984 Band Aid single "Do They Know It's Christmas?" and then with the "global jukebox" Live Aid, both aimed at relieving the Ethiopian famine. Organizer Bob Geldof achieved the impossible—he marshaled a cast of chart stars like Queen and Elton John to perform an intercontinental telethon. The Philadelphia and London shows —watched by 1.5 billion people— were less remarkable for their rock dinosaur reunions, brash sets by then-unknowns like U2. Band Aid's success inspired the

charity single "We Are the World" by USA for Africa, an array of 1980s stars who were asked to leave their egos at the door. A host of spin-offs followed, including "Sun City," an anti-apartheid single with a harder urban edge than USA for Africa's gloppy ballad, and Burt Bacharach's ballad "That's What Friends Are For," which benefited AIDS charities. Not every effort was a success. The online-based NetAid, a concert advocating debt relief for Africa, was an under-attended flop in 2000.In 2005, Geldof reprised his efforts for the impoverished African nations on an even larger scale. Twenty years after Live Aid, Live 8 featured ten concerts held around the world. This time, the headliners—Paul McCartney, Coldplay, Björk, Green Day, Jay-Z, and Madonna—weren't asking for money but, instead, online signatories to a petition urging the G8 nations to offer debt relief, medical aid, and fair trade. World leaders agreed to increase aid, too. Rock won't solve the world's problems. But, then again, every little bit helps.

Fans at London's Wembley Stadium at the Live Aid Concert. July 13, 1985.

Left: Cover of the album *We Are the World* (1985).

Duos:
Who sang with whom?

Answer

1. Sonny and Cher.
2. Jack White and Meg White, The White Stripes.
3. Serge Gainsbourg and Jane Birkin.
4. Tina and Ike Turner.
5. Bob Dylan and Joan Baez.
6. Annie Lennox and Dave Stewart, Eurythmics.
7. Eric and Stone Charden.
8. Paul Simon and Art Garfunkel.
9. John Lennon and Yoko Ono.
10. Amadou Bagayoko and Mariam Doumbia.

U2

• *WAR* (1983), *THE UNFORGETTABLE FIRE* (1984), *THE JOSHUA TREE* (1987), *ACHTUNG BABY* (1991), *ZOOROPA* (1993), *ALL THAT YOU CAN'T LEAVE BEHIND* (2000), *HOW TO DISMANTLE AN ATOMIC BOMB* (2004)...
• FORMED IN 1976
COLDPLAY, DOVES, PETER GABRIEL, HOTHOUSE FLOWERS, INXS, MIDNIGHT OIL, SINÉAD O'CONNOR, THE POLICE, SIMPLE MINDS, STING, THE STONE ROSES, THE VERVE, THE WATERBOYS

U2 in Malibu, California, 1985.
From left to right: Bono (vocals), The Edge (guitar), Adam Clayton (bass), and Larry Mullen, Jr. (drums).

Right:
Bono during the Elevation Tour. Miami, March 26, 2001.

Since becoming the biggest band on Earth with 1987's *The Joshua Tree,* the Irish band U2 have worked harder than anyone to stay that way. They challenge themselves with each new record, play electrifying and inspirational live shows and, thanks to their mouthy front man Bono, have integrated themselves into global politics. Even Pope John Paul II liked them.
The band's basic elements have always remained the same. Bono polemicizes in a dramatic tenor about desire and injustice, trying to throw his arms around the world.

The Edge doesn't so much play the guitar as put it through a series of electronic treatments to create clipped rhythms and ambient effects. Stone-faced bassist Adam Clayton and ageless drummer Larry Mullen, Jr. carry the melody and provide the rock thrust. When U2 first started, only their mullets and leather trousers made them stand out from the post-punk pack. *War* (1983) turned Ireland's political troubles into hit singles. But their boldest move was to submit themselves to sonic experiments of Bowie/Talking Heads collaborator Brian Eno. The producer created atmospheric settings for their anthems that made them sound unlike any band around. In the post-"We Are the World" era, U2 became a universal jukebox, throwing in covers of the Righteous Brothers and Bob Dylan while singing about issues like apartheid as if they could succeed where the politicians failed. The experimental shift of *Achtung Baby* (1991), which deconstructed their pretensions, kept U2 from succumbing to rock 'n' roll pomposity. *All That You Can't Leave Behind* (2000) found the band regrouping when their experiments in irony began to confuse their fans. If the album sounded overly familiar, it also found a band whose first album was called *Boy* (1980) dealing with becoming men. They've become comfortable with their responsibilities. Bono now hobnobs with presidents as he tries to end poverty and was even nominated for the Nobel Peace Prize twice in two years (2003 and 2005). The other band members stick to saving rock music.

?

What group's debut album features a picture of the Hindenburg disaster?

Madonna

• *LIKE A VIRGIN* (1984), *TRUE BLUE* (1986), *LIKE A PRAYER* (1989), *BEDTIME STORIES* (1994), *RAY OF LIGHT* (1998), *MUSIC* (2000), *CONFESSIONS ON A DANCE FLOOR* (2005)...
• 1958
PAULA ABDUL, CHRISTINA AGUILERA, MARIAH CAREY, GLORIA ESTEFAN, DEBBIE GIBSON, JANET JACKSON, CYNDI LAUPER, GEORGE MICHAEL, KYLIE MINOGUE, RU PAUL, JESSICA SIMPSON, BRITNEY SPEARS, SPICE GIRLS

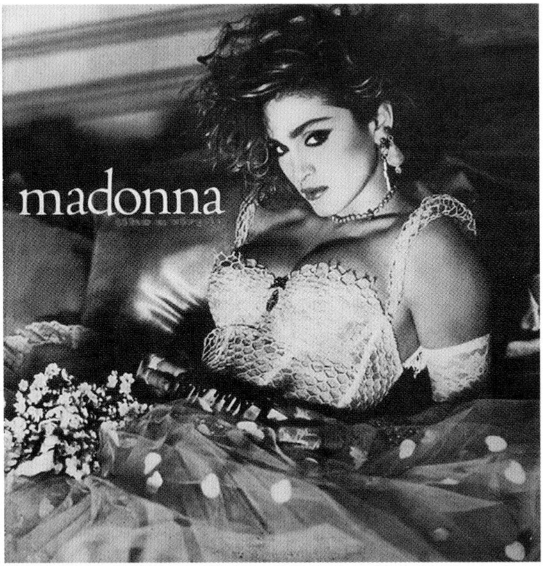

It's tempting to consider what Madonna might have been in another era, and the American pop singer has provided plenty of suggestions—all through her music videos. The boy toy of "Like a Virgin"; the glamorous film star of "Material Girl"; the great emancipator of "Express Yourself"; or a beatific "Ray of Light," hurtling through the accelerated century—Madonna has somehow been and done it all. She is the greatest icon of the video era, establishing a stardom that doesn't depend on singles or best-selling albums.

Madonna Louise Ciccone trod an artist's route, arriving in New York from Detroit, where her Catholic childhood would inform her canny manipulation of iconography. She starved, hung out with the painter Basquiat, visited Paris, posed nude, and eventually began singing the streetwise dance-pop prevalent in nighteries like the Mudd Club and Danceteria. Her voice on those early recordings is an unremarkable squawk. Put her in front of a camera, though, and Madonna was a star.

The singer quickly understood that being the subject of the male gaze was actually empowering. She became the woman of a thousand faces, a modern-day La Gioconda. Denounced as a slut, she donned a wedding dress for "Like a Virgin," then fishnets for "Open Your Heart," playing a stripper whose customers were implicated in the spectacle as much as she was. Madonna made her fans invisible accomplices in her

! Led Zeppelin.

sexcapades—bedding Sean Penn, Warren Beatty, and even John F. Kennedy, Jr.—like the blonde Moreau lost in a debauched funhouse she incarnated in "Justify My Love."

The controversial "Like a Prayer" video, with its black Jesus, burning crosses, and Madonna's faux-naif pilgrim costume, ended with a hint of the real woman beneath the facade: she exuberantly joins a gospel choir and likens herself to salvation's balm. It's a cousin to her innocent hit "Holiday," with music being the transcendent vehicle. The music got better and more honest as the videos became more contradictory. Madonna used dance-floor trends the same way she did the camera's eye. On *Ray of Light* (1998), she remade herself into an ambient techno guru, while *Music* (2000) was a more grown-up version of "Holiday's" feckless dance diva. Her two weakest albums—*Erotica* (1992) and *American Life* (2003)—were a result of placing momentary sensation over pop's power.

The modern Madonna is a dilemma for her fans. She has haplessly pursued an acting career, become a mother, and written children's books. Today, her Kabbalah-inspired pilgrimage to Israel and insistence that the public call her "Esther" is somehow as outrageously daffy as her steel-bound *Sex* book seemed in 1992.

When those early nude photos were first published, Madonna's idea of damage control was to say, "So what?" Her creed is still the same. It's her world; we're just watching it.

Madonna on stage during a U.S tour. June 1990.

Left: Cover of Madonna's *Like a Virgin* (1984).

Prince

• *1999* (1983) *PURPLE RAIN* (1984), *AROUND THE WORLD IN A DAY* (1985), *PARADE* (1986), *SIGN 'O' THE TIMES* (1987), *DIAMONDS AND PEARLS* (1991), *N.E.W.S* (2003), *MUSICOLOGY* (2004), *1321* (2006)...
• 1958
2PAC, THE BANGLES, CAMEO, GEORGE CLINTON, BOOTSY COLLINS, SHEILA E., MISSY ELLIOTT, RICK JAMES, JAY-Z, ALICIA KEYS, CHAKA KHAN, LENNY KRAVITZ, MADONNA, MORRIS DAY AND THE TIME, SEAL, SINÉAD O'CONNOR

Prince, The Artist, Jamie Starr, Alexander Nevermind, Victor, Camille, Skipper, Sexy MF. Prince Rogers Nelson is so much larger than life that it's no wonder he needs more than that one persona. He's made enough hit records to fuel whole labels. There are also the movies, but let's put those aside. His albums would bare the forbidding credit, "Produced, composed, arranged, and performed by Prince." With Bambi-like eyes and a unique

fashion sense, the Minneapolis Maestro let his libido lead him, whether it was to a pocketful of Trojan horses in "Little Red Corvette" or to "Darling Nikki" and her dirty magazines on *Purple Rain,* the 1984 soundtrack to his hit autobiographical movie. Prince's stagecraft was straight from the book of James Brown, combined with Jimi Hendrix-like flourishes and the rawness of porn star John Holmes thrown in. You never knew what he would do for an encore. Threaten an arena's foundations with another axe solo like he did in *Purple Rain?* Cuddle up to the mike to beg, "Do Me, Baby?" Could his band the Revolution literally funk all night?

With hits like "When Doves Cry"—the first American No. 1 of the rock era with no bass line—along with the videos, tours, and films, Prince achieved the mega-stardom status of Michael Jackson or Madonna. In 1987, he cast away the Revolution for his most personal album to date—the extraordinary *Sign 'O' the Times* (1987). The double album suggested nothing was beyond Prince's ability. There were protest songs, hard dance jams, psychedelic trifles, jazzy excursions, and a ballad called "Adore" that was part prayer, part sex manual. Prince simply did it all. *The Black Album* (1994) was put aside after Prince scared himself with the darker muse he awakened, and his vaults are said to be crammed with gems only he has heard.

From his Paisley Park studio, Prince masterminded his career and others with varying success. He wrote hits for Chaka Khan and the Bangles that were tailor-made to match the musicians' personalities—so much so, in fact, that the listener would never detect Prince's handiwork. The leftover ballad "Nothing Compares 2 U" made Sinéad O'Connor's career. Now a committed Jehovah's Witness, Prince no longer sings dirty songs and, instead, spends afternoons knocking on neighbors' doors offering salvation. But, he's left us with the tantalizing prospect of not knowing where the next masterpiece might come from.

Prince in concert. Detroit 1986.

Left:
Prince in concert in Rotterdam. August 1988.

How are Maria Bethânia and Caetano Veloso related?

Raï

- CHABA FADELA, CHEB KADER, CHEB MAMI, CHEIKHA REMITTI, FAUDEL, KHALED, RACHID ET FETHI BABA AHMED, RACHID TAHA...
- FRANCE
- 1930S—

Cover of the album Les *Princesses du Raï* (2004) with Cheb Khaled, Cheb Ali & Electric Rai Land, Cheb Karim, Djamel Benyelles, Haim, and others.

Right:
Cover of Cheb Mami's *Dellali* (2001).

By the twentieth century, the Algerian city of Oran had separate Spanish, French, Jewish, and Arab quarters; this hedonistic melting pot gave raï music its main characteristics. The word "raï" is a street exclamation, indicating an expressive opinion. Naturally, t was put into great use by street musicians who attacked the French colonials with their songs. Based on Bedouin folk music, it's also extremely adaptable. It incorporates goat-skinned drums, as well as Western instruments like the saxophone, accordion, and flamenco guitar. Even reggae and rap can be absorbed into raï.

Besides Cheikh Kali and Cheikh Hamada, the first great raï star was Cheikha Remitti. Although Oran women were subject to strict rules of conduct, *cheikhas,* like Remitti, performed bawdy songs at women-only wedding celebrations. To the disapproval of the colonial government and orthodox Muslims, the husky-voiced singer recorded those ribald tunes, making private lust public. Joining the cheikhas were male singers, who would take the title *cheb* ("young") or *cheikh* ("old"), depending on their specific life experience.

Raï was suppressed with Algeria's independence in 1962, but the music experienced a revival in the late 1970s spearheaded by producer Rachid Baba Ahmed. Faced with a lack of slick session musicians in Oran, he turned to pre-programmed beats and played all the instruments himself to create a slick raï sound. Singer Chaba Fadela recorded the huge hit "Ana ma h'lali ennoum" with him, and pop raï was born. Pop raï dominated the 1980s and Ahmed became a one-man hit factory for the raï rebels, who would sing evocatively over an echo-drenched melody before the chunky disco beat kicked in. New stars,

! They are brother and sister.

like musician Khaled, bloomed. Khaled, the so-called "King of Raï" radically replaced the violins in his band with electric guitars. In the 1990s, many raï stars left Algeria to escape the civil war. Those who stayed, like Ahmed, were killed. Another victim was Cheb Hasni, who created the sentimental genre of "lovers raï." His light voice also challenged government censorship, and fundamentalists assassinated him in 1996. France rapidly became the raï capital, and Cheb Kader established himself as the new "Prince of Raï" with his songs about the immigrant's woes. Raï remains immensely popular in Algeria (where it is begrudgingly tolerated by the authorities) and France—where several raï musicians, like Rachid Taha and Khaled, have immigrated—but has yet to make an international breakthrough, although the self-styled Crown Prince of Raï, Cheb Mami, graced the Sting hit "Desert Rose" with his falsetto and Faudel, who is nicknamed "The Little Prince of Raï," promises to lead a new generation of like-minded singers.

Auction:

What was the auction price of Spice Girl Geri Halliwell's minidress?

Answer

Approximately $72,000. The item sold on September 16, 1998, at Sotheby's in London. Geri Halliwell wore the dress during the 1997 Brit Awards.

Minimalism

- JOHN ADAMS, PHILIP GLASS, CHARLEMAGNE PALESTINE, STEVE REICH, TERRY RILEY...
- EUROPE, UNITED STATES
- 1960S–

Minimalism is classical music stripped down to its barest essentials. Inspired by North Indian ragas, it emphasizes repetitive chords and phrases, which slowly evolve over the piece's lengthy duration. As avant-garde as it sounds, minimalism became a popular variant of classical music in the 1970s and 1980s because of its return to traditional chords, transcendent qualities, and use in movie soundtracks.

California's Terry Riley has been called the inventor of minimalism. A student of Indian classical music, he placed

raga-derived melodic lines over repeating riffs and drones. The 1964 album *In C* used fifty-three separate interlocking musical "loops"—hectic snatches of melody—played over a constant piano pulse. The steady underlying harmony created a static sense of ease that would also turn up in New Age and Ambient music. Inspired by non-Western music, others were drawn to minimalism's cyclical and cumulative effects. Steve Reich was fiddling around with tape recordings he had made of a San Francisco street preacher when he let two identical loops slip out of phase with each other. The disjunctive effect of "phasing" became the basis for 1966's *It's Gonna Rain,* where Brother Walter's sermon about Noah is distorted until it became syllables of pure sound breaking against each other. With 1971's *Drumming,* Reich applied the technique to instruments. Bongos, marimbas, glockenspiel, and vocalists all repeated the same rhythmic pattern. Over four parts and ninety minutes long, its shifting rhythms and timbres made a familiar phrase evolve into new forms.

Philip Glass is a New York composer who felt like he had hit a dead end until he was asked to transcribe the improvisations of sitar player Ravi Shankar. His analysis led him to start using short rhythmic phrases and unvarying harmonies. Although he has written dance pieces and operas, Glass became famous for his 1981 soundtrack for *Koyaanisqatsi,* a documentary about modern life. The use of Glass's music in films like *The Thin Blue Line* (1988) and *The Hours* (2002) gained minimalism popular acceptance. The repetitive minimalist principles were taken up by David Bowie on his 1977 *Low* album (which Philip Glass later used as the basis of a symphony) and even Detroit techno DJs. It has since evolved into the post-minimalism of composer John Adams—whose works like *Shaker Loops* (1990) and *Harmonielehre* (1993) subject the repetitive melodies to dramatic climaxes and changes in tone and dynamics. Another contemporary of Glass is Charlemagne Palestine, whose *Strumming Music* (written in 1974 but released in 1991) features over forty-five minutes of Palestine forcefully playing two notes in rapid succession. Heavily influenced by the Jewish Hazanout, Palestine stretched minimalist themes into works of pure, joyous abstraction with *Sine Wave Study* and *Open Closing* (both 1965).

Cover of John Adams's *Strong* (1987).

Left: Philip Glass in New York, 1985.

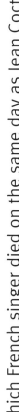

Which French singer died on the same day as Jean Cocteau?

Ladies of Jazz

• BETTY CARTER, ELLA FITZGERALD, INTERNATIONAL SWEETHEARTS OF RHYTHM, DIANA KRALL, NORAH JONES, ABBEY LINCOLN, PEGGY LEE, MADELEINE PEYROUX, NINA SIMONE, SARAH VAUGHAN, CASSANDRA WILSON...
• UNITED STATES
• 1930S

Women have played a larger role in the development of jazz than is commonly acknowledged and were among those playing and writing ragtime songs at the beginning of the twentieth century. During the age of the speakeasy, all-women bands, like the International Sweethearts of Rhythm, were in great demand. But women left their biggest mark as jazz vocalists.

Every big band featured a singer to perform a few numbers, and the canniest learned to use their voice as an instrument in its own right. With her trumpet-like cadences, Billie Holiday showed female singers how to shape a phrase like a musician. Working with bop players like Charlie Parker and Dizzy Gillespie, however, gave singers like Ella Fitzgerald and Sarah Vaughan the confidence to start performing dexterous scat solos of their own.

Fitzgerald's voice was said to have a range so wide you needed an elevator to go from the bottom to the top. She treated the Gershwin and Porter standards, recorded as part of her *Songbook* albums (1956–1964), with reverence. But in concert, she could ebulliently out-sing and out-swing almost any other member of the band. Lady Ella's three-octave voice gave lift to songs like "Air Mail Special" and hit notes as nimbly as a Parker solo.

Edith Piaf. Both died on October 11, 1963.

Singing for big bands demanded versatility. Fitzgerald recorded samba and gospel songs as well as jazz tunes. During the 1960s, she even sang songs by the Beatles. Having a jazz background let singers like Peggy Lee and Nina Simone cross over into pop territory. Lee breathed sensuous life into the slinky "Fever." Simone poured her soul into everything from the Hebrew anthem "Hava Nagila" to her impassioned protest song, "Mississippi Goddamn."

Other singers went in the opposite direction. Betty Carter used her husky tone to reinvent her material. In improvisations that might last nearly half an hour, she could completely alter a song's tempo and dynamic. Born in 1930, the fiercely independent singer only attained recognition late in life. By then, however, she had influenced a whole new generation of singers, led by Cassandra Wilson.

Wilson kept the jazz vocal tradition alive during the early 1990s with hit albums like *Blue Light 'Til Dawn* (1993). Against spare musical backdrops, her woozy alto voice stretched pop songs by Bob Dylan and the Monkees into impressionistic pieces. Others have followed this effective template. Following the tradition of Billie Holiday, Abbey Lincoln performs every song with an emotional intensity rare among today's soft-spoken Norah Jones and Madeleine Peyroux—two gifted singers who prefer a hushed atmosphere to Lincoln's sensual style. Regardless of their styles of singing, these women, and the countless others before them, continue to inspire the lives and careers of future jazz women. A woman's voice is now firmly part of the band.

Ella Fitzgerald in London, 1971.

Left:
(left)
Norah Jones in concert in Amsterdam. October 13, 2002.

(right)
Diana Krall in concert, 2003.

Alternative Rock

• THE CURE, HÜSKER DÜ, JANE'S ADDICTION, MINISTRY, NIRVANA, PIXIES, R.E.M., RADIOHEAD, THE REPLACEMENTS, THE SMITHS, SONIC YOUTH, THE WHITE STRIPES ...
• GREAT BRITAIN, UNITED STATES
• 1980s–

This Page:
(top)
Cover of The Smith's album *The World Won't Listen* (1987).

(bottom)
Robert Smith, lead singer of the Cure. Bath, April 1996.

Right:
R.E.M. in concert in Milan. January 15, 2005.

The definition of alternative rock drastically changed in the twenty years after the punk rock rebellion. In the 1980s, it was a label given to bands determined to play guitars, but shun the mainstream market, dominated by commercial heavy metal. After Nirvana topped the charts with *Nevermind* in 1991, however, alternative rock *became* the mainstream.

The punk explosion created the circumstances that let alternative rock thrive: in America, there was a fierce sense of fan allegiance and respect for independence, combined with a conservative political climate that demanded resistance. Punk's do-it-yourself ethic expressed itself in the proliferation of independent labels like Dischord and SST, the alternative rockers' handmade album art, and their conscious lack of image. Compared to metal's garish performers, these musicians looked like hardware store owners. Although the guitar was the prominent instrument, alternative rock embraced a range of sounds. There was the Byrds-ian twelve-string jangle and inscrutable poetry of R.E.M., Hüsker Dü, and the Pixies, who wailed about romance and UFOs over a hurricane of guitar noise pop. Ministry's industrial sound used guitars like a hip-hop

producer might use samples. Jane's Addiction played heavy funk-rock, but their decadent lyrics and artwork invited censure from the authorities. Closely allied with burgeoning music scenes in their native cities, these bands' marginality made them hip. In Britain, alt.rock coexisted with its populist equivalent. Independent labels were respected and melancholy bands like the Smiths and the Cure attracted intense devotion, adoring press coverage, and regular radio airplay. As in the U.S., alternative rock was especially popular in colleges, which provided the groups with regular places to play. It was also possible for their 45s to crack the Top 40 charts. R.E.M. and Minneapolis barroom rockers the Replacements experienced chart success; the touring Lollapalooza festival began in 1991 to unite the alternative nation around its diverse line-ups, but Nirvana's sudden rise upset the entire scene. Major labels descended and marketed alt.rock as fiercely as they had heavy metal. R.E.M.'s folk-rock sound became café-friendly listening, while the art-rock of Sonic Youth was less palatable. Grunge's popularity inspired its own backlash, and "alternative" became "indie," named after the independent labels where these bands found refuge.

There still exist bands at the extremes making oddball noises, but groups that might once have been called alternative—such as the noisy blues of the White Stripes or Radiohead's experimental rock—are both popular and cutting edge. The world of alt. rock music has been so drained of meaning that the Pixies can embark on a lucrative reunion tour without a glimmer of irony. Whatever comes next will need to be an alternative to the alternative.

What American song did Caetano Veloso quote in his Brazilian hit "Baby"?

Mbaqanga

• DARK CITY SISTERS, LADYSMITH BLACK MAMBAZO, MAHLATHINI AND THE MAHOTELLA QUEENS, SPOKES MASHIYANE ...
• SOUTH AFRICA
• 1950S

In 1984, the New York singer-songwriter Paul Simon was handed an album called *Gumboots: Accordion Jive Hits, Volume II.* He was instantly taken with its naïve pleasure, which reminded him of the 1950s rock 'n' roll he had grown up with. Two years later he released *Graceland,* an album inspired by this effervescent sound, and turned South Africa's *mbaqanga* (" township jive") into a world music. Simon's amateur musicology wasn't far off the mark. *Mbaqanga* was born out of pennywhistle jive, a rural style that, in the early 1950s, became the music of choice for Afrikaans juvenile delinquents known as "ducktails." The sound of a whistle playing a melodic line over the harmony of three or four others was South Africa's answer to rock 'n' roll, a music that many thought spelled the end of civilization. Police arrested the young street corner jivers for creating a public disturbance. Like rock, it was popular: in 1954, Spokes Mashiyane's "Ace Blues" became the biggest tune in Africa. Pennywhistle jive became *mbaqanga*

! Paul Anka's "Diana."

Joseph Shabalala, lead singer of the group Ladysmith Black Mambazo, with Zulu dancers. South Africa, 1993.

Left: English musician Johnny Clegg dancing during a Zulu wedding. South Africa, in the 1990s.

in 1958, when Spokes turned in his whistle for a saxophone and recorded the all-conquering "Big Joe Special." The jazz community dismissed this sacrilegious defilement as "homemade." The sax's broad sound, however, let more instruments in on the act. Soon the repetitive riffs were fleshed out by pumping melodic electric bass, guitars playing high and bright notes, and a percussion that could draw quite a township crowd.

Vocals entered the mix, too. South African singing groups like the Dark City Sisters added a twist to the American 45s that inspired them. Instead of four vocalists, these groups had five members, with the tenor voice split into a high and low part. The bass singer was known as a "groaner," and soon stepped forward as the lead. The good news was that gravel-voiced groaners like Simon "Mahlathini" Nkabinde, backed by the honeyed sound of the Mahotella Queens, were showmen as arresting as James Brown or Tom Waits.

Appearing alongside the mbaqanga groups on Graceland was Ladysmith Black Mambazo, a veteran a cappella—or *iscathamiya*—group that became international stars under Simon's patronage. Leader Joseph Shabalala created the group in 1974 after experiencing a vision—a choir with seven bass voices, an alto, a tenor, and himself singing lead. To their melodies he added a high keening and emphatic grunt accompanied by a stamp associated with the Zulu tribe.

Mbaqanga was hit by the rise of disco and reggae music, which inspired South African imitators like the Movers and Lucky Dube. And while Paul Simon's *Graceland* did its part to end apartheid, the lifting of the embargo has buried the national sound beneath a flood of countless American imports.

THE MUSIC PAGES

GOSSIP AND SCANDAL

Chet Baker

Chesney H. Baker had movie-star looks. On a sad May night, the fragile-voiced angel fell from his hotel window in Amsterdam. He influenced his times like no other jazz trumpet player, save for his famous rival, Miles Davis. (*Libération*, 1988)

• **This Note's for Me!**
Neil Young has recalled two hundred thousand copies of *Comes a Time* at his own expense after discovering that the album's missing several high frequencies. To ensure they are never released, he fired a rifle into each case of LPs. (1978)

• **Holy Cow!**
After "Nothing Compares 2 U" went to No. 1, Sinéad O'Connor tore up a picture of the pope on TV. The shaven-headed singer has since declared herself a lesbian, become a priest of the Latin Tridentine Church, and repeatedly retired from show business. (1992)

• **Longevity**
In 1999, the sitar player Ravi Shankar held the record for longest career, having given his first concert in 1939 in New York. Shankar continues to play today and is one of the best-known Indian musicians across the world. In 1969, he participated in Woodstock.

• **Hip-Hop**
On September 7, 1996, at the end of a Mike Tyson boxing match, the rap artist 2Pac Shakur drove his BMW toward Club 662 in Las Vegas, to join Tyson's victory celebration. A white Cadillac pulled up alongside his car on the road. Four men on board opened fire. The rapper died a few days later. Suspects include 2Pac's rival Notorious B.I.G, who was murdered six months later. (*Libération*)

• **Concert**
During a concert in Dallas in 1978, the bass player John Ritchie, aka Sid Vicious, carved, "Gimme a fix" on his chest with a razor. (*Libération*, 1979)

CURRENT EVENTS AND NEWS IN BRIEF

• Auctions

John Lennon's Rolls Royce Phantom V was sold at Sotheby's in New York to an anonymous buyer for $2,229,000 on June 29, 1985.

• Record

The title of Fiona Apple's 1999 album was no less than ninety words long:

When the Pawn Hits the Conflicts He Thinks Like a King / What He Knows Throws the Blows When He Goes to the Fight / And He'll Win the Whole Thing 'Fore He Enters the Ring / There's No Body to Batter When Your Mind is Your Might / So When You Go Solo, You Hold Your Own Hand / And Remember That Depth Is the Greatest of Heights / And If You Know Where You Stand, Then You Know Where to Land / And If You Fall it Won't Matter, Cuz You'll Know That You're Right.

• Rap Hymn in the Bronx

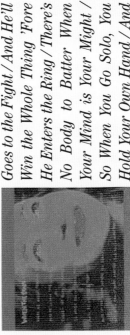

In 1982, the rap artist Grand Master Flash wrote "Message," one of the greatest hits of early rap. The lyrics went: "Don't push me, cause I'm close to the edge / I'm trying not to loose my head / It's like a jungle sometimes, it makes me wonder / How I keep from going under." (*Libération*)

West African Music

- KING SUNNY ADE, SALIF KEITA, YOUSSOU N'DOUR, ORCHESTRA BAOBAB, ALI FARKA TOURE ...
- FRANCE, GUINEA, MALI, NIGERIA, SENEGAL
- 1970S–

Youssou N'Dour. Paris 1998.

Right:
Ali Farka Toure at The Festival in the Desert, Essakane, Mali. January 2003.

In West Africa singers, have a special status. In Mali, they're known as the praise-singing *jali.* In Senegal, they're called *griots.* Having been colonized (and enslaved) by the British, French, and Germans, West Africa is no stranger to foreign influence. The biggest sound in Africa is, in fact, native music crossed with Latin rhythms, which first arrived in Senegal and elsewhere through visiting sailors. In the Senegalese capital of Dakar, Orchestra Baobab mixed rumba with punchy sax solos, bubbling guitars, and *griot* singing in the tribal Wolof tongue. The Afro-Cuban hodgepodge made for a dance music that sounds both ancient and modern at the same time —and it is irresistible.

Baobab's rivals were the Star Band, whose griot leader Youssou N'Dour created his own musical style. *Mbalax* was named after the sound made by Senegal's *mbung mbung* drum. N'Dour made African drums play an elastic rumba beat. The charismatic singer added a unique vocal style—part scat, part rap, part muezzin cry—that made him one of Africa's true idols. He's used his position to challenge accepted beliefs, singing on behalf of women's rights.

N'Dour has remained true to his roots in Dakar, but many musicians, like the sandy-voiced singer Salif Keita, moved to Paris in search of crossover success. A member of Malian royalty, Keita had already crossed several borders to become a musician. With the band Les Ambassadeurs, he had traveled West Africa playing Malian music crossed

with Zairian *soukous*. In Paris, he incorporated R&B, jazz, and other styles, while sending lyrical missives to his fans oppressed beneath his homeland's dictatorship.

In Nigeria, the story is the same. *Juju* is a dance music played by accordions, electric guitars, and a wall of talking drums —whose pitch can be adjusted to mimic the tonal language of the Yoruba people. West Africa is renowned for its intense interband competition, and the fierce rivalry between *juju* stars King Sunny Ade and Chief Commander Ebenezer Obey found them adding even more exotic instruments, like the Hawaiian guitar until Obey's band numbered nearly twenty musicians.

This African amalgamation should ultimately come as no surprise. Rumba, jazz, R&B, even rock all have roots in West Africa. The musical traffic between continents has found artists like Ry Cooder, Peter Gabriel, Paul McCartney, the Rolling Stones, and Paul Simon crossing songlines with African musicians. No matter what it sounds like or where it comes from, the cradle of twentieth-century music is still rocking.

?

What song did Paul Anka rewrite and give to Frank Sinatra as "My Way"?

Gangsta Rap

• 2PAC, 50 CENT, DMX, DR. DRE, JA RULE, JAY-Z, ICE-T, MOBB DEEP, N.W.A., NAS, THE NOTORIOUS B.I.G., P. DIDDY, SALT-N-PEPA, SNOOP DOGG, WU-TANG CLAN ...
• UNITED STATES
• 1990S

Gangsta rap served notice that the party started in 1979 with "Rapper's Delight" was over. Inspired by Ice-T, a rapper who drew on pimp novelist Iceberg Slim's explicit prose for melodramatic crime narratives, acts like N.W.A. (Niggaz With Attitude) rhymed about what they knew—the genocide of black youth occurring on their streets through gang wars, drugs, and police intimidation, among other topics. They introduced to rap extreme

! Claude Francois' "Comme D'habitude."

violence, profanity, and the mythical figure of the gangster.

Taking their cue from Public Enemy's apocalyptic shuffle, N.W.A.'s music resounded with the gunshots heard in their Compton neighborhood, a noted Los Angeles war zone. On 1988's underground smash *Straight Outta Compton* (1989), sawed-off shotguns and AK-47s went off in a world where everyone—cops, gangstas, and "bitches"—was a threat. Public Enemy's Chuck D called rap "CNN for black people," and his assessment seemed spot-on. MTV banned the group, and the FBI wrote their record label an intimidating letter, but suburban kids ate it up like picnickers watching the distant carnage of the battle of Waterloo.

The group had broken up by 1992, when the Rodney King riots tore through Los Angeles. Ice-T had come under fire that year for recording a heavy metal track called "Cop Killer." Dr. Dre had left N.W.A. to start Death Row Records and overhaul his sound. His debut *The Chronic* (1992) set gangsta lyrics to loping Parliament-Funkadelic samples and the laidback rhymes of his young protégé Snoop Dogg. When Dogg's *Doggy Style* (1993) became the first debut album to enter the U.S. chart at No. 1, the so-called "G-funk" became endemic. G-funk's whining organs and R&B choruses dominated the decade. The gangsta became less of a ghetto fact of life than a superhero. Snoop Dogg blurred fact and fiction when

Graffiti portrait of 2Pac in New York, 1996.

Left: Snoop Dogg. December 1999.

he was arrested for a drive-by shooting and released a single called "Murder Was the Case." N.W.A. lyricist Ice Cube, however, combined abrasive threat with an unusual sensitivity on solo tracks like "Dead Homiez," in which he rues fallen comrades. Gangsta rap went from refusing compromise to begging for pity.

The twin shooting deaths in 1994–1995 of gangsta superstar 2Pac and his rival Notorious B.I.G. didn't stop the music. In the "Dirty" South, a score of 2Pac imitators sprung up, rapping violent tirades and sorrowful songs. In New York, Nas and Jay-Z did verbal acrobatics around gangsta imagery. Nas made his rep rapping from the perspective of a bullet in the chamber of a gun.

Gangsta rap turned hip-hop into the most popular music in America, and Ice-T and Ice Cube have turned their notoriety into successful acting careers. Both have even played the policemen they once lambasted. Like any craven hustler, they're doing what any right-thinking gangsta would do—following the money.

Gypsy Music

• BOBAN MARKOVIC ORKESTAR, GORAN BREGOVIC, FANFARE CIOCARLIA, THE GIPSY KINGS, TARAF DE HAÏDOUKS, PACO DE LUCÍA, DJANGO REINHARDT ...
• EUROPE
• 1900S–

Django Reinhardt (c. 1950).

Right: Cover of Fanfare Ciocarlia's *Iag Bari* (2001).

The story of Gypsy music is one that unfolds across time and space. It follows the Gypsy journey from Rajasthan in northwest India across the Middle East and Europe. With each stop the Roma made in their migration, their musicians played to feed their families, picking up the regional sounds on the way. As a result, there are now as many varieties of Gypsy music as there are Roma communities across the globe. The Gypsies adopted the instruments of their new homes. Gypsies who played in Turkish brass bands formed groups of their own, making trumpets, saxophones, and clarinets swing in their own manner. The guitar became a popular "Gypsy" instrument, and Django Reinhardt's unorthodox manner of playing made him the pre-eminent jazz guitarist of the 1930s and 1940s. In Spain, Gypsies created the flamenco style on their guitars, absorbing influences from their fellow Moorish and Jewish migrants to summon up the mysterious power of *duende*.

Gypsy music is meant to be played while one is at the height of intoxication or in the depths of the following day's hangover. Wailing vocals often sound a note of complaint; the lyrics frequently refer to their nomadic lives of suffering. But there is no celebration like a Gypsy celebration—the eleven-member brass band Fanfare Ciocarlia have been known to play for thirty hours at a time in their native Romania, letting dazzling solos ripple over a steady beat provided by two tubas and a kettle drum.

In the twentieth century, France's Gypsy Kings and the movies of Serbian director Emir Kusturica introduced the music to a new generation. The Gypsy Kings are neither Gypsies nor kings, but their slick flamenco sound and canny covers of old songs like "Volare" and even "Hotel California" earned them a devoted following.

Composer Goran Bregovic became an international concert hall staple due to his work on Kusturica's *Time of the Gypsies* (1988) and *Underground* (1995). Bregovic's soundtracks often feature the frenzied trumpet of Serbian bandleader Boban Markovic fused with tango and classical styles, but many Gypsies despise the Sarajevo-born rock musician for what they see as a hodgepodge of their culture. Similarly, the Algeciran guitarist Paco de Lucía angered flamenco purists by collaborating with jazz guitarists and working with orchestras.
In the highways of Europe, however, you can still find the true Romany spirit. A pair of Belgian tourists discovered the Taraf de Haïdouks band living in a tiny Romanian village. Named after a band of thieves, their members—aged from twenty to seventy-eight—have gone on to play with Swiss pop stars and classical ensembles. Their performances are often chaotic affairs. The Haïdouks play from the heart, and are incapable of letting their *cimbalom* and fiddles sing the same tune twice. Despite its ancient origins, Gypsy music continues to sound perennially youthful. It carries the spirit of a culture, which refuses to bow to any rules.

?

Who is Jacques Brel buried next to on the island of Hiva Oa?

Nirvana

• *BLEACH* (1989), *NEVERMIND* (1991), *IN UTERO* (1993), *MTV UNPLUGGED: LIVE IN NEW YORK* (1994) ...
• FORMED IN 1987 AND DISBANDED IN 1994
50 FOOT WAVE, ALICE IN CHAINS, THE BREEDERS, BUSH, DINOSAUR JR., FOO FIGHTERS, PJ HARVEY, HOLE, L7, THE OFFSPRING, PEARL JAM, PIXIES, RADIOHEAD, SCREAMING TREES, SOUNDGARDEN, THE VINES

The American rock trio Nirvana brought punk music into the mainstream. They had all the hallmarks of a successful pop group. Moody singer Kurt Cobain was also a gifted songwriter. Bassist Krist Novoselic and drummer Dave Grohl were capable of playing with tremendous power. But the band was ambivalent about the success they experienced in the early 1990s. On the one hand, they wanted to appeal to listeners as disaffected as they were with what life had to offer. On the other, Cobain couldn't deal with the consequences of mass acceptance—that the very people he despised might love his music. The members of Nirvana were part of a Seattle scene where bands played a slow and heavy take on Black Sabbath's sludgy heavy metal sound. What Cobain brought to grunge music was a keen sense of pop dynamics. Some of Nirvana's best songs would lure the listener in with a quietly rumbling or choppy riff. When the chorus arrived, it unleashed a torrent of noise. It was a formula that only coalesced on the band's second album *Nevermind* (1991), when producer Butch Vig made the music kick in radio speakers with its rebellious frenzy. *Nevermind* knocked Michael Jackson off the top of the charts in 1992, jokingly dubbed "the year punk broke." Nirvana weren't hedonists like their fellow rockers Guns N' Roses. Cobain was the product of a broken home who loved obscure music and knew what it was like to be an outsider. Now the very jocks who rejected him at school crowded Nirvana's explosive shows—shows that often ended in frustration and smashed instruments. He performed in dresses and publicly dismissed his band as "corporate rock whores." Cobain's lyrics oscillated between self-loathing and appealing to the alienated. The band's smash single "Smells Like Teen Spirit" caught the mood of the listless twenty-somethings novelist Douglas Coupland—dubbed Generation X—with its lyric, "Here we are now, entertain us." Soon after Cobain married Courtney Love, lead singer of the band Hole, Nirvana released *Insecticide* (1992), a odds-and-ends

! Paul Gauguin.

Nirvana in London
(c. 1990)

Left:
Portrait of
Kurt Cobain, 1992.

compilation that rose to No. 39 on the U.S. charts and 14 in the U.K. On the group's third album *In Utero* (1993), however, Cobain tried to undo everything he had achieved. The working title for the abrasive record was *I Hate Myself and I Want t o Die,* and its best song was the mournful "All Apologies."

Heroin helped ease Cobain's mind and the constant stomach pains that bedeviled him. In 1994, after several overdoses, he committed suicide, leaving behind a note quoting a Neil Young lyric, "It's better to burn out than fade away." The fragile-sounding *Unplugged* (1994) was an epitaph that hinted at what Nirvana might have achieved. The acoustic setting exposed Cobain's emotional fragility and the intense melodic intelligence behind his primal screams. You couldn't say, "Nirvana rocked." They were brilliant.

Grunge

• ALICE IN CHAINS, BUSH, CREED, HOLE, L7, THE MELVINS, MUDHONEY, NIRVANA, PEARL JAM, SCREAMING TREES, SILVERCHAIR, SOUNDGARDEN, STONE TEMPLE PILOTS, TEMPLE OF THE DOG ...
• UNITED STATES
• 1990S

Grunge was a sluggish form of rock music, which became popular in the 1990s following the success of Nirvana's *Nevermind*. Although it grew up around the band's central base of Seattle in the Pacific Northwest, the sound soon clogged the American charts. Its feedback-saturated riffs were first called "grunge" by Mike Arm, whose band Mudhoney were a key group in the movement.

The grunge rockers were all fans of bands from the 1980s alternative rock scene. Around Seattle, fans would see gigs by the likes of Sonic Youth and Black Flag. When they started their own bands, they imitated those groups' penchant for dirty guitar noise. Their antiestablishment outlook was similar to punk rock, but the grunge rockers played at a more deliberate pace.

The 1991 success of Nirvana's *Nevermind* forced musicians

Courtney Love's hardcore glamour as seen by Gilles Bensimon for *Elle*. November 2003.

Right:
Eddie Vedder, lead singer of Pearl Jam, in concert in the 1990s.

to reassess themselves. Local favorites became stars almost overnight, and tried to distinguish themselves from the pack. Soundgarden, named after a Seattle sculpture, emerged from Nirvana's shadow with 1994's *Superunknown,* which hinted at a Led Zeppelin-like epic ambition. Alice in Chains boasted a morbidly obsessed singer and guitar wizard. It was dour stuff, but Mudhoney was happy to be the scene's clowns with songs like "Touch Me, I'm Sick." The lyrical content was a mixture of self-obsessed whining and the exaggerated anxiety of Black Sabbath. Unlike punk rock, grunge was not a social music. It privileged the lonely listener over the community. Pearl Jam wrote "Jeremy" about a student who commits suicide to shame the bullies who torment him. Alice in Chains' "Would" was about life after rehab, and drug references were common lyrical currency. The suicide of Nirvana's lead singer Kurt Cobain in 1994 shook the entire scene. Alice in Chains' singer Layne Staley eventually overdosed himself, and heroin took the lives of many grunge rockers or sidelined them at critical points in their careers. Pearl Jam's stadium-friendly sound made them Nirvana's natural heirs, but they lacked Cobain's dangerous edge and became a bland touring machine. More importantly, music labels soon began manufacturing post-grunge groups who were happy to give Seattle's coarse sound a more melodic spin. The radio waves became so flooded with grunge it became impossible to tell one band from another. Loud guitars continue to prevail in American rock, but they no longer carry the exhilarating feel of identity that they used to.

What was the rain made out of in the film *Singin' in the Rain?*

French Techno

- AIR, CASSIUS, ETIENNE DE CRECY, DAFT PUNK, DIMITRI FROM PARIS, LAURENT GARNIER, ALEX GOPHER, MANU LE MALIN, ST. GERMAIN ...
- FRANCE
- 1990S

! A combination of water and milk.

French pop music has always been an undervalued commodity. Although one-offs like Gainsbourg and Sacha Distel have crossed over into the global consciousness, the majority of contemporary French music is seen as either too derivative or paradoxically too French to win popular audiences. That changed with the mid-1990s popularity of French techno: a type of electronica that a group of musicians gave their own Gallic stamp.

French techno was sexy, thoughtful, and atmospheric. It was also pillaged from a variety of styles. Daft Punk named their first album *Homework* (1997) in tribute to the house music they fell in love with. St. Germain combined the rigid beat of a drum machine with jazzy improvisations, using sampled upright basses and trumpets to create the sound of “café cool.” In another time, Air might have been called easy listening,

their music nodding along to both lounge guru Burt Bacharach and synth pioneer Jean-Jacques Perrey. These artists brought a much-needed sense of style to music that could very easily have become monotonous. Air and Daft Punk, along with techno duo Cassius, had all been in bands and applied their song-craft to grooves played on antique synthesizers. While Daft Punk dismantled beats, Air could drop the rhythm for a celestial madrigal played by a church organ.
Guest vocalists gave the music added personality—although the English lyrics were distorted with vocoders.
It was the 1990s equivalent of Erik Satie's "furniture music," and it soon turned up in the background of advertisements, movie soundtracks, and TV shows. French techno gave anything an instant touch of sophistication, combined with the retro-futurism of Godard's *Alphaville* (1965). Daft Punk dressed up as robots before releasing an album called *Human After All* (2005). Master magpies, they mocked the folly of the "new," embracing anachronistic kitsch. Air even wore capes onstage like a 1970s progressive rock band.
With the twenty-first century finally here, it remains to be seen how the first wave of French techno will adjust. Most of Air and Daft Punk's followers, like Etienne de Crecy and Cassius failed to emulate their success, and DJs like Laurent Garnier have been stricken by dance music's ebbing fortunes. Nowadays people at least smile at French music for the right reasons.

Still from the Japanese animated film *Interstella 5555: The 5tory of the 5ecret 5tar 5ystem,* written in 2003 by the members of Daft Punk.

Left: Air in Paris, 1998.

Lyrics and music
Who sang what?

Sinéad O'Connor,
"Nothing Compares 2 U"

Janet Jackson, "Together Again"

Simon & Garfunkel,
"The Sound of Silence"

The Doors, "Light My Fire"

Murray Head, "Say It Ain't So, Joe"

Peter Gabriel, "Shock the Monkey"

Eminem, "My Name Is"

The Bee Gees, "How Deep Is Your Love"

The Rolling Stones, "Paint It Black"

Nancy Sinatra, "Bang Bang!"

Eminem

• *THE SLIM SHADY LP* (1999), *THE MARSHALL MATHERS LP* (2000), *THE EMINEM SHOW* (2002), *ENCORE* (2004) ...
• 1972
50 CENT, MC PAUL BARMAN, BUCK 50, BUSTA RHYMES, CYPRESS HILL, D12, EAZY-E, THE GAME, JAY-Z, METHOD MAN, OBIE TRICE, OL' DIRTY BASTARD, SNOOP DOGGY DOG, TWISTA, KANYE WEST

Eminem is the Elvis Presley of hip-hop. He is a white performer who has revitalized a black style. Rap was already popular before the Detroit MC, born Marshall Mathers, came along. But with his flair for controversy and undoubted lyrical prowess, he shook up the entire music scene by reminding everyone of the power of the word. At its best, his songs capture the frustrations of the disenfranchised while making listeners laugh nervously at his very outrageousness. Early on in his career, Eminem created a second persona for himself. This so-called Slim Shady could say anything

Cover of Eminem's *Encore* (2004).

Right:
Eminem in concert at the Palazzo Sant Jordí in Barcelona. MTV Europe Music Awards, November 14, 2002.

he liked. On his *The Slim Shady LP* (1999) debut, the twenty-seven-year-old let rip. Within the first two verses of his debut single “My Name Is,” he claimed to stick nails through his eyelids, admitted taking drugs, and imagined mutilating the *Baywatch* starlet Pamela Anderson. Unlike the gangsta rappers who reveled in sexual fantasies, his lyrics focus on hate and violence. In “Kim,” he rapped about killing his wife in front of his daughter. The listener constantly had to consider what was true and what was false, and Eminem merrily fooled with their confusion, rhyming, “I am / Whatever you say I am.”

Accept everything he rhymes about at face value, and Eminem is sexist, sadistic, homophobic, homicidal, drug addicted, and foulmouthed. In print interviews, however, he paints himself as a reclusive family man. Other songs painfully draw on his mother’s neglect. Few performers are so conscious of living life in stardom’s glare. After making his name by attacking celebrities from the position of someone who had been let down by them, he subjected himself to the same treatment on “Stan,” a song about a psychotic love letter from a fan found on *The Marshall Mathers LP* (2000). None of this would matter if Eminem wasn’t so good at what he does. He adjusts the rhythm of his voice to almost any beat, usually provided by his mentor Dr. Dre or more increasingly by himself. He can breathlessly spit out syllables or turn his voice into a threatening growl to enhance a track. And he has a gift for audacious rhyme making. In “Lose Yourself,” he sketches in two lines the picture of a nervous rapper: “His palms are sweaty, knees weak, arms are heavy/There’s vomit on his sweater already, mom’s spaghetti.” It’s these glimpses of vulnerability that make Eminem so compelling and propel his chart-topping albums to sell in the millions. He flirted with movies—playing a somewhat autobiographical character in *8 Mile* (2002)—but it’s a preeminence he seems weary of. In one of the inside photos from his latest album *Encore* (2004), Eminem prepared to turn a gun on his audience. Being a fan of Eminem’s music could be just as challenging as being Eminem.

What Velvet Underground song was inspired by a Leopold von Sacher-Masoch novel?

The Lilith Scene

- TORI AMOS, TRACY CHAPMAN, PJ HARVEY, SARAH MCLACHLAN, ALANIS MORISSETTE, LIZ PHAIR ...
- UNITED STATES
- 1980S–1990S

The singer-songwriter movement of the 1970s gave women an important voice while keeping them separate from the male-dominated province of rock music. In the late 1980s and 1990s, the tradition of the singer-songwriter revived with an important difference. This time it was a post-feminist music that wasn't afraid to strap on that musical symbol of male potency, the electric guitar.

As well as settling scores with old lovers and dealing with the legacy of sexual freedom left for them by their forebears, this new wave of women in rock had to cope with religious upbringings and broken families. There was also a new vocabulary to deal with them. When Joni Mitchell framed her musings in vivid verse, the lyrics could read like the transcript of a therapy session or a postcard from an ashram.

Tracy Chapman rescued the acoustic guitar from the 1980s onslaught of synthesizers with her self-titled 1988 debut. Its songs were similar to Bruce Springsteen's stories of working-class survival, but her vulnerable voice and delicate strumming reminded women there was a medium for them beyond Madonna's dance-pop.

Throughout the 1990s, the archetype of the girl with a guitar regained a popularity unseen since the days of Joni Mitchell—so much so that Canadian singer-songwriter Sarah McLachlan could launch a popular touring cavalcade known as the Lilith Fair.

"Venus in Furs." The book chronicles an S&M relationship.

Two songwriters saw the seamier side of the love about which Chapman sang with so much yearning. On 1993's *Exile in Guyville,* Liz Phair took on the male hegemony by structuring an "answer record" to the Rolling Stones' *Exile on Main Street.* She played the cock rockers at their own game with songs that chronicled a promiscuous but lonely existence. Teasing, growling, and at times singing like an angel, the flame-haired Tori Amos sang of her triumph over rape and the church while warning, "Just because you can make me cum / That doesn't make you Jesus."

Amos's piano prettified her confessions, but Phair's serrated rock guitar was as much part of her identity as her jaded drawl. PJ Harvey, while considered her British equivalent, was also compared to rock legend Nick Cave. She sang about rejection in painfully intimate terms over scraping riffs. Harvey's subsequent career has been like a kid playing dress-up with mommy's wardrobe: Jezebel ballroom gowns, neon pink bikinis, and a willingness to expose her scrawny body confronted men with what a rock chick should look like.

The confessional, the sexual, and the embrace of rock found its chart apotheosis with Alanis Morissette, a Canadian teen singer whose "You Oughta Know" was the angriest Dear John letter to make it to the Hit Parade. Morissette was smart, fierce, and, compared to Phair and Harvey, safe. Her multiplatinum success, however, completed the transformation: women were free to shout and scream with the best of the boys.

Photograph of Alanis Morissette, a popular songwriter during the mid-1990s.

Left: Tori Amos in Paris. April 2005.

Works of Art: *Which musician painted what?*

Answer

1. David Bowie, *The Rape of Bigarschol*, 1996.
2. Charlelie Couture, *The Basic*, 1991.
3. Astrud Gilberto, *Magya*, 1996.
4. Dee Dee Ramone, *Forced*, 2001.

1

2

DAVID BOWIE

•

ASTRUD GILBERTO

•

CHARLELIE COUTURE

•

DEE DEE RAMONE

3

4

Electronica

• APHEX TWIN, THE CHEMICAL BROTHERS, FATBOY SLIM, LIL' LOUIS, MOBY, THE ORB, THE PRODIGY, UNDERGROUND RESISTANCE, UNDERWORLD ...
• GREAT BRITAIN, UNITED STATES
• 1980S

Illustration of Moby by Gina Miller, 2004.

Right:
Cover of Underworld's *United Underworld* (2004).

Republica was a one-hit-wonder band who had little in common with electronica aside from their use of a synthesizer. In 1996, however, the British music paper *Melody Maker* used the word "electronica" to describe their sound. Ever since, the blanket term refers to a club-oriented genre where the music generated by computers outweigh those made by more organic instruments.

When disco collapsed at the end of

the 1970s, dance music retreated into underground regional scenes clustered around synthesized electronica records. Inspired by the tracks they were playing, many DJs tried to replicate the sounds they heard for themselves. They bought sequencers and samplers. The only familiar element on an electronica record might be a gospel-like vocal or an excitable piano.

In New York, this new music became known as garage, after the soulful-sounding records played at the Paradise Garage. In Chicago, house music took its name and feel from the mix of disco and electro played at the Warehouse. In Detroit, DJs and musicians made gloomy techno from old analogue synthesizers and drum machines. Although Americans ignored this movement, electronica crossed over into European clubs in the late 1980s and these pioneers assumed heroic status.

There are now dozens of subgenres with names like gabba and happy hardcore, but electronica is music to dance to. Mixing electronica with hip-hop samples, British DJs Fatboy Slim and the Chemical Brothers created a rowdy, song-oriented "big beat" suited for moving the sweaty masses. While America and MTV braced for an electronica invasion led by them and the punky group Prodigy, darker sounds like the frenetic drum loops and militant bass of jungle rocked England's underground clubs.

Electronica can also be ambient,

similar to Brian Eno's wallpaper-like "music for airports." The Orb fashioned elaborate sound-scapes from drone-like tones and vocal samples, culminating in "The Blue Room," at forty minutes the world's longest single. American DJ Moby's samplings of old-time blues vocalists in sedate synthetic settings achieved a wide crossover success.

Eccentrics still abound in the now mainstream style. Aphex Twin uses harsh bursts of atonality and tempo-shifts like a bipolar Schoenberg, and the young British MC Dizzee Rascal performs a mutant version of jungle called garage. But in the wrong hands, electronica can be tedious and worse, anonymous. While the elated kitsch of trance has come to dominate clubs, electronica has retreated before a new wave of rock bands and hip-hop's rhythmic personality. With groups like Radiohead and Postal Service incorporating its textures into their music, electronica has become just another sound.

Who was rumored to have bought the Père Lachaise gravesite next to Edith Piaf?

Björk

- *DEBUT* (1993), *POST* (1995), *HOMEGENIC* (1997), *VESPERTINE* (2001), *MEDÚLLA* (2004) ...
- 1965

AIR, MADONNA, MASSIVE ATTACK, MÚM, BETH ORTON, PIZZICATO FIVE, PORTISHEAD, PRIMAL SCREAM, SAINT ETIENNE, SIGUR RÓS, STEREOLAB, TRICKY

Though her voice was once described as "an ice pick through concrete," no artist has quite managed to be pop and avant-garde in the same way as Björk. She has made music and videos that push at the very possibilities of both art forms. Her albums flirt with the sound of disco and classical music. She appeared at the Academy Awards dressed as a swan, complete with a purse that laid an egg. Her voice screeches, coos, breaks, and seems as incandescent as the Northern Lights.

! Cher.

Björk Guomundsdóttir's artistic urges were evident from an early age. She recorded her first album, a collection of Icelandic folk songs, when she was only eleven. By 1986, she had helped form the Sugarcubes. On their hit single "Birthday," she whooped over the atmospheric guitars like a child with an opera diva's lungs.

Björk moved from Reykjavik to London and became immersed in the booming club scene there. Her 1993 solo album *Debut* was filled with wide-eyed wonder and dance-friendly songs like "Big Time Sensuality." But the early tendency toward something different could be heard deep within the grooves. Amid *Debut*'s disco abandon were otherworldly duets with saxophones and a cover of "Like Someone in Love" where Björk's whisper was accompanied by just a harp.

Subsequent albums found her moving slowly toward music's fringes. *Post* (1995) was filled with skittering electronics and raging anthems like "Army of Me." *Homogenic* (1997) was scored for both techno beats and a string quartet. By the time she recorded 2004's *Medúlla,* Björk had decided that "instruments are so over." The album was recorded completely a cappella, employing choirs and rhythmic beat-boxers to create its pillowy acoustics. The resulting sound was similar to a Philip Glass composition. Björk's music videos have also become displays of her complex personality:

Björk. London 1997.

Left: Cover of Björk's third album, *Homogenic* (1997).

"Big Time Sensuality's" ecstatic trip through New York; "It's Oh So Quiet's" eye-popping musical tribute to Jacques Demy's *The Umbrellas of Cherbourg* (1964); "Bachelorette's" autobiographical story of a woodland sprite whose story is appropriated by the media; and "All Is Full of Love's" contradictory scene of two robots making tender love.

Vibrancy, tenderness, hurt, and love are key elements to her art. Even before *Medúlla,* Björk was recoiling from fame, following the suicide of a besotted fan and her brawl with a journalist. She seems to have found her peace with filmmaker Matthew Barney, and her 2001 album *Vespertine* was a sensual celebration of domesticity. In Lars von Trier's movie *Dancer in the Dark* (2000), she shared the saintly despair that Maria Falconetti brought to *The Passion of Joan of Arc* (1928). Björk is music's last armor-clad innocent.

Teen Pop

• 2BE3, CHRISTINA AGUILERA, ALLIAGE, ALIZÉE AND LORIE, BACKSTREET BOYS, DEBBIE GIBSON, MENUDO, NEW KIDS ON THE BLOCK, *NSYNC, JESSICA SIMPSON, BRITNEY SPEARS, SPICE GIRLS, TAKE THAT, t.A.T.u, TIFFANY, WESTLIFE...
• EUROPE, UNITED STATES
• 1950S

Popular music and teenagers have had a close relationship ever since the 1950s when rock 'n' roll made a distinction between being young and being an adult. Of course, the first internationally well-known teen idol was the pelvis-gyrating Elvis Presley. His rebellious movements and sound represented the kind of freedom and fun every teen longed for. Once the industry's bigwigs realized they could market music written by teens for teens, they hit gold. Every decade since has featured a handful of artists who performed almost exclusively for young audiences. In the 1970s, the Osmonds, a Mormon family pop group, sparked "Osmondmania," a prepubescent version of "Beatlemania."

But it was at the end of the 1980s that the "teen pop" phenomenon really took off. Prefabricated boy bands like New Kids on the Block and Take That created record buying frenzies among boy-crazy girls that prompted the existence of other like-minded (and similarly dressed) groups: the Backstreet Boys, Westlife, and *NSYNC. There were even French versions: 2Be3 and Alliage. The lifespan and success of each of these bands lasted as long as the musicians' adolescence did. Proving that girls can do anything boys can do, another teenybopper trend emerged at the end of the century: the "Lolitas," i.e. the girl groups, which featured fresh-faced singers with whom young girls could

The Spice Girls in Tokyo, 1996.

Left:
(left)
The singer Beyoncé at the Heineken Music Hall in Amsterdam, November 2003.

(right)
Britney Spears at the premiere of Tamra Davis's *Crossroads* (2002). Los Angeles, February 11, 2002.

easily identify with and idolize. "Wannabe," the Spice Girls' 1997 single, jumpstarted the careers of the five singers: Mel B ("Scary Spice"), Mel C ("Sporty Spice"), Emma ("Baby Spice"), Victoria ("Posh Spice"), and Geri ("Sexy Spice"), as well as rivalry among other Lolitas to get on the top of the hit lists worldwide. Britney Spears won huge notoriety with her R&B hit ". . . Baby One More Time," an explicit song accompanied by a video of her in a school uniform. Christina Aguilera and Jessica Simpson came in her wake, each sporting even more suggestive outfits. Despite parental complaints, teenagers' T-shirts began creeping up and up, revealing pierced belly buttons en masse. The phenomenon spread to all countries. Russia's most popular export was t.A.T.u, a hot duo that teased audiences with suggested lesbianism; France's version was Alizée and Lorie.

Though sex plays a larger role today than it did during the heyday of Tiffany and Debbie Gibson's innocence, the recipe for building a successful teen pop sensation hasn't changed in decades. First, create light, danceable pop music with simple lyrics. Find artists that have good media presence (this is even more important than talent). Then, churn out a passable single. Repeat. Finally! A musical format that suits a weekly allowance.

?

What was the first rap song to win an Academy Award, in 2003?

Japanese Pop

• BOREDOMS, CORNELIUS, DIR EN GREY, FANTASTIC PLASTIC MACHINE, GLACKT, GUITAR WOLF, PIZZICATO FIVE, PUFFY AMIYUMI...
• JAPAN
• 1980S

! Enimem's "Lose Yourself," from the *8 Mile* soundtrack.

Describing his brand of Japanese pop, Cornelius invokes the Zen Buddhist concept of *ton-chi.* He describes it as the act of looking at life from a different perspective, taking it for something different than it is. There is no better way to describe the topsy-turvy world of Japanese pop music, which might be made of familiar elements but somehow sounds utterly different.

A career in "J-pop" (the term that originated with the radio station J-WAVE) that lasts longer than a decade is a rarity. But the sugar rush sound of J-pop is inescapable in Japan. It's used in TV shows, anime movies, video games, commercials, store sound systems, and anything else requiring insanely catchy and addictive noise. Momentarily delightful and instantly forgettable, it's the perfect sound for a culture where consumption is king, and everything is there to either be discarded or repackaged.

That's the philosophy behind the *shibuya-kei* scene Cornelius is part of, along with Pizzicato Five and Fantastic Plastic Machine. Named after Tokyo's chic shopping district, shibuya-kei groups take their fascinations and overlay and juxtapose at will like a boutique owner constructing a window display. You can reel off a list of their hipper-than-thou obsessions—the Beach Boys, bossa nova, French pop, feedback-drenched indie music, and lounge sounds—but can't possibly imagine how they're blended into a stylish whole without hearing it. Appropriately, these groups see shopping as just another art form, and many have extended their quirky brands into their own fashion labels and stores.

At the furthest reaches of style are the *visual-kei* bands who look like they could have stepped straight out of an outlandish anime or an old print by fin-de-siècle artist Aubrey Beardsley. Androgynous in their makeup and ornate costumes, the artists of *visual-kei* are closer to poseable action figures than the flagrantly camp rock stars they pose as. The music is similar to glam metal, but the stars cultivate an air of eccentricity. Many keep their names secret, and the epicene Glackt insists he was born in 1540. These groups are particularly adored by teenage girls, who dress up as their favorite band members.

For years, J-rock was thought of as a pale imitation of the American version, called "cover pop," but that derisively changed with the Boredoms. Led by vocalist Eye Yamatsuka, who during the heat of one concert drove a backhoe through the venue, their cacophony sounds like an exorcism in a construction site, assuming your eardrums hold out long enough to make sense of it all. Their compatriots Guitar Wolf prefer to turn up the volume on greasy raunch 'n' roll sounds, reminiscent of a soundtrack to a sped-up biker movie. Unlike their cut-and-paste *shibuya-kei* cousins, these bands make their mark by substituting passion for style.

This Page
(top)
Maki Nomiya and Yasuharu Konishi of Pizzicato Five, 1999.

(bottom)
Cover of Pizzicato Five's *SAERA* (2001).

Left:
Guitar Wolf at the Transmusicales Festival in Rennes, 2002.

Names: *What are their real names?*

Answer

1. Paul Hewson, aka Bono.
2. Vincent Furnier, aka Alice Cooper.
3. Olufemi Sanyaolu, aka Keziah Jones.
4. Norman Cook, aka Fatboy Slim.

Bono

Alice Cooper

NORMAN COOK

•

VINCENT FURNIER

•

PAUL HEWSON

•

OLUFEMI SANYAOLU

Keziah Jones

Fat Boy Slim

Britpop

• BLUR, THE BOO RADLEYS, COLDPLAY, ECHOBELLY, ELASTICA, MANIC STREET PREACHERS, OASIS, RADIOHEAD, SAINT ETIENNE AND THE SLEEPERS, SUEDE, SUPERGRASS, SUPER FURRY ANIMALS, THE VERVE ...
• GREAT BRITAIN
• 1990S

In 1993, the great tradition of British pop was in danger of extinction. Although it enjoyed a heritage that stretched back to the Beatles, the Kinks, and the Who, the English manner of combining strong guitar-based tunes with wry lyrics was under attack by colorless dance music, mopey American grunge, and painfully aesthetic "shoegazing" groups who shyly whispered into a storm of feedback.

Two very different London-based bands armed themselves with tradition and fought back. Suede adopted the limp-wristed glam rock of David Bowie and Marc Bolan, singing about the British institutions of the suburbs and gay sex. The art-school-educated Blur turned to the catchy riffs of the British invasion, dissecting village green life and making the post-Imperialist claim, "Modern life is rubbish."

They awoke a sleeping beast. Soon the music papers were filled with "Britpop" bands who sang in their native accents and dressed up tidy three-minute songs in mod suits and pub sing-along choruses. A "Cool Britannia" scene grew around these new bands, which included British art stars like Damian Hirst and the rising political force of Tony Blair's Labour Party.

It came to a head on August 14, 1995, when Blur and Oasis both released singles on the same day, and the race was on to see who would reach No. 1. It was a telling competition. Blur's album *Park Life* (1994) had become an essential Britpop document. But their songs about the BBC's shipping news and package holidays hid a darkly satiric streak. (They even sang in French!) Oasis were an unashamedly triumphalist band from Manchester, whose aspiring anthems boasted nonsense lyrics and the Sex Pistols-like snarl of singer

Noel Gallagher and Paul Arthurs, members of Oasis. Photograph taken during the British TV show *The White Room*. April 1995.

Left:
Blur, 1994. From left to right: Graham Coxon, Dave Rowntree, Alex James, and lead singer Damon Albarn (seated).

Liam Gallagher. To the working-class Oasis, the bourgeoisie Blur were anathema. The media treated the showdown like it was a World Cup final and the entire nation held its breath on the outcome.

Blur won the battle. Their single "Country House" topped the charts. They also lost the war. Led by the ballad "Wonderwall," Oasis' album *(What's the Story) Morning Glory?* (1995) became an international success. Unlike their Britpop peers, Oasis had a knack of appealing to the rest of the world with their simple songs and tabloid-friendly antics. They became the biggest British band since the Beatles, but Britpop became a casualty. Suddenly everyone wanted to sound like Oasis, and the music lost its individuality. Drugs and alcohol also laid waste to the scene. Britpop's hedonistic legacy sidelined many of its leading lights.

Nearly a decade later, Britpop's legacy is still being felt. Blur and Pulp resurrected the literate pop tradition. Britpop was also very open to women. Groups like Elastica, Saint Etienne and the Sleepers were all led by commanding females. The leading British exports continue to make the same delicate ballads in the mold of "Wonderwall." And while Oasis are still with us, Blur finally got their global hit with "Song 2" and its "whoo-hoo!" chorus. Contrary to the last, it sounded like the Yankee grunge Blur once despised.

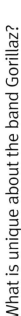

What is unique about the band Gorillaz?

Pop Idols

- *AMERICAN IDOL, MONGOLIAN COW SOUR YOGURT SUPERGIRL CONTEST, NASHVILLE STAR, OBJETIVO FAMO, POP IDOL, PROJECT SUPERSTAR, ROCK STAR: INXS, STAR ACADEMY, SUPER STAR ...*
- INTERNATIONAL
- 2001–

Talent competitions have been around since Orpheus plucked his lute to win Persephone's heart, but there has never been one like *Pop Idol*. The British program first aired in October 2001. Since then, it has spun off a host of similar TV programs around the world—ranging from the United States to the farthest reaches of China—and launched the careers of hundreds of would-be chart stars.

The *Pop Idol* process is simple. A team of judges oversees the initial auditions. The aspirants are a mix of impassioned singers, the tone deaf, and fame-seekers, all performing hits in an emotive manner. The most promising enter a TV studio. Each week they perform a song of their choice and are scrutinized by the judges.

The group is whittled down to ten finalists. With each episode, the audience votes for their favorite. The least popular singer leaves the show until only one is left. The remaining "idol" wins a coveted record contract.

The format is so popular that more people voted in America's version—American Idol—final

than in the 2000 presidential election. In Singapore, the spin-off Project Superstar actually determines its winner based on which finalist's single sells more.

Sometimes fans' passions for their favorites run high. When one contestant was voted off in the Lebanese show *Super Star*, a riot broke out among his supporters outside the Beirut studio.

The imitations have made subtle changes to the established format. The French *Star Academy* sends its contestants to a kind of musical boot camp, with cameras capturing their every move onstage and off. Perhaps the most

! The group is entirely made up of animated characters.

Poster for the *Star Academy* Concert, France.

Left:
The *Star Academy for Lebanon*: *Al-Academia*. The show airs on the private television station LBCI (2004).

curious show, however, is China's *Mongolian Cow Sour Yogurt Super Girl Contest*. Originally broadcast on a rural channel, the competition became a sensation that attracted four hundred million viewers. How to account for an audience bigger than the combined populations of America and Canada? Perhaps it's because the show allowed an entire generation of Communist music lovers to vote for the first time in their lives. Forget the singers. The *Idol* formula works because it gives audiences a collective voice.

Appendixes

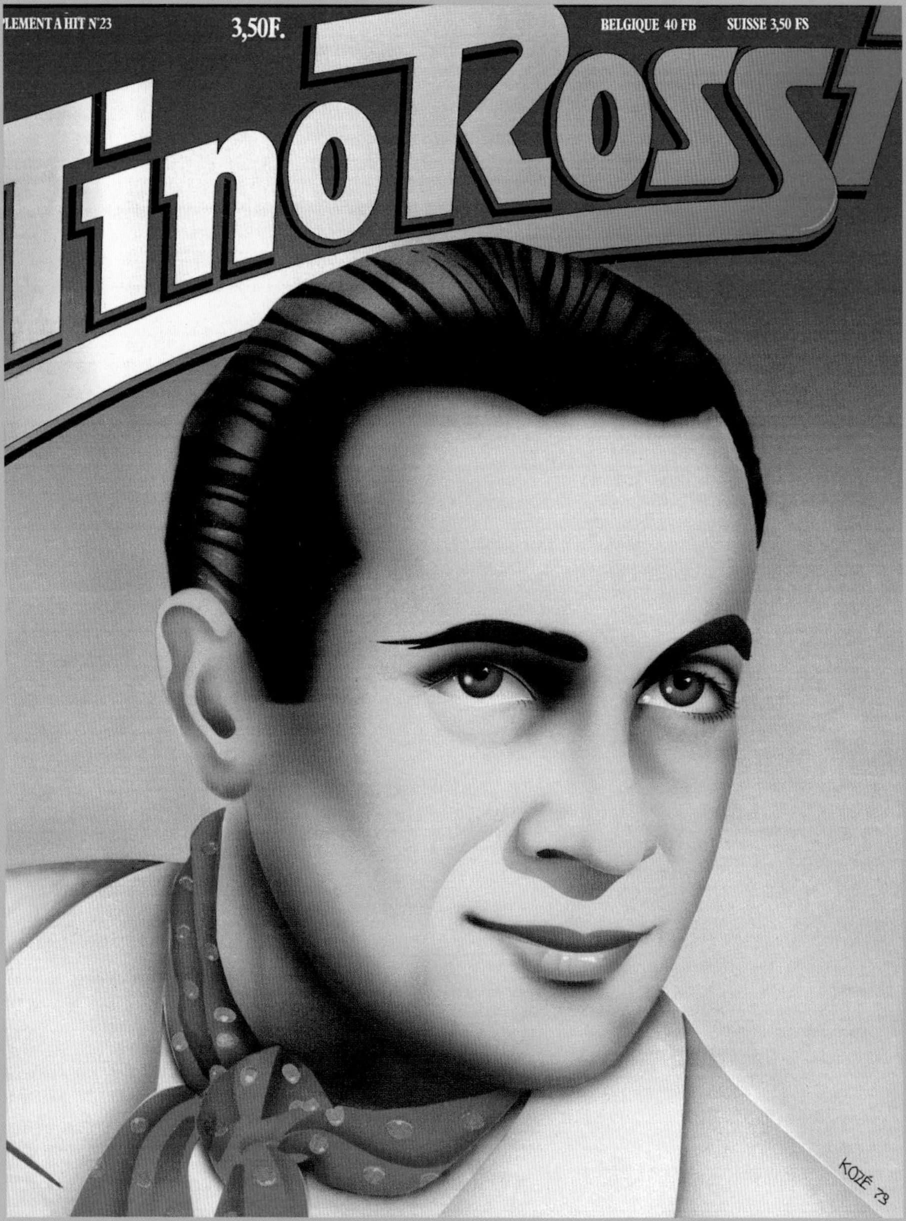
PLEMENT A HIT N°23
3,50F.
BELGIQUE 40 FB
SUISSE 3,50 FS
Tino Rossi
KOZÉ 73

Glossary

A CAPELLA
Choral singing without instrumental accompaniment.

ACOUSTIC
Acoustic music generally refers to music produced by instruments that are not electronic.

ALLEGRO
An Italian term (literally "lively") indicating the tempo at which a piece must be played. The allegro is also the first movement of a sonata.

BANDONÉON
A small, accordion-like instrument, invented in 1840 by Heinrich Band and first used in Germany in Protestant temples. It arrived in Latin America in 1865 and became one of the indispensable instruments of tango. In the twentieth century, its name was often coupled with the Argentine composer Astor Piazzolla.

BARBERSHOP HARMONY
A type of close, four-part harmony, often with chromatic passing notes, that was popular in America at the turn of the century.

BARITONE
A term used for deep, low sounds, it is used both to designate a type of male voice and certain wind instruments. It refers to the *tessitura* of the voice of an opera singer, an intermediate pitch between bass and tenor. Dietrich Fischer-Diskau and José Van Dam are among the great baritone singers. The term has the same definitions when applied to instruments. The baritone saxophone is, therefore, between the bass and tenor saxophone.

BEL CANTO
Italian term referring to the art of "beautiful song," as exemplified by the finest Italian singers of the eighteenth and nineteenth centuries. It is the opposite of the declamatory style of singing brought into prominence by Richard Wagner.

CLASSICAL MUSIC
Colloquially, any serious artistic music, as opposed to popular or folk music.

CLUBBING
From jazz clubs in the 1950s to the discotheques of our time, nightclubs are emblematic of nightlife. Clubbing means going to a club to dance or to listen to music.

DA CAPO
An Italian term, abbreviated as D.C. on sheet music, which indicates that the musical piece must be played again from the start.

DANCE MUSIC
Emerging in the 1990s, dance music borrows from techno, raga, and hip-hop. It is characterized by melodies that are easy to remember and a rhythm particularly suitable for dancing. The bands 2 Unlimited, Corona, and Ace of Base were icons of the genre in the 1990s. Pioneers include Cher and Kylie Minogue in the late 1980s.

DIXIELAND
An American jazz style that began around 1915 and that became prominent in the 1920s. The instruments typically featured in a Dixieland band are the trumpet (or cornet), clarinet, piano, banjo, and drums, and the style is characterized by collective improvisation, dotted rhythms, and syncopation. Dixieland enjoyed a revival after World War II and continues to experience occasional popularity. The Original Dixieland Jass Band (in mid-1917, the spelling was changed to "Jazz") was a New Orleans band which, in 1917, was the first ever to make a jazz recording.

DRUM MACHINE
An electronic synthesizer specifically designed to simulate different types of percussion sounds. It is usually outfitted with some type of built-in sequencer that allows the musician to save and store rhythmic patterns so they can be played at a later time. Early drum machines were often referred to as "rhythm machines."

ELECTRONIC MUSIC
A body of compositions created out of a new, resourceful method of tone production by electronic means. The earliest electronic instrument, the theremin, was developed by the Russian inventor of the same name in 1919. The most advanced electronic instruments are synthesizers, capable of generating any desired pitch, scale, rhythm, tone color, or volume. Examples of early innovators in this field are Pink Floyd, Kraftwerk, and Tangerine Dream.

ELEVATOR MUSIC
A colloquial term for "muzak." Muzak is the trade name for the first U.S. company to have license to produce, distribute, and transmit background

music for public consumption. One of the many public places muzak is heard is in elevators, hence its more popular name.

EXPERIMENTAL MUSIC
Music that strays from the usual conventions of style, form, and genre that have developed throughout history. Its proponents begin with Erik Satie and Charles Ives and move through and beyond the works of John Cage and Cornelius Cardew.

FALSETTO
The highest of the vocal registers.

FEEDBACK
In any audio system, feedback, an echo effect, is due to the proximity of the transmitter (microphone or instrument) and the amplifier. The piercing sounds were used as early as the 1960s by guitarists like Jimi Hendrix.

FILMI
Filmi music is a fundamental element of popular Indian cinema. In both small and large Bollywood productions, filmi music is often available before the release of the movie as promotion for the film. It is sometimes even its main ingredient. Since 1992, the composer A.R. Rahman has been rejuvenating filmi, combining technology and traditional instruments. Although not directly related to traditional ancestral music, filmi is an essential part of Indian culture, and India has the most productive movie industry in the world.

FINGERPICKING
A style of guitar-playing in which a musician picks strings with the tips of his or her fingers (or with steel metal picks placed on the fingers) rather than strumming the strings. This style is commonly heard in acoustic blues, folk, and soft-rock music.

FRENCH OVERTURE
A type of overture developed in France in the eighteenth century, during the Baroque period. It consists of three sections: the first is in a slow tempo, the second is rather quick, and the third is slow. Examples can be found in the opening movement of each of Johann Sebastian Bach's orchestral suites, and as openings to many oratorios by George Frideric Handel (including *Messiah*); the sixteenth movement of Bach's *Goldberg Variations* is a French overture in miniature.

FURNITURE MUSIC
A description coined by Erik Satie (as *musique d'amueblement*) to denote background music, it is a precursor to the term "muzak".

GAGAKU
Japanese term literally meaning "elegant enjoyment," it is orchestral music of the Japanese court dating back to the twelfth century whose instruments include the *shinobue* (transverse flute), *hichiriki* (shawn), *sho* (mouth organ), and *taiko* (barrel drums).

GAMELAN
This term designates both the players of the traditional Indonesian instrument and the orchestra itself, which consists entirely of percussion instruments. Metallophones, xylophones, and cymbals carry cyclical melodies, which are often opened and closed by a gong. Many kinds of gamelans are found in Indonesian territory and are part of major social and cultural events, like marriages and other religious ceremonies. In the 1950s, the British composer Benjamin Britten introduced the gamelan into Western contemporary music, in which it still can be heard today.

GESAMTKUNSTWERK
German term meaning "total artwork," it is attributed to Richard Wagner and refers to a restoration of the unity of the arts of music, literature, and painting as they were believed to have originally existed in Greek practices.

GLOCKENSPIEL
This percussion instrument, meaning "chime" in German, belongs to the idiophone family, along with the xylophone and vibraphone. Originally made with bells, the glockenspiel today consists of small metal bars that are played with wooden sticks. Its clear tones greatly resemble chimes. It is used in classical orchestrations, especially in certain passages of Mozart's *Magic Flute* (1791). It has also drawn the attention of rock stars like Bruce Springsteen, Tom Waits, and independent groups like Godspeed You Black Emperor.

GOLD RECORD
A gold record is awarded to an artist whose single—in the past known as a 45"—has sold five hundred thousand copies. The idea of an award came to the fore in 1905 when the British company Grammophone gave the violinist Marie Hall a

gold bracelet incrusted with seven small albums, symbolic of the seven hits of her success. Today, silver, platinum, and diamond records are also given and represent different numbers of sales in different countries. In Germany, an artist is awarded a platinum record after three hundred thousand albums are sold, whereas in New Zealand, ten thousand is enough.

HARMONICA
A set of graduated metal reeds mounted in a narrow frame, blown by the mouth, and producing different tones on exhalation and inhalation. It is also called a "mouth harmonica," "mouth organ," or, more colloquially, the "Mississippi saxophone." Commonly used in blues and folk music, it's also found in jazz, classical music, rock.

HARPSICHORD
A keyboard string instrument in which the strings are plucked by quills or bits of hard leather. A predecessor to the piano, it was popular both as a solo and as an ensemble instrument in the eighteenth century. Dimitri Shostakovich (*Hamlet*, 1964) and Alfred Schnittke (Symphony no. 8, 1998) used the harpsichord as part of orchestral texturing.

IMPRESSIONISM
A term used to describe modern French compositions of the early twentieth century in which subtle impressions are conveyed through the use of ethereal harmonies in free form (or in modulation) and with colorful instrumentation. The influence of Impressionistic thought extends (most famously) to the world of painting as well as to that of literature. Famous musical Impressionists include Claude Debussy, Frederick Delius, and Maurice Ravel.

IMPROVISATION
A term that refers to the spontaneous performance of music without previous preparation, practice, or written notes. During the Middle Ages, singers often improvised additional lines to liturgical chant; in the Renaissance and Baroque periods, musicians improvised over written chords. In the twentieth century, jazz and bluegrass musicians were celebrated for their improvisational skills. Today, rap has embraced improvisation, too.

INDUSTRIAL
Industrial music exists at the crossroads of electronic music and experimental music. From the start, its evolution has been linked to avant-garde and underground music. Incorporating everything from futuristic concepts to John Cage's experiments, industrial music took root as early as the 1970s. As its name suggests, industrial music expresses the world around us, combining political awareness with musical experimentation. Using electronic sound, urban noise, and non-musical elements like video or bits of text, it develops a postmodern aesthetic which is extreme and which is often considered shocking. The visual performances given by pioneers like Throbbing Gristle or Cabaret Voltaire are noteworthy. Generating sub-genres like electro-industrial, metal-industrial, or noise music, industrial music mostly attracts audiences who follow its development. The 1980s Berlin group Einstürzende Neubauten is currently one of the most current representatives of the genre.

IPOD
A portable digital media player designed and marketed by Apple Computer. Devices in the iPod family provide a simple user interface designed around a central scroll wheel. As of September 2005, the lineup consisted of the fifth-generation iPod, which can play videos; the iPod Nano, which has a color screen; and the iPod Shuffle.

ITUNES
Apple Computer's bundled software used for uploading music, photos, and movies to an iPod. The music jukebox application stores a comprehensive library of music on a user's computer.

JAM SESSION
Happening generally in bars or clubs, a jam session is a period of musical improvisation bringing together amateurs and professionals. Often applied to jazz, the term is used in rock as well. The idea of jamming developed in the 1940s, when improvised music like bebop emerged. Jam sessions with Dizzy Gillepsie or Charlie Parker resulted in many jazz hits, which have today become standards.

JAZZ
A term covering a wide variety of African-American styles: ragtime, blues, Dixieland, swing, bebop, cool, third stream, free jazz, funk, jazz-rock, and other styles that lack a specific category. Most are characterized by improvisation and a "swinging"

beat, composed of a steady, prominent meter and dotted or syncopated rhythms.

JAZZ-ROCK

A style of the late 1960s and 1970s that merges the electric amplification and the heavy beat of rock with some of the more sophisticated improvisatory features of jazz. It is also called "jazz fusion."

KAPELLMEISTER

A German term for the conductor of an orchestra or choir.

KAZOO

A toy-like instrument consisting of a short tube with membranes at one end, into which a player hums, producing a whimsical nasal tone. It is also known as "mirliton," and in the seventeenth century, it was called a flute-eunuque ("eununch flute"). The Original Dixieland Jazz Band 1921's recording of "Crazy Blues" features a kazoo solo by drummer Tony Sbarbaro. In the early 1920s, the Mound City Blue Blowers had a number of hit kazoo records (with Dick Slevin on metal kazoo and Red McKenzie on comb and tissue paper kazoo.)

KEYBOARD INSTRUMENTS

Term for instruments such as the organ, piano, clavichord, and harpsichord, which are sounded through the use of a set of keys. These keys are laid out in such a way that the white keys are the keys of the C major scale, and all the semitones in the chromatic scale are produced by depressing the black keys.

KITHARA

An ancient Greek instrument of the lyre family, consisting of several strings stretched over a soundbox.

KLANGFARBENMELODIE

This term literally means "melody of tone colors." Invented by Arnold Schoenberg in his text on harmony, *Harmonielehre* (1911), it describes the technique of altering the tone color of a single note or musical line by switching from one instrument to another in the middle of that note or line.

LAMELLAPHONES

Also called "thumb pianos," these are a class of handheld musical instruments indigenous to Africa whose sound is produced by the vibration of thin tongues of metal or wood plucked by the thumbs. Well known versions are the mbira and the kalima.

LUTE

A general term for a variety of plucked, stringed instruments.

LYRICS

A colloquial term for the text of a popular song or stage musical.

MEDLEY

Very popular in the 1980s, a medley brings different pieces of music together into a single title. It generally borrows standards from one or from a variety of artists. "Aquarius/Let the Sunshine In" is a medley of the songs "Aquarius" and "The Flesh Failures (Let the Sunshine In)," from the musical *Hair*. This song was originally released by The Fifth Dimension as a single, which held the No. 1 position on the U.S. charts for six weeks in 1969.

METRONOME

The familiar timekeeper for musicians or, more appropriately, for music students. It is a double pendulum moved by clockwork, with a slider on a scale that marks the number of beats the metronome makes per minute. "M.M." stands for "Maelzel's Metronome," after the reputed inventor, Maelzel of Vienna (1816). The number following such an indication in a score, as in "M.M. = 60," instructs the player to perform at a moderate temp of sixty beats per minute.

MIDI (MUSICAL INSTRUMENT DIGITAL INTERFACE)

The digital language used for connecting computers, synthesizers, sequencers, and other modern electronic musical instruments so that they may "communicate with" (send data to) each other. Almost all music recordings today utilize MIDI as a key enabling technology for recording music. In addition, MIDI is used to control hardware, including recording devices as well as live performance equipment such as stage lights and effects pedals.

MODAL MUSIC

Like other kinds of music (Indian, Eastern, etc.), modal music is distinguished by its structure and system of notation, in which notions of mode and tone are fundamental. Fundamentally, there are seven modes, each one designating the manner in which octave notes are arranged. Medieval music is largely modal, as are Gregorian polyphonies. At the end of the sixteenth century, music theory and music notation evolved. Only two modes, known as "minor" and "major," remained, but the range of tonalities increased. Thus, the foundation of classical music was established. Melodies played simultaneously had to respect the chosen key. In this way, tonal harmony replaced the modal harmonies of the polyphonies. Later, composers like Claude Debussy and Arnold Schoenberg used other systems to contrast with the tonal system. Aleatoric, concrete, and serial music, upon which contemporary music is based, stems from these innovations.

MODERATO
The Italian term for "moderate," indicating the tempo at which the piece must be played. Moderato is slower than allegro and faster than adagio.

NEW AGE
A generic name given to soft, often acoustic music which attempts to convey spiritual themes or mystical perspectives.

NEW WAVE
A musical genre that grew out of the New York City punk scene during the late 1970s and early 1980s. Artistically inclined bands like Talking Heads were leaders in this style, their music featuring poetic, oblique lyrics and intentionally simple melodies and accompaniments.

NOISE POP
A kind of pop that is defined by its extreme quality. It is also called "shoegaze," because some groups who play it look down at their shoes. Noise is a stylistic form of rock or grunge, as represented by the group Sonic Youth. Noise groups seek to destroy commonplace musical structures. Since 1990, groups like My Bloody Valentine have to this end layered distorted guitar and inaudible lyrics over pop, making it less accessible.

OPERA
A form of drama of Italian origin in which both vocal and instrumental music are essential and predominant. The several dramatic acts of a "grand opera," usually preceded by instrumental introductions, consist of vocal scenes, songs, arias, duets, trios, choruses, etc., accompanied by the orchestra. A "comedy" opera is a versified comedy set to music, and a "comic" opera has spoken interludes.

OPERETTA
This term literally means "little opera," which is the precursor to the modern musical company. Similar to an opera, an operetta generally deals with less serious topics; music is light and lively, often interrupted by dialogue.

OPUS
A Latin word for "work," often written "Op." or "op." In music, pieces are given opus numbers, which generally run in order of publication.

PERCUSSION
Percussion instruments are played by being struck, shaken, rubbed, or scraped. Instruments of percussion are drums, tambourines, cymbals, bells, triangle, etc., as well as the dulcimer and the pianoforte. They are considered the oldest instruments, with exception of vocals. Percussion instruments play not only rhythm but also melody and harmony.

PHRASING
Just as punctuation makes a text readable, musical notation allows Western music to be decoded. On sheet music and with precise indications, phrasing indicates the way in which a musical phrase is to be played and also offers suggestions for its performance. The nuances of phrasing go from legato ("linked") to staccato ("detached"). It is, therefore, possible to create different musical phrases with the same group of notes. Melody and the structure of the piece are built on the arrangement of these musical phrases.

PLAYER PIANO
Trade name of a mechanical piano in which the keyboard action is produced by a rotating perforated roll. An early example was the Pianista, developed by Henri Fourneaux in 1863, though ultimately the best known was the Pianola, created by Edwin Scott Votey in 1895. Igor Stravinsky composed for it, and, more recently, Conlon Nancarrow has written a series of highly original works for the instrument.

PLECTRUM
A small wooden, ivory, or metal instrument generally held between the thumb and index finger, and specifically used for string instruments. More commonly known as a "pick" by guitarists and mandolin players, the plectrum can be employed for different instruments. Sometimes every finger is needed for its use.

PODCASTING

A term used to describe a collection of technologies for automatically distributing audio programs over the Internet. It differs from earlier online collections of audio works because it automatically transfers the files to the user's computer for later use and enables independent producers to create self-published "radio shows."

POP(ULAR) MUSIC

A general term to denote a wide variety of musical styles, generally characterized by their easy accessibility to wide audiences. Pop songs are usually of modest length, with prominent and memorable melodies and lyrics and a simple, unassuming harmonic language.

POTPOURRI

A kind of musical medley in which all kinds of tunes, or parts of tunes, are connected in an arbitrary manner.

QUOTATION MUSIC

Music that parodies another work or works, presenting them in a new style or guise.

QUICKSTEP

A form of International Style ballroom dance that follows a 2/4 or 4/4 beat, similar to a fast fox-trot. The dance evolved in the 1920s from a combination of the fox-trot and the Charleston as bands started to play music that was too quick to allow for the large open leg movements which the fox-trot required.

QUINTET

A quintet can be a genre, a musical work, or a group of five musicians for which such a work is written. The English term often designates a jazz orchestra, whereas its French equivalent, the quintette, is more often a term used to describe classical groups. Schubert's famous work *The Trout*, written for piano, violin, viola, and bass, is classified as a quintet. In jazz, Miles Davis's 1955 quintet included John Coltrane on the saxophone and Red Garland on the piano.

RAGA

Raga is a Sanskrit term, meaning attraction, color, or passion, and also refers to a style of sacred melody structured by a set of precise rules. Specific to classical Indian music, this system is above all founded upon ancient Vedic theories. Because its origins derive from sacred texts, raga mostly plays a religious role and can be compared to western liturgical hymns. There are more than four thousand known ragas. However, only ragas from the north (Hindustani music), influenced by Islam, and ragas from the south (Carnatic music) have retained their former classification.

RAGTIME

Ragtime, a musical genre that emerged in the United States at the end of the nineteenth century, originated in saloons. Often played on piano, guitar, or banjo, ragtime can also be performed by a single instrument or by fanfare bands. In ragtime (as in "ragged time") a characteristic rhythm is played in sync with a melody. Scott Joplin, one of the inventors of classic ragtime, found fame in 1899 with his song "The Maple Leaf Rag." Ragtime experienced a revival in 1973 when music adapter Marvin Hamlisch used Joplin's music as the featured soundtrack for George Roy Hill's *The Sting*. The film swept the 1973 Oscars, winning "Best Musical Score." The genre continues to thrive today in the work of composers like William Bolcom and Trebor Tichenor.

RAPSODIE

A rhapsody. Generally, in an instrumental fantasia based on folk songs or on motives taken from primitive national music.

RAVE

Emerging in Great Britain in the 1960s along with the first examples of electronic music, raves are techno parties that often take place in unusual spots, like fields, forests, or abandoned buildings. Not as clandestine as "free parties," raves are nonetheless countercultural and are closely monitored by authorities. Today, they sometimes have the same commercial ambitions as clubs. In Europe, Teknivals (ad hoc techno festivals) have a more subversive style.

REMIX

A remix is a new version of a previously recorded song. It's replayed by a DJ live in concert or in a club. A remix can also appropriate a piece from an entirely different genre. Techno remixes have transformed soul hits, like Aretha Franklin's "Respect," into club dance music.

RIFF

A riff is an easily identifiable, short musical phrase that is often more rhythmic than melodic. In the past, it was usually associated with jazz, but today, the term has been entirely assimilated into rock jargon.

The opening bars of "Satisfaction" by the Rolling Stones or of Deep Purple's "Smoke on the Water" are some famous examples of riffs.

ROCKABILLY

A 1950s-era style of music that combined a rock 'n' roll beat with country music sentiments. It was revived in the 1970s, primarily in England and Europe. Elvis Presley's 1954 Memphis sessions for Sam Phillip's Sun Records produced the first rockabilly recordings. Carl Perkins, who also recorded for Sun, is another performer who helped define the genre. "Blue Suede Shoes," witten by Perkins, is considered a classic of the style. And, the early recordings of Jerry Lee Lewis, Johnny Cash, Dale Hawkins, Charlie Feathers, and Roy Orbison are also considered essential.

SAMPLE

A sample is a borrowed and reused sound or melody. Often very short and made with a sampler, it was a fundamental element of 1980s hip-hop and remains so today. It is also widely incorporated into electronic music and pop.

SCANSION

In poetry, scansion refers to the scanning a verse, that is, giving diction rhythm and meter. Therefore, by extension, in musical compositions or in songs, it involves putting text to a beat.

SCAT

Scat literally means "hum," but actually consists of imitating an instrument's melody by using voice and onomatopoeia. Legend has it that during a Hot Five jam, Louis Armstrong entirely improvised the song "Heebie Jeebies," forgetting the lyrics in order to scat. Ella Fitzgerald also distinguished herself in the genre. Since, scatting can be heard in rock. In particular, it was used by Bob Marley in his 1977 "Punky Reggae Party."

SEQUENCER

An electronic device that supplies a sequence of determined voltages in sound synthesis or processing. It is commonly used to record short melodic or rhythmic patterns, which are then played back in a repeating loop through a synthesizer or through another device. Drum machines often feature built-in sequencers, because rhythm patterns tend to repeat through popular songs.

SITAR

The sitar, an Indian pluck instrument, consists of a hemispherical resonating chamber and an arm with frets. Originally, it was a fundamental instrument in *khyal*, classical music from the north of India. It arrived in the West in the 1970s, through the popularity of psychedelia. It is heard in songs by The Beatles and The Rolling Stones, and, since the 1990s, in Goa Trance and Psychedelic Trance electronic music. The sitar is emblematic of Indian culture as interpreted by the West.

SOUNDBOX

The body of a stringed instrument that amplifies its sound.

STACCATO

Staccato is an Italian term meaning "detached" and opposes the legato, meaning "linked." Indicated by a dot over a note, it specifies that the note must be played separately from the previous one and that it must be strongly accented.

STURM AND DRANG

A term that literally means "storm and stress." It is a literary term borrowed by music theorists and critics to describe a highly emotional minor key style of composition that emerged during the early classical period (1770s), particularly in Germany.

SWING

Swing is a technical term for a kind of delayed rhythm that cannot be easily transcribed onto sheet music, and it is a very intuitive manner of interpreting jazz. It is also a genre that emerged in the 1910s, better known as the fox-trot, which is a dance that is closely linked to ragtime. Jelly Roll Morton, a major figure of swing in the 1920s, opened the way for improvisation in jazz in the decades that followed.

TAARAB

Emerging in the nineteenth century, *taarab* is the Arab word for "emotion." Musically, its richness derives from the various influences that inform the history of Zanzibar, where it originated. Traditional music based on female choirs singing in Swahili, *taarab* borrows from Arab, Egyptian, Western, and Indian music alike. At first, it was played among members of high society as well as for the Sultan and his entourage. It is conducive to meditation as well as to entertainment and bridges music with traditional and modern poetry.

TESSITURA

Tessitura designates the range of sounds (from low to high) that can be emitted without difficulty. It is a way of classifying voices and instruments into large categories: soprano, mezzo soprano, alto, tenor, baritone, and bass.

THEME SONG

The most prominent song in a musical, or a movie, calculated to express the abiding sentiment of the entire production.

THEREMIN

A forerunner of electronic instruments and invented in 1919 by Léon Theremin in Russia, the instrument consists of an electronic box and two metal rods. The first controls the pitch of the note, and the other controls the volume. The player varies the sound by changing his physical distance from the instrument. Functioning by magnetic stimulation, it doesn't require any physical contact (the opposite of a hammer action keyboard). A symbol of technological progress for the USSR, the instrument today draws attention from pop and electronica musicians. It has been used by, among others, the Beach Boys, Portishead, and Jean-Michel Jarre.

TIMBRE

Timbre designates the specificity of a voice or of an instrument. A consideration of timbre must not only include pitch, intensity, and duration, but also listening conditions. It is hugely difficult for theoreticians and acousticians to study it scientifically and to define it precisely.

TONIC SOL-FA

A method of teaching vocal music, invented by Sarah Ann Glover of Norwich, England, in about 1812. Pupils are taught to recognize the tones of a scale by observing the mental impressions peculiar to each tone. It is based on the "moveable do" system and uses the syllables doy, ray, me, fah, soh, lah, and te.

UNEQUAL VOICES

Voices different in compass and quality; mixed voices.

UPRIGHT PIANO

A piano standing vertically with its strings arrange cross-wise (diagonally) along the vertical soundboard, as distinguished from a grand piano in which the strings and the soundboard are horizontal.

VIOLA

A tenor violin. A bowed string instrument with its four strings tuned one fifth lower than the violin.

VIRTUOSO(A)

A highly proficient instrumentalist or vocalist.

WASHBOARD

A percussion instrument that comes out of Louisiana Cajun music, the washboard is, along with the fiddle and guitar, one of the main components of country music. As its name indicates, it was first a simple, striated washing board that was rubbed with a thimble. It has since become a genuine instrument, and today's models come with cymbals and bells. In Skiffle, an Anglo-Saxon music that combines jazz, folk, and blues, the washboard replaces the drum. The Quarrymen, John Lennon's first group, was a skiffle band.

WAH-WAH

The wah-wah sound was first developed by jazz trumpet players who blocked and unblocked their instruments with a mute. The "open-close" effect that causes sound fluctuation is the principle behind the wah-wah pedal used by bass players and guitarists. Wah-wah gives instruments a warmer tonality, similar to groove and reminiscent of its jazz origins.

WEST COAST JAZZ

This jazz style developed in the 1950s, featuring small groups of mixed timbres playing contrapuntal improvisations. Some of the major pioneers of West Coast jazz include Chet Baker, Dave Brubeck, Paul Desmond, and Gerry Mulligan.

WOODWIND

The woodwind family is less homogeneous in construction and sound production than the string family; it includes the piccolo, the flute, the oboe, the English horn, the clarinet, and the bassoon. The saxophone is a more recent woodwind instrument that is frequently heard in jazz.

WORLD BEAT

A collective term for popular Third-world music, ethnic and traditional music, and eclectic combinations of Western and non-Western music. Also called "ethno-pop."

XYLOPHONE
An instrument consisting of a row of flat wooden bars fastened horizontally to two stretched boards, tuned to the tones of a scale, and struck with two mallets. Some xylophones also have resonating chambers placed below each bar to amplify tone.

YANGQIN
A Chinese hammered dulcimer with a trapezoidal sound box and metal strings that are struck with bamboo sticks.

YODEL
A technique that consists of vocalization moving from the head voice to the chest voice, producing a characteristic quavering. Originally, the yodel was a way for mountain dwellers to communicate. It combines the folklore of alpine regions with bluegrass and country music. In the early years of the twentieth century, pioneers like Hank Williams and Jimmie Rodgers were masters of a kind of yodeling that today is very different from its European equivalent.

ZARZUELA
A type of Spanish opera that includes spoken dialogue.

ZEITROPER
German operas of the 1920s and 1930s that had distinct sociopolitical themes.

ZITHER
Family of string instruments with a sound box over which strings are stretched; the strings may be plucked or bowed. Zithers appear in many shapes and are common in traditional music throughout Europe, Asia, and Africa.

ZIGEUNERMUSIK
Another word for Gypsy music.

Festivals

WOMAD
A series of festivals around the world that introduces international audiences to international performers.
Various
www.womad.org

AUSTRALIA

BIG DAY OUT
Annual antipodean tour of international alt.rock acts.
January
Australia and New Zealand
www.bigdayout.com

BRUNSWICK MUSIC FESTIVAL
Festival of world music held at Brunswick Town Hall.
March–April
Brunswick
+61 3 9387-3376
www.brunswickmusicfestival.com.au

EARTHCORE
A series of outdoor dance music festivals held in forest settings with bands and DJs.
Victoria
November
+61 3 9527-1444
www.earthcore.com.au

FALLS FESTIVAL
Annual three-day music and youth culture festival held in two locales during the New Year.
Lorne, Victoria and Marion Bay, Tasmania
December–January
www.fallsfestival.com

GLOBAL CARNIVAL
Multicultural arts festival celebrating Australia's cultural diversity.
September-October
Bellingen, New South Wales
+61 2 6655 3024
www.globalcarnival.com

HAWKESBURY NATIONAL FIDDLE FESTIVAL
Features workshops, concerts, contests, and busking.
April
Clarendon, New South Wales
+61 2 4576 7023
www.fiddlefestival.com

LIVID
Australia's longest running outdoor festival, with local and international DJs, artists, and bands.
October
Sydney, Melbourne, Brisbane
www.livid.com.au

MANLY INTERNATIONAL JAZZ FESTIVAL
Australia's biggest jazz festival, set alongside Sydney Harbour. And it's free!
October
Manly, New South Wales
+61 2 9976 1430
www.manly.nsw.gov.au/minisites/main.asp?ms=27

NYMAGEE OUTBACK MUSIC FESTIVAl
Three-day event celebrating outback music and culture.
October
+612 6837 3667
Nymagee, New South Wales
www.geocities.com/nymageefestival

TOTALLY HUGE NEW MUSIC FESTIVAl
Biennial showcase for new chamber music, electronica, radiophonics, multimedia, and sound art.
September–October
Perth
+61 8 9380 6996
www.tura.com.au

AUSTRIA

SALZBURG FESTIVAL
Classical music festival held in Mozart's birthplace. Begun in 1920 by Richard Strauss, Max Reinhardt, and Hugo von Hofmannsthal.
Summer
Salzburg
+43 662 804 5500
www.salzburgfestival.com

WIENER FESTWOCHEN
Hundreds of shows and concerts make up this feast of art, dance, opera, and music.
May–June
Vienna
+43 1 589 22 22
www.festwochen.at

BELGIUM

JIGSAW CIRCUS
Festival of music videos held around Belgium.
February
+32 9 228 33 03
www.jigsawcircus.com/main_mx.html

PUKKELPOP FESTIVAL
Alternative music festival with more than 180 bands and DJs held over five stages.
August
Hasselt
+32 11 40 22 67
www.pukkelpop.be

QUEEN ELISABETH INTERNATIONAL MUSIC COMPETITION OF BELGIUM
Open to musicians beginning their careers, with a closing concert held at the Palais des Beaux-Arts.
June
Brussels
+32 2 507 82 00
www.concours-reine-elisabeth.be

ROCK WERCHTER
Belgium's largest music festival. Headliners have included Faithless, Metallica, and Massive Attack.
Werchter
June–July
www.rockwerchter.be

SFINKS
World music festival with over fourty bands performing on six stages.
July
Boechout
+32 3 455 69 44

CANADA

CANADIAN MUSIC WEEK
A showcase of Canadian bands in association with the music industry's trade fair.
March
Toronto, Ontario
www.cmw.net

COME TOGETHER MUSIC FESTIVAL
A three-day outdoor festival of jam bands.
September
Waterford, Ontario
1-519-717-4665
www.cometogethermusicfest.ca

QUEBEC CITY SUMMER FESTIVAL
Ten-day festival of world music.
July
Quebec City, Quebec
1-418-523-4540
www.infofestival.com

FOLK ON THE ROCKS MUSIC FESTIVAL
Two-day event held underneath the midnight sun in Canada.
July
Yellowknife, Northwest Territory
1-867-920-7806
www.folkontherocks.com

FRANCO FOLIES DE MONTRÉAL
Ten-day event celebrating francophone music.
June
Montreal
1-514-876-8989
www.francofolies.com

GREAT CANADIAN TOWN BAND FESTIVAL
Three-day annual band festival featuring a military parade and concerts.
July
Orono, Ontario
1-800-294-1032
www.townbandfestival.com

MONTREAL INTERNATIONAL JAZZ FESTIVAL
Twelve-day long jazz/blues/salsa/swing love-fest held around the Place des Arts with over two thousand performers.
June-July
Montreal, Quebec
1-514-871-1881
www.montrealjazzfest.com

NORTH BY NORTHEAST
Canadian showcase for new rock music, held in over thirty bars around Toronto.
June
Toronto, Ontario
1-416-863-6963
www.nxne.com

ROYAL CANADIAN BIG BAND MUSIC FESTIVAL
Celebration of bygone big band music and the legacy of bandleader Guy Lombardo.
September
Port Elgin, Ontario
1-800-387-3456
www.canadianbigband.ca

WINNIPEG FOLK FESTIVAL
Featuring over three hundred performers of blues, Celtic, bluegrass, world, gospel, and more.
July–August
Winnipeg, Manitoba
1-204-231-0096
www.winnipegfolkfestival.ca

CROATIA

MUSIC BIENNALE ZAGREB
International festival of contemporary music, including opera, ballets, and dance projects.
April
Zagreb
info@biennale-zagreb.hr
www.biennale-zagreb.hr

DENMARK

COPENHAGEN JAZZ FESTIVAL
A ten-day festival of jazz music with nearly 100 concerts daily.
July
Copenhagen
+45 3393 2013
http://festival.jazz.dk

RIVERBOAT JAZZ FESTIVAL
Four-day festival featuring sixty-five different acts performing in the heart of Jutland.
June
Silkeborg
+45 8680 1617
www.riverboat.dk

ROSKILDE FESTIVAL
One of Europe's most celebrated summer rock festivals.
June–July
Roskilde
+45 4636 6613
www.roskilde-festival.dk

FINLAND

KALOTTJAZZ & BLUES FESTIVAL
The largest jazz celebration in the far north, held on the border between Finland and Sweden.
June–July
Tornio
+358 40 5140630
www.kalottjazzblues.net

KEITELE JAZZ FESTIVAL
Weekend jazz festival happy to take risks with its line-up.
July
Äänekoski
+358 40 5106 795
www.aanekoski.fi/keitelejazz

OULU MUSIC VIDEO FESTIVAL & AIR GUITAR WORLD CHAMPIONSHIPS
City-wide event celebrating music and video, as well as a competitive display of "air guitar."
August
Oulu
+358 8 5700 500
www.omvf.net

PORI JAZZ FESTIVAL
Weeklong festival of jazz and R&B held in venues around this port city.
July

Pori
+358 2 6262 200
www.porijazz.fi

TAMPERE JAZZ HAPPENING
Weekend-long festival of intimate contemporary jazz concerts.
October-November
Helsinki
+358 3 3146 6751
www.tampere.fi/jazz

FRANCE

FESTIVAL D'AIX-EN-PROVENCE
Summer festival of music boasting operas, theatre plays, concerts, and recitals.
June—July
D'Aix-en-Provence
+33 442 17 34 00
www.festival-aix.com/index.asp?lng=en

FESTIVAL DE JAZZ DE SOUILLAC
Weeklong series of jazz concerts held around the church of Ste-Marie.
July
Souillac
info@souillacenjazz.net
www.souillacenjazz.net

FESTIVAL DES INROCKUPTIBLES
Rock music concerts held throughout Paris, sponsored by the music magazine.
November
Paris
+33 1 4952 5310
www.lesinrocks.com

INTERNATIONAL GUITAR FESTIVAL OF VENDÔME
Balzac's hometown pays host to guitarists from around the world for four spring days.
April
Vendôme
+33 2 5489 4401
www.vendomeguitarfest.com

ORCHESTRADES UNIVERSELLES
Festival for young classical music enthusiasts, with local and international ensembles.
August
Brive
+33 4 7835 8714
www.orchestrades.com

FESTIVAL DES VIEILLES CHARRUES DE CAHRAIX
Summer festical of Breton rock and pop.
Juillet
Carhaix
+33 820 890 066
www.vieillescharrues.asso.fr

EUROCKÉENNES DE BELFORT
Festival of rock, pop, and easy listening.
Juillet
Belfort
www.eurockeennes.fr

LES FRANCOFOLIES DE LA ROCHELLE
Festival of francophone music similar to its equivalent in Montreal.
Juillet
La Rochelle
+33 5 46 28 28 28
www.francofolies.fr

TRANSMUSICALES DE RENNES
International festival of new rock and pop.
Décembre
Rennes
+33 2 99 31 12 10
www.lestrans.com

LA ROUTE DU ROCK
International festival of rock and pop.
Août
Saint-Malo
+33 2 99 54 01 11
www.laroutedurock.com

LE PRINTEMPS DE BOURGES
The oldest French festival of music, literature, and cinema.
Avril
Bourges
+33 2 48 27 40 40
www.printemps-bourges.com

GERMANY

LOVE PARADE
Techno/house pageant which started in Berlin in 1989 and which is now held around the world.
July
Berlin
+49 30 284 620
www.loveparade.de

MAYDAY
Germany's biggest rave party, held the day before Mayday and continuing into the early hours.
April 30
Dortmund
+49 30 327 9160
www.mayday.de

MUNCHENER BIENNALE
Opera music event with an emphasis on experimentation.
May
Munich
+49 89 280 5607
www.muenchenerbiennale.de

SCHLESWIG-HOLSTEIN MUSIK FESTIVAL
Highlights the classical music of a different country each year.
July–August
Lubeck
+49 451 389 570
www.shmf.de

SUMMERJAM
Festival of reggae and world music.
July
Stuttgart
+49 711 2385 050
www.summerjam.de

ZAPPANALE
Four day event dedicated to Frank Zappa's music, featuring former cohorts and tribute bands.
August
Bad Doberan
mail@zappanale.info
www.zappanale.de

ICELAND

ICELAND AIRWAVES
Five days of Icelandic and international rock acts.
October
Reykjavik
+354 552 0380
www.icelandairwaves.com

REYKJAVIK ARTS FESTIVAL
Dedicated to promoting Icelandic culture through concerts, dance, and opera performances.
May–June
Reykjavik
+354 561 2444
www.artfest.is

IRELAND

DUBLIN INTERNATIONAL ORGAN AND CHORAL FESTIVAL
A triennial ten-day event celebrating the versatility of the pipe organ.
June
Dublin
+353 1 633 7392
www.dublinorganfestival.com

FLEADH CHEOIL
Ireland's largest festival, with an emphasis on traditional music, held in a new location each year.
August
+353 74 9125133
www.fleadh2005.com

GUINNESS JAZZ FESTIVAL
Five days of jazz music on Ireland's scenic southern coast.
Cork
October
+353 21 427 8979
www.corkjazzfestival.com

ISRAEL

RED SEA JAZZ FESTIVAL
International performers are invited to this festival held on the Red Sea shore.
August
Eilat
www.redseajazz.com

ITALY

CLASSICAL GUITAR COMPETITION
Awarded to the most promising young guitarist. Since 1968.
September
Alessandra
+39 0131 25 12 07
www.pittaluga.org

SANREMO SONG FESTIVAL
Italian popular song contest has launched many of the country's biggest acts.
March
Sanremo
www.sanremo.rai.it/sanremo

JAMAICA

JAMAICA OCHO RIOS JAZZ FESTIVAL
Eight days during which Jamaican jazz musicians play alongside international guests.
June
Ocho Rios
1-866-649-2137
www.ochoriosjazz.com

JAPAN

FUJI MUSIC FESTIVAL
Japan's biggest rock festival.
July
Naeba Ski Resort
info@smash-jpn.com
www.fujirockfestival.com

LITHUANIA

KAUNAS JAZZ
Festival of local and international musicians. Since 1991.
Kaunas
Spring
+370 37 750145
www.kaunasjazz.lt

VILNIUS JAZZ FESTIVAL
Four-day Baltic event with an emphasis on new and progressive jazz.
September
Vilnius
office@vilniusjazz.lt
www.vilniusjazz.lt

MALAYSIA

RAINFOREST WORLD MUSIC FESTIVAL
Three days of music from around the globe, held in the Sarawak Cultural Village's "living museum."
July
Sarawak
+60 82 423600
www.rainforestmusic-borneo.com

MALI

FESTIVAL IN THE DESERT
Three-day festival of world music modeled on traditional gatherings and celebrations of the Tuareg people.
Essakane
January
info@festival-au-desert.org
www.festival-au-desert.org

MOROCCO

FES FESTIVAL OF WORLD SACRED MUSIC
Celebrating the sacred music of monotheistic religions, including Christianity, Judaism, Islam, and Sufism.
June
Fes
+212 55 74 05 35
www.fesfestival.com

NEPAL

KATMANDU JAZZ FESTIVAL
Weeklong event of music and workshops held in the Nepalese capital.
Katmandu
November
info@jazzmandu.com
www.kathmandujazzfestival.com

NEW ZEALAND

WELLINGTON INTERNATIONAL JAZZ FESTIVAL
Citywide festival, opening with a parade featuring a jazz bus and amok musicians.
October
Wellington
+64 4 385 9602
www.jazzfestival.co.nz

NORWAY

MOLDE INTERNATIONAL JAZZ FESTIVAL
Weeklong series of performances held both in intimate clubs and on a large outdoor stage.
July
Molde
+47 71 20 31 50
www.moldejazz.no

ÖYAFESTIVALEN
Four-day indoor/outdoor festival featuring a host of alternative rock acts from around the world.
August
Oslo
www.oyafestivalen.no

POLAND

ALEKSANDER TANSMAN INTERNATIONAL COMPETITION OF MUSICAL PERSONALITIES
Musical competition for performers of the violin, cello, piano, guitar, oboe, and voice.
November
+48 42 657 86 66
www.tansman.lodz.pl

INTERNATIONAL PADEREWSKI PIANO COMPETITION
Open to pianists of all nationalities.
Bydgoszcz
November
+48 52 327 02 91
www.konkurspaderewskiego.pl

RUSSIA

INTERNATIONAL TCHAIKOVSKY COMPETITION
One of the most prestigious classical music competitions in the world, for pianists, violinists, vocalists, and cellists. Takes place every four years.
June
Moscow
+7 095 248 3494
www.tchaikovsky-competition.ru

SOUTH AFRICA

SPLASHY FEN
Annual weekend musical festival and South Africa's answer to Woodstock.
April
KwaZulu-Natal
+27 33 701 1932
www.splashyfen.co.za

SPAIN

FESTIVAL INTERNACIONAL DE BENICÀSSIM
Alternative pop and rock festival held near the north shore of Spain.
August
Benicàssim
www.fiberfib.com
info@fiberfib.com

HEINEKEN JAZZALDIA
One of Europe's oldest jazz festivals, it also includes flamenco performances.
July
San Sebastian
+34 943 440 034
www.jazzaldia.com

SWITZERLAND

JAZZ FESTIVAL WILLISAU
Jazz festival originally inaugurated as a memorial for John Coltrane. Since 1977.
Lucerne
August–September
+41 970 27 31
www.jazzwillisau.ch

MONTREUX JAZZ FESTIVAL
Since 1969, the festival has offered an eclectic program at the foot of the Alps, mingling jazz performances with other music.
June–July
Montreux
+41 21 966 44 44
www.montreuxjazz.com

THE NETHERLANDS

BLUES ESTAFETTE
European festival for "roots" blues and R&B performers.
November
Utrecht
+31 30 231 4544
www.bluesworld.com/Estafette.html

DUTCH INTERNATIONAL VOCAL COMPETITION
Open to vocalists thirty and under. Since 1954.
+31 73 6900999
www.ivc.nu

DYNAMO OPEN AIR
Annual one-day metal music festival.
Eindhoven
May
+31 70 385 6001
www.dynamo.nl

METROPOLIS FESTIVAL ROTTERDAM
One-day festival featuring international rock bands from all ends of the spectrum.
July
Rotterdam
+31 10 4341 684
www.metropolisfestival.nl

SUMMER JAZZ BICYCLE TOUR
Annual citywide festival designed to be experienced via bicycle.
August
Reitdiep valley
bimbus@zjft.nl
www.zjft.nl

UNITED KINGDOM

ALL TOMORROW'S PARTIES
Artists "curate" weekend festivals of indie rock during the off-season at a seaside resort.
Camber Sands
www.atpfestival.com

BBC YOUNG MUSICIAN OF THE YEAR
Competition for keyboard, percussion, string, brass, and woodwind players aged eighteen years and under.
May
London
+44 020 8895 6143
www.bbc.co.uk/youngmusician

CREAMFIELDS
Day-long festival of dance acts and world class DJs in Northern England.
August
Liverpool
http://www.cream.co.uk

EDINBURGH INTERNATIONAL HARP FESTIVAL
Concerts, workshops, and exhibitions celebrating Scotland's oldest musical instrument.
April
Edinburgh
+44 131 478 8446
www.harpfestival.co.uk

EDINBURGH MELA
Scotland's biggest intercultural festival, with music, dance, fashion, and food. Since 1995.
Edinburgh
September
+44 131 557 1400
www.edinburgh-mela.co.uk

GLASTONBURY
England's premier pop and rock event. A three-day festival held in the Vale of Avalon.
June
Glastonbury
+44 1458 834 596
www.glastonburyfestivals.co.uk

KING'S LYNN FESTIVAL
Two-week long celebration of classical music, first held in 1951.
King's Lynn
July
+44 1553 767557
www.kl-festival.freeserve.co.uk

NOTTING HILL CARNIVAL
The largest street festival in the world, with sound systems and live acts attracting 1.5 million partygoers annually.
London
August
+44 870 059 1111
www.lnhc.org.uk

T IN THE PARK
Weekend series of concerts which annually draws the cream of British rock and international headliners.
July
Balado
+44 8701 53 53 53
www.tinthepark.com

V FESTIVAL
Sedate family-friendly weekend festival of Top 40 acts held in two separate locations.
August
Chelmsford and Staffordshire
+44 870 405 0447
www.vfestival.com

UNITED STATES

BEALE STREET MUSIC FESTIVAL
Blues, rock, gospel, R&B, alternative, and soul music at the home of rhythm and blues.
April–May
Memphis, Tennessee
info@thebealestreetmusicfestival.com
www.thebealestreetmusicfestival.com

BEN & JERRY'S FOLK FESTIVAL
Four days of folk and roots music. Famous for being the festical at which Bob Dylan scandalized purists by "going electric."
August
Newport, Rhode Island
info@fpiny.com
www.newportfolk.com

BONNAROO
Three days of alternative rock, classic rock, and "jam band" performers. Since 2002.
June
Manchester, Tennessee
info@bonnaroo.com
www.bonnaroo.com/2005

CMJ MUSIC MARATHON
Convocation of college radio bands and rising acts held throughout New York City.
September
New York, New York
1-917-606-1908
www.cmj.com/marathon

CMA MUSIC FESTIVAL
Musical jamboree, where country's biggest stars meet and greet fans.
June
Nashville, Tennessee
1-800-CMA-Fest
www.cmafest.com

COACHELLA VALLEY ART AND MUSIC FESTIVAL
Two-day alternative festival held in the Californian desert.
April
Indio, California
info@coachella.com
www.coachella.com

FUSE-IN DETROIT'S ELECTRONIC MUSIC FESTIVAL
Three-day festival of electronic music produced by techno legend Kevin Saunderson.
May
Detroit, Michigan
1-313-758-0833
www.fuse-indetroit.com

JVC JAZZ FESTIVAL NEWPORT
Four-day festival features jazz artists performing on three stages in Fort Adams State Park.
August
Newport, Rhode Island

401-847-3700
www.festivalproductions.net

MICHIGAN WOMYN'S MUSIC FESTIVAL
Woman-only celebration of culture and community held in 650 acres of Michigan woodlands.
August
Walhalla, Michigan
1-231-757-4766
www.michfest.com

MONTEREY JAZZ FESTIVAL
The second-oldest jazz festival in the world, held on seven stages at the Monterey Fairgrounds. Since 1958.
September
Monterey, California
1-925-275-9255
www.montereyjazzfestival.org

MOSTLY MOZART FESTIVAL
One of the best classical music festivals, held inside and outside around New York.
July–August
New York, New York
1-212-875-5000.
www.lincolncenter.org

NEW ORLEANS JAZZ AND HERITAGE FESTIVAL
Weeklong event celebrating the city's legacy as the birthplace of jazz music.
April–May
New Orleans, Louisiana
1-504-522-4786
www.nojazzfest.com

SOUTH BY SOUTHWEST
Thousands of acts perform on over fifty different stages during this music industry conference. Open to the public.
March
Austin, Texas
1-512-467-7979
2006.sxsw.com

VAN CLIBURN INTERNATIONAL PIANO COMPETITION
For young pianists. Held every four years at the Bass Performance Hall.
May–June
Fort Worth, Texas
1-817-738-6536
www.cliburn.org

VANS WARPED TOUR
Popular touring festival which presents a day of punk and skate-oriented performances for one low price.
June–August
Various locations
www.warpedtour.com

WAYSIDE BLUEGRASS FESTIVAL
Convention of old-time and bluegrass musicians held in the Blue Ridge Mountains.
September
Stuart, Virginia
1-276-692-5239
www.waysidepark.com

WEST COAST A CAPELLA SUMMIT
"Festival of vocal virtuosity" for amateur and professional a capella singers.
November
San Rafael, California
1-415-472-3500
www.singers.com/summit.html

YELLOW PINE HARMONICA FESTIVAL
Weekend of mouth-harp music.
August
Yellow Pine, Idaho
1-208-633-3300
www.harmonicacontest.com

Awards

Grammys

Since 1959, the Grammy Awards have annually celebrated the best artists and technicians in music. Votes are cast by the Recording Academy, a committee of music professionals who award the honors during a ceremony. The event takes place every year in February in a major American city. In 2005, they were held in Los Angeles. The awards are broadcast live on CBS.

There are more than one hundred Grammies given, including Special Merit Awards, which are prizes honoring lifetime achievements in music or major contributions by American companies. Since 2000, the Recording Academy has devoted a special ceremony to Latin music artists, known as the Latin Grammy Awards.

Visit: www.grammy.com.

2006
Record of the Year: U2 – "Sometimes You Can't Mike It On Your Own"
Album of the Year: U2 – *How To Dismantle An Atomic Bomb*

2005
Record of the Year: Ray Charles & Norah Jones – "Here We Go Again"
Album of the Year: Ray Charles – *Genius Loves Company*

2004
Record of the Year: Coldplay – "Clocks"
Album of the Year: OutKast – *Speakerboxxx/The Love Below*

2003
Record of the Year: Norah Jones – "Don't Know Why"
Album of the Year: Norah Jones – *Come Away With Me*

2002
Record of the Year: U2 – "Walk On"
Album of the Year: Various artists – *O Brother, Where Art Thou?*

2001
Record of the Year: U2 – "Beautiful Day"
Album of the Year: Steely Dan – *Two Against Nature*

2000
Record of the Year: Santana – "Smooth"
Album of the Year: Santana – *Supernatural*

1999
Record of the Year: Celine Dion – "My Heart Will Go On"
Album of the Year: Lauryn Hill – *The Miseducation of Lauryn Hill*

1998
Record of the Year: Shawn Colvin – "Sunny Came Home"
Album of the Year: Bob Dylan – *Time Out of Mind*

1997
Record of the Year: Eric Clapton – "Change the World"
Album of the Year: Celine Dion – *Falling into You*

1996
Record of the Year: Seal – "Kiss from a Rose"
Album of the Year: Alanis Morissette – *Jagged Little Pill*

1995
Record of the Year: Sheryl Crow – "All I Wanna Do"
Album of the Year: Tony Bennett – *Unplugged*

1994
Record of the Year: Whitney Houston – "I Will Always Love You"
Album of the Year: Various artists – *The Bodyguard*

1993
Record of the Year: Eric Clapton – "Tears in Heaven"
Album of the Year: Eric Clapton – *Unplugged*

1992
Record of the Year: Natalie Cole & Nat King Cole – "Unforgettable"
Album of the Year: Natalie Cole – *Unforgettable*

1991
Record of the Year: Phil Collins – "Another Day in Paradise"
Album of the Year: Quincy Jones – *Back on the Block*

1990
Record of the Year: Bette Midler – "Wind Beneath My Wings"
Album of the Year: Bonnie Raitt – *Nick of Time*

1989
Record of the Year: Bobby McFerrin – "Don't Worry, Be Happy"
Album of the Year: George Michael – *Faith*

1988
Record of the Year: Paul Simon – "Graceland"
Album of the Year: U2 – *The Joshua Tree*

1987
Record of the Year: Steve Winwood – "Higher Love"
Album of the Year: Paul Simon – *Graceland*

1986
Record of the Year: USA for Africa – "We Are the World"
Album of the Year: Phil Collins – *No Jacket Required*

1985
Record of the Year: Tina Turner – "What's Love Got to Do With It?"
Album of the Year: Lionel Richie – *Can't Slow Down*

1984
Record of the Year: Michael Jackson – "Beat It"

Album of the Year: Michael Jackson – *Thriller*

1983
Record of the Year: Toto – "Rosanna"
Album of the Year: Toto – *Toto IV*

1982
Record of the Year: Kim Carnes – "Bette Davis Eyes"
Album of the Year: John Lennon & Yoko Ono – *Double Fantasy*

1981
Record of the Year: Christopher Cross – "Sailing"
Album of the Year: Christopher Cross – *Christopher Cross*

1980
Record of the Year: The Doobie Brothers – "What a Fool Believes"
Album of the Year: Billy Joel – *52nd Street*

1979
Record of the Year: Billy Joel – "Just the Way You Are"
Album of the Year: Various artists – *Saturday Night Fever*

1978
Record of the Year: The Eagles – "Hotel California"
Album of the Year: Fleetwood Mac – *Rumours*

1977
Record of the Year: George Benson – "This Masquerade"
Album of the Year: Stevie Wonder – *Songs in the Key of Life*

1976
Record of the Year: Captain & Tennille – "Love Will Keep Us Together"
Album of the Year: Paul Simon – *Still Crazy After All These Years*

1975
Record of the Year: Olivia Newton–John – "I Honestly Love You"
Album of the Year: Stevie Wonder – *Fulfillingness' First Finale*

1974
Record of the Year: Roberta Flack – "Killing Me Softly With His Song"
Album of the Year: Stevie Wonder – *Innervisions*

1973
Record of the Year: Roberta Flack – "The First Time Ever I Saw Your Face"
Album of the Year: Various artists – *The Concert for Bangla Desh*

1972
Record of the Year: Carole King – "It's Too Late"
Album of the Year: Carole King – *Tapestry*

1971
Record of the Year: Simon & Garfunkel – "Bridge Over Troubled Water"
Album of the Year: Simon & Garfunkel – *Bridge Over Troubled Water*

1970
Record of the Year: 5th Dimension – "Aquarius/Let the Sunshine In"
Album of the Year: Blood, Sweat & Tears – *Blood, Sweat & Tears*

1969
Record of the Year: Simon & Garfunkel – "Mrs. Robinson"
Album of the Year: Glen Campbell – *By the Time I Get to Phoenix*

1968
Record of the Year: 5th Dimension – "Up, Up and Away"
Album of the Year: The Beatles – *Sgt. Pepper's Lonely Hearts Club Band*

1967
Record of the Year: Frank Sinatra – "Strangers in the Night"
Album of the Year: Frank Sinatra – *Sinatra: A Man and His Music*

1966
Record of the Year: Herb Alpert & the Tijuana Brass – "A Taste of Honey"
Album of the Year: Frank Sinatra – *September of My Years*

1965
Record of the Year: Stan Getz & Astrud Gilberto – "The Girl from Ipanema"
Album of the Year: Stan Getz & Joao Gilberto – *Getz/Gilberto*

1964
Record of the Year: Henry Mancini – "Days of Wine and Roses"
Album of the Year: Barbra Streisand – *The Barbra Streisand Album*

1963
Record of the Year: Tony Bennett – "I Left My Home in San Francisco"
Album of the Year: Vaughn Meader – *The First Family*

1962
Record of the Year: Henry Mancini – "Moon River"
Album of the Year: Judy Garland – *Judy at Carnegie Hall*

1961
Record of the Year: Percy Faith – "Theme from 'A Summer Place'"
Album of the Year: Bob Newhart – *The Button–Down Mind of Bob Newhart*

1960
Record of the Year: Bobby Darin – "Mack the Knife"
Album of the Year: Frank Sinatra – *Come Dance With Me*

1959
Record of the Year: Domenico Modugno – "Nel Blue Dipinto di Blu"
Album of the Year: Henry Mancini – *The Music from Peter Gunn*

Awards

Brit Awards

Launched in 1977 by the Brit Awards Academy, the Brit Awards annually celebrate British and international artists. The list of winners is established by the Academy, which includes more than one thousand artists and music professionals. Nevertheless, some of the voting is left to the general British public, via the BBC web site. The ceremony is broadcast live and always takes place on February 20 at Earl's Court in London. In May 2000, the Brit Award Academy inaugurated the first ceremony of Classical Brit Awards, which honors international classical artists.
Visit: www.brits.co.uk

2006
British Single:Coldplay – "Speed Of Sound"
British Album: Coldplay – *X&Y*

2005
British Single: Will Young – "Your Game"
British Album: Keane – *Hopes and Fears*

2004
British Single: Dido – "White Flag"
British Album: The Darkness – *Permission to Land*

2003
British Single: Liberty X – "Just a Little"
British Album: Coldplay – *A Rush of Blood to the Head*

2002
British Single: S Club 7 – "Don't Stop Movin'"
British Album: Dido – *No Angel*

2001
British Single: Robbie Williams – "Rock DJ"
British Album: Coldplay - *Parachutes*

2000
British Single: Robbie Williams – "She's the One"
British Album: Travis – *The Man Who*

1999
British Single: Robbie Williams – "Angels"
British Album: Manic Street Preachers – *This Is My Truth Tell Me Yours*

1998
British Single: All Saints – "Never Ever"
British Album: The Verve – *Urban Hymns*

1997
British Single: Spice Girls – "Wannabe"
British Album: Manic Street Preachers – *Everything Must Go*

1996
British Single: Take That – "Back for Good"
British Album: Oasis – *(What's the Story) Morning Glory*

1995
British Single: Blur – "Parklife"
British Album: Blur – *Parklife*

1994
British Single: Take That – "Pray"
British Album: Stereo MC's – *Connected*

1993
British Single: Take That – "Could It Be Magic"
British Album: Annie Lennox – *Diva*

1992
British Single: Queen – "These Are the Days of Our Lives"
British Album: Seal – *Seal*

1991
British Single: Depeche Mode – "Enjoy the Silence"
British Album: George Michael – *Listen Without Prejudice, Vol. 1*

1990
British Single: Phil Collins – "Another Day in Paradise"
British Album: Fine Young Cannibals – *The Raw and the Cooked*

1989
British Single: Fairground Attraction – "Perfect"
British Album: Fairground Attraction – *First of a Million Kisses*

1988
British Single: Rick Astley – "Never Gonna Give You Up"
British album: Sting – *Nothing Like the Sun*

1987
British single: Pet Shop Boys – "West End Girls"
British album: Dire Straits – *Brothers in Arms*

1986
British single: Tear for Fears – "Everybody Wants to Rule the World"

1985
British single: Frankie Goes to Hollywood – "Relax"
British album: Sade – *Diamond Life*

1984
British Single: Culture Club – "Karma Chameleon"

1983
British Single: Dexy's Midnight Runners – "Come On, Eileen"
British Album: Barbra Streisand – *Love Songs*

1982
British Album: Adam + the Ants – *Kings of the Wild Frontier*

1977
British single: Queen – "Bohemian Rhapsody"/Procol Harum – "Whiter Shade of Pale"
British album: The Beatles – *Sgt. Pepper's Lonely Hearts Club Band*

Awards

Victoires de la Musique

The Victoires de la Musique not only celebrates musicians but also the musical events that have made the year special. They were launched in 1986 by the Association des Victoires, composed of four committees of music professionals. For each session, the association selects three thousand artists, producers, distributors, critics, and record dealers to make up the list of nominees and prizewinners in ten categories. Votes are cast once, by a limited group, and are supervised by the association. However, the choice of best singer, best song, and best web site are subject to a people's choice vote, which takes place on the night of the ceremony. It is broadcast live and is viewed by several million television viewers.
Visit: www.lesvictoires.com

2006
Original Song of the Year: Raphel – "Caravane"
Breakout Album of the Year: Camille – *Le Fil*

2005
Original Song of the Year: Calogero – "Si seulement je pouvais lui manquer"
Breakout Album of the Year: Daniel Darc, Crève Coeur and Ridan – *Le rêve ou la vie*

2004
Original Song of the Year: Mickey 3D – "Breathe"
Breakout Album of the Year: KYO – *The Way*

2003
Original Song of the Year: Renaud and Axelle Red – "Manhattan Kaboul"
Breakout Album of the Year: Vincent Delerm – *Vincent Delerm*

2002
Original Song of the Year: Garou – "Sous le vent"
Breakout Album of the Year: Laurent Voulzy – *Avril*

2001
Original Song of the Year: Daniel Levi – "L'Envie d'aimer"
Breakout Album of the Year: Henri Salvador – *Chambre avec vue*

2000
Original Song of the Year: Zebda – "Tomber la chemise"
Breakout Album of the Year: Johnny Hallyday – *Sang pour sang*

1999
Original Song of the Year: Notre Dame de Paris – "Belle"
Breakout Album of the Year: Alain Bashung – *Fantaisie Militaire*

1998
Original Song of the Year: Noir Desir – "L'Homme presse"
Breakout Album of the Year: IAM – *L'Ecole du micro d'argent*

1997
Original Song of the Year: Khaled – "Aicha"
Breakout Album of the Year: Eddy Mitchell – *Mr. Eddy*

1996
Original Song of the Year: Celine Dion – "Pour que tu m'aimes encore"
Breakout Album of the Year: Alain Souchon – *Defoule sentimentale*

1995
Original Song of the Year: Enzo Enzo – "Juste quelqu'un de bien"
Breakout Album of the Year: Francis Cabrel – *Samedi soir sur la Terre*

1994
Original Song of the Year: Alain Souchon – "Foule sentimentale"
Breakout Album of the Year: Eddy Mitchell – *Rio Grande*

1993
Original Song of the Year: Pow Wow – "Le Chat"
Breakout Album of the Year: Laurent Voulzy – *Caché Derrière*

1992
Original Song of the Year: William Sheller – "Un homme heureux"
Breakout Album of the Year: William Sheller – *Sheller en solitaire*

1991
Original Song of the Year: Julien Clerc – "Fais-moi une place"
Breakout Album of the Year: Alain Souchon – *Nickel*

1990
Original Song of the Year: Alain Souchon – "Quand j'serai KO"
Breakout Album of the Year: Francis Cabrel – *Sarbacane*

1988
Song of the year: Maxime le Forestier – "Né quelque part"
Breakout Album of the Year: Claude Nougaro – *Nougayork*

1987
Original Song of the Year: Michel Sardou – "Musulmanes"
Breakout Album of the Year: Rita Mitsouko – *The No Comprendo*

1986
Original Song of the Year: Laurent Voulzy – "Belle-Île-En-Mer Marie-Galante"

1985
Original Song of the Year: Michel Jonasz – "La Boîte de Jazz"

Awards

Internet

···> POPULAR MUSIC

African Music Encyclopedia
www.africanmusic.org
Search artists by name or by country for biographical information and cool photos.

Afro Cuba Web
www.afrocubaweb.com
A clearing house for news and reviews about Afro-Cuban music.

All About Jazz
www.allaboutjazz.com
One of the Web's best jazz sites.

All Music Guide
www.allmusic.com
Database of artists, albums, songs, and genres, from Aaron Copland to ZZ Top.

All Hip-Hop
www.allhiphop.com
Hip-hop site, with news, reviews, gossip, and rumors.

Björk
www.bjork.com
Chock-full and currently the best Internet resource.

Bossa Nova Guitar
www.bossanovaguitar.com
History, chords, and MP3s for bossa nova, samba, and MPB.

The British Library Sound Archive Catalogue
www.bl.uk/catalogues/sound.html
Online listing of the British Library's 3.5 million holdings.

The Brush Creek Follies
www.umkc.edu/lib/spec-col/Follies/main.htm
Step back in time with this online archive of a 1930s country music radio show.

Country Music Television
www.cmt.com
Plenty of news and interviews with country music's finest.

Electronic Musical Instruments 1870–1990
www.obsolete.com/120_years
Online museum of electronic instruments.

God of Guitar
www.godofguitar.com
Site that teaches "how to pose as a god of guitar."

Head Heritage
www.headheritage.co.uk
Dedicated to "obscure and/or lost rock 'n' roll," run by The Teardrop Explodes' Julian Cope.

Heathen World's Origins of Band Names
www.heathenworld.com/band-name
What does R.E.M. mean? Find out the origin of your favorite band's name here.

iTunes
www.itunes.com
The Internet's leading digital music emporium.

J-Pop
www.jpop.com
A portal for the frenzied world of Japanese music and culture.

Jazz Discography Project
www.jazzdisco.org
This site is for obsessives only, and features discographies for jazz labels, large and small.

Jazz Online
www.jazzonln.com
Still confused? This site provides a handy "Jazz 101."

Motown Historical Museum
www.motownmuseum.com
An online compendium of Motown artists.

MTV.com
www.mtv.com
Site for the music video channel; contains an excellent news section.

National Music Museum
www.usd.edu/smm
Take a virtual tour through over ten thousand instruments from around the world.

Nippop
www.nippop.com
Excellent guide to Japanese chart stars, with pictures and biographies.

The Official U.K. Charts Company
www.theofficialcharts.com
The official U.K. charts, with an audio snippet of every No. 1... ever!

The Old-Time Music Home Page
www.oldtimemusic.com
Remembering music performed before the rise of radio, hosted by an old-time fiddler.

Paul Really Is Dead
www.james-paul-mccartney.150m.com/fc1.html
Did Paul McCartney really die in the late 1960s? Review the evidence and decide for yourself.

Pitchfork Media
www.pitchforkmedia.com
Opinionated site for alternative rock news, reviews, and interviews.

Planet Salsa
www.planetsalsa.com
Sexy site for salsa and mambo, with a guide to musical events in your area.

Pollstar
www.pollstar.com
Comprehensive listings of who's on tour, where, and when.

Popjustice
www.popjustice.co.uk
Online shrine to the glory of contemporary British pop.

Robert Christgau
www.robertchristgau.com
Online library for the works of the "dean of rock criticism."

Rocklist
www.rocklist.co.uk
All the "best of" lists you can read without seriously reorganizing your album collection.

Slipcue E-Zine: French Pop Music Guide
www.slipcue.com/music/pop/france/froghop.html
Entertainingly biased introduction to French pop music in English.

Songfacts
www.songfacts.com
Trivia, facts, and quizzes about a variety of songs.

Soulful Kinda Music
www.soulfulkindamusic.net
Dedicated to the U.K. soul scene, with biographies, discographies, and club histories.

Stax Museum of American Soul Music
www.soulsvilleusa.com
Online home of Memphis's Stax Museum. Includes a virtual tour.

Tango
www.todotango.com
Information on musicians, dancers, poets, sheet music, and a daily dose of Carlos Gardel, the enormously popular tango singer.

Vintage Tips
www.vintagetips.com
A guide to CD reissues, with an emphasis on the era before The Beatles and Star Wars.

The Vinyl Exchange
www.vinylexchange.com
An online forum and swap-meet for lovers and users of hip-hop vinyl records.

Woodstock '69
www.woodstock69.com
Festival museum with photos, memories, and set lists.

The Yé-Yé Girls Web Site
members.tripod.com/ye_ye_girls/home.html
Informed introduction to the button-cute pop Lolitas of the 1960s.

··› CLASSICAL MUSIC

All About Opera
www.allaboutopera.com
Handy compendium of the latest operatic scuttlebutt from around the Web.

Composition Today
www.compositiontoday.com
Resources for the composer, with concert listings and interviews.

Lichtensteiger
www.lichtensteiger.de
Bilingual site (English and German) on experimental music and literature with pages on Ligeti, Reich, and Boulez.

Sequenza 21
www.sequenza21.com
CD reviews, music calendar, and a forum where contemporary composers duke it out.

··› ARTISTS

Arnold Schoenberg Center
www.schoenberg.at
Everything you need to know about the serialist composer/painter/modernist gadfly.

BBC Music/Profiles—Debussy
www.bbc.co.uk/music/profiles/debussy.shtml
A snappy guide to the Impressionist, with sound-clips and a list of what to hear and read.

Billie Holiday
www.ladyday.net
Her life, lyrics to her songs, and even the file the FBI kept on the tragic singer.

Bing Crosby Internet Museum
www.kcmetro.cc.mo.us/pennvalley/biology/lewis/crosby/bing.htm
News, lyrics, even streaming excerpts from the crooner's popular radio shows.

Bird Lives
www.birdlives.co.uk
Fan site dedicated to Charlie Parker, telling his life story in text, photos, and memorabilia.

Bob Dylan
www.bobdylan.com
Features new and vintage MP3s, tour news, and a lyrics database.

Bob Marley at Thirdfield
www.thirdfield.com
Lyrics, links, photos, videos, speeches, and much more.

The Can Lyrics Project
mitglied.lycos.de/canlyricsproject
What exactly is Damo Suzuki singing about? You might get a clue here.

David Bowie
www.davidbowie.com
David Bowie houses an entire online community on his site, including news and fan blogs.

Divina
www.callas.it
Maria Callas's official Web site, featuring a catalog of the diva's performances.

Edith Piaf
www.lehall.com/galerie/piaf/index.htm
Entertaining animated guide in French to Piaf's life and loves—but mostly her loves.

Ella Fitzgerald, 1917–1996
www.museum.media.org/ella
The first lady of song is remembered with essays, discography, and audio interviews.

Ellington on the Web
www.ellingtonweb.ca
A great overview of the various Web sites devoted to Duke Ellington.

Elvis Presley
www.elvis.com
Photos, a virtual tour of Graceland, and plenty of Presley memorabilia.

Erik Satie
www.af.lu.se/~fogwall/satie.html
Facsimiles of the composer's manuscripts and MP3s of his work.

Fela Kuti Project
www.felaproject.net
Biography, quotes, and images—a great leaping off point to learn more about the Afro-beat master.

Foundation Jacques Brel
www.jacquesbrel.org
Brel's official site (in French), featuring a giant biography and notes on his work as an actor and director.

George and Ira Gershwin
www.gershwin.com
Information on their shows and movies. Includes an online jukebox of their songs.

The Glenn Gould Archive
www.collectionscanada.ca/glenngould/index-e.html
Featuring a virtual exhibition drawn from Gould's papers and numerous audio recordings.

Harmolodic
www.harmolodic.com
Free jazz pioneer Ornette Coleman's colorful site explains his "harmolodic" philosophy.

Howlin' Wolf
www.furious.com/perfect/wolf
Interesting articles and a comprehensive discography of the blues belter.

Igor Stravinsky
w3.rz-berlin.mpg.de/cmp/stravinsky.html
A biography, photos, and an in-depth look at his ballet, *Petruschka*.

The Internet Beatles Album
www.beatlesagain.com
Nicely navigable guide to the Fab Four and their ephemera.

The Internet Nirvana Fan Club
www.nirvanaclub.com
Lots of interviews and fan discussion about the Seattle band and tributes.

James Brown—The Godfather of Soul
www.godfatherofsoul.com
Boasts interviews, a list of his chart hits, and a photo of Brown with the Pope.

John Cage
www.newalbion.com/artists/cagej
Features an interesting autobiographical "statement" and discussion group.

Johnny Hallyday
www.johnny14.com
Fan site in French, bursting with images, ticket stubs, news, and lyrics.

Karlheinz Stockhausen
www.stockhausen.org
News on the German visionary and a special section on how he influenced The Beatles.

KCET presents the Buena Vista Social Club
www.pbs.org/buenavista
A public TV site accompanying

the Wim Wenders film that introduces the Club's personalities and music.

Kurt Weill Foundation for Music
www.kwf.org
News, performance schedules, and audio files for the composer and his wife/muse Lotte Lenya.

Led Zeppelin
www.led-zeppelin.com
Fan site that charts the current movements of ex-Zeppelin members and that posts old concert reviews.

Little Richard
www.littlerichard.com
Keep up with the architect of rock 'n' roll and visit this informative site.

The London News Review
www.lnreview.co.uk/music/blog
Erudite and super-smart blog about music.

Madonna
www.madonna.com
The ray of light's very own version of *Pravda*—telling you only what you need to know.

Miles Davis
www.milesdavis.com
Somewhat skimpy site does offer a handful of MP3s and a tour of Davis' artwork.

MJJ Source
http://mjjsource.com
Where the elusive King of Pop Michael Jackson puts up his latest decrees.

Muddy Waters
www.muddywaters.com
The blues giant's official site has candid snaps and his recipe for "Ham Hocks, Muddy Style."

Philip Glass
www.philipglass.com
Minimalist site for the minimalist genius, with a "Glass Engine" guide to over sixty of his works.

Prince
www.prince.org
Fan forum and news resource for everything going on with His Purple Majesty.

Queen
www.queenonline.com
For regular updates on the fabled opera-rockers, visit this comprehensive site. A Queen expert is also on hand to answer questions.

Radiohead
www.radiohead.com
The English band's official site is one of the most original creations on the Internet.

The Robert Johnson Notebooks
xroads.virginia.edu/~MUSIC/rjhome.html
An academic look at the lyrics of the mysterious Delta bluesman.

The Rolling Stones
www.rollingstones.com/home.php
The "virtual ticket" section of the site features performances from their latest tour.

Satchography
www.satchography.com/sidemen.html
Nicely laid-out guide to Louis Armstrong's recordings and the musicians he worked with.

The Smile Shop
www.thesmileshop.net
Comprehensive investigation into the Beach Boys' "lost" album.

Sondheim
www.sondheim.com
News, essays, and community for fans of the Follies composer.

U2
www.u2.com
Official site allows users to download tracks, stream videos, and view an in-studio Webcam.

Uum Kulthum
almashriq.hiof.no/egypt/700/780/umKoulthoum
Nice introduction to the Egyptian diva, with lyrics, film clips, and academic articles.

Velvet Underground
members.aol.com/olandem/vu.html
Scrappy but comprehensive fan site contains interviews and old press clippings.

Youssou N'Dour
www.youssou.com
Site in French and English for the mbalax singer, with online radio, biography, and testimonials.

BLOGS

Arts Journal
www.artsjournal.com
Blog compendium features observations on music, dance, and culture from noted critics.

Because They Are Dead
www.paulbaileyensemble.org/blog
"Alternative classical garage

band" blog about the alternative classical garage trend.

Blissblog
blissout.blogspot.com
"Rockist-raveist-grimiest" blog plots close-to-the-edge musical entertainment.

David's Journal
www.davidbyrne.com/journal/current.php
Talking Heads supremo David Byrne records his thoughts here.

Hip-Hop Music
www.hiphopmusic.com
Hip-hop commentary and streaming mixes from WBAI's Underground Railroad show.

Links Clips Notes
www.lacunae.com
Portland-based critic and Dark Beloved Cloud label boss Douglas Wolk blogs about popular culture.

Michaelangelo Matos
m-matos.blogspot.com
Seattle Weekly critic Matos crams in all his non-print stuff and archives old articles here.

New York London Paris Music
www.freakytrigger.co.uk/nylpm
Reviewing pop the way you should: track by track, hit by hit, and minute by minute.

Parterre Box Presents La Cieca
www.parterre.com
An opera director whose blog has been described as "the Matt Drudge of opera."

Plan B Magazine
www.planbmag.com/blogs/everett/index.php
The 1990s critic/grunge warrior Everett True's blog is worth battling the lousy design to read.

Renewable Music
renewablemusic.blogspot.com
Four composers blog it up about "music made for the long while and the world around that music."

The Rest Is Noise
www.therestisnoise.com
The blog of the *New Yorker's* classical music critic boasts the best writing on the Internet.

S/FJ
www.sashafrerejones.com
The *New Yorker* pop music critic's life in bloggy commentary and photographs.

Sieglinde's Diaries
balconybox.blogspot.com
An opera buff keeps a beady eye on diva doings.

Stereogum
www.stereogum.com
Hilarious music and media blog, which revels in the minutiae and gossip about the stars.

Things Twice
www.dylanchords.com/blog
Eyolf Østrem gets obsessive about Bob Dylan and related topics in his blog.

Twang Twang Twang
harpist.typepad.com
A prize-winning harpist blogs about the sordid life of a working musician.

Vilaine Fille
vilainefille.blogs.com
The blog of a writer and opera fan. The title comes from Serge Gainsbourg's song.

What I Like About . . .
musicviews.blogspot.com
Isaac Watras is on a mission—to write an opinion on every selection in the two volume, twelve CD *Norton Recorded Anthology of Western Music.*

Zoilus
www.zoilus.com
Toronto Globe & Mail critic Carl Wilson is your guide to the world of rock music.

MP3 BLOGS

45blog
www.45blog.com
Relive the crackling excitement that comes from hearing obscure sounds on 45 rpm singles.

Blogio Oddio
oddiooverplay.blogspot.com
Taking part in the business of human happiness with a range of delightful (and obviously odd) MP3s.

Blowupdoll
blow-up-doll.blogspot.com
Sweet girl-oriented MP3s accompanied by great photographs.

Bubblegum Machine
www.bubblegum-machine.com/culchah.html
An MP3 blog for bubblegum pop—meaning handclaps, tambourines, and harmonies that could rot your teeth.

Cocaine Blunts and Hip-Hop Tapes
www.cocaineblunts.com/new
Posting hip-hop MP3s with plenty of informed commentary.

Copy, Right?
copycommaright.blogspot.com
An MP3 blog dedicated to cover songs. Need to hear Don Ho singing Peter Gabriel? Here it is.

Fingertips: The Intelligent Guide to Free and Legal Music on the Web
www.fingertipsmusic.com
Sorts the good from the bad of online MP3s so you don't have to.

Garage Hangover
users.rcn.com/cbishop/GarageHangover/index.html
The great greasy rock explosion of the 1960s remains alive.

Good Rockin' Tonight
homercat.blogspot.com
Musical MP3s from the past are given historical context and put into themed playlists.

Mr. Barf's Rock and Soul a Go-Go!
mrbarf.blogspot.com
This MP3 blog mixes love for 1960s punk and boogaloo soul with an impure go-go aesthetic.

Mod-ified Music
modcentric.blogspot.com
Obscure audio delights (Bollywood, indie rock, French kitsch, etc.).

No. 1 in Belgium
wearerestaurant.free.fr/number1
MP3 blog resource for fans of old school hip-hop, 1960s chicks, and pop music.

Soul Strut
www.soulstrut.com
Covering the crate diggers—DJs and hip-hop heads—with features, beats, and downloadable mixes.

Too Good to Be Bad
toogoodtobebad.blogspot.com
Swedish-based MP3 blog besotted with yé-yé stars and girl groups.

Weave in They Hair Weed in They Purse
gelandweave.blogspot.com
Hip-hop blog with emphasis on music coming from the "Dirty" south. Interviews and MP3s.

ODDITIES

All-Time Best of the Worst Country Song Titles!
www.downstream.sk.ca/country.htm
Sample: "Hand Me the Pool Cue and Call Yourself an Ambulance."

Bedazzled!
bedazzled.blogs.com
An Aladdin's cave of musical ephemera—bootlegs, trailers, radio ads, and everything you've gotta have.

Clubbo Records: Music to Believe In
www.clubbo.com
The archive of a possibly made-up independent record label.

Frank's Vinyl Museum
www.franklarosa.com/vinyl
A collection of bizarre novelty records. How about Muhammad Ali fighting tooth decay . . . in song?

Garota de Ipanema
www.garotadeipanema.com.br
Official Web site of Helô Pinheiro, the girl from Ipanema.

Guitar Geek
www.guitargeek.com
See the guitar rigs used by the stars of alternative rock.

Joe Bussard's Vintage 78
www.vintage78.com/siteCF
The legendary record collector offers compilations made from vintage "old-time" music 78s.

Rock 'n' Roll Minor Planets
cfa-www.harvard.edu/iau/special/rocknroll/RockAndRoll.html
A list of planets named after rock and pop stars by their astronomer fans.

MAGAZINES

Billboard Magazine
www.billboard.com
Features the world-renowned Billboard 200 album charts and the Hot 100 singles.

Downbeat
www.downbeat.com
Daily jazz news and archived gems from the last seventy years.

FMQB
www.fmqb.com
Chart the changing landscape of American radio with this online newsletter.

The Guardian
www.guardian.co.uk
The British newspaper's arts and pop section is second to none.

Guitar Part
www.guitar.fr
Site for the French monthly devoted to the current music scene. Also offers playing tips and sheet music.

Les Inrockuptibles
www.lesinrocks.com
Site for the weekly French culture magazine. Filled with information about the current music scene. There are also tour dates, classifieds, and contests.

Jazz Magazine
www.jazzmagazine.com
Site for the monthly magazine that specializes in jazz and that was launched in 1954. There are reviews and articles about the history of jazz as well as event listings.

New Musical Express
www.nme.com
The Web site for the U.K.'s leading music magazine, with hysterical news and fervid reviews.

No Depression
www.nodepression.net
Site for the alternative country magazine, which gave the scene its name.

Nova Magazine
www.novaplanet.com
Site for *Radio Nova* and *Nova Magazine,* the media monthly.

The Peel Tapes
www.jonhorne.co.uk/jptapes/jptapes.html
A selection of recordings from the late DJ John Peel, including extracts from his famed sessions.

Rock & Folk
www.rocknfolk.com
Site for the rock magazine launched in 1966. Includes articles by Patrick Eudeline, the musician and influential 1970s rock critic.

Rolling Stone
www.rollingstone.com
Online version of the magazine allows you to search their reviews back to 1967.

Technikart
www.technikart.com
Site for the monthly culture and society magazine.

Playlist

13th Floor Elevators – "You're Gonna Miss Me"
2Pac – "California Love"
50 Cent – "In Da Club"
A.R. Rahman – "Roja Jaaneman"
Aaron Copland – Piano Variations
AC/DC – "Back in Black"
Adam Ant – "Goody Two Shoes"
Aerosmith – "Sweet Emotion"
a-ha – "Take On Me"
Air – "Kelly Watch the Stars"
Al Jolson – "Toot, Toot, Tootsie, Goodbye"
Alain Bashung – "Madame rêve"
Alain Chamfort – "Manureva"
Alain Souchon – "Foule sentimentale"
Alanis Morissette – "You Oughta Know"
Alban Berg – "Altenberg Leider, collection of 5 songs for voice & orchestra, Op. 4"
Albert Ayler – "Ghosts"
Albert Roussel – "Padmåvatî, opera, Op 18"
Alex Gopher – "Super Disco"
Alex North – *A Streetcar Named Desire*, film score
Ali Farka Toure – "Saukare"
Alice Coltrane – "Ptah, the El Daoud"
Alice in Chains – "Would?"
Alicia Keys – "Fallin'"
Alizée – "Moi ... Lolita"
Amina – "Mektoubi"
Amon Düül – "Wolf City"
András Schiff – Aria from *The Goldberg Variations*, BWV 988
Andrew Lloyd Webber – "Don't Cry for Me Argentina"
Angela Gheorghiu – "Casta Diva...Ah! Bello a Me Ritorna," from *Norma*
Aníbal Troilo – "Orlando Goñi"
The Animals – "The House of the Rising Sun"
Antonio Carlos Jobim – "One Note Samba"
Aphex Twin – "Windowlicker"
April March – "Chick Habit"
Aretha Franklin – "You Make Me Feel Like a Natural Woman"
Arnold Schoenberg – Pierrot lunaire, melodrama for voice and chamber ensemble, op. 21
Arsenio Rodriguez – "Mami Me Gusto"
Art Blakey – "Moanin'"
Arthur Freed – "Singin' in the Rain"
Arthur Honegger – Pacific 231, symphonic movement for orchestra, H53
Artie Shaw – "Stardust"
Asha Bhosle – "Dukhbhare Din," from *Mother India*
Astor Piazzolla – "Balada para un Loco"
Astrud Gilberto – "The Girl from Ipanema"
Baaba Maal – "Lam Tooro"
Backstreet Boys – "I Want It That Way"
Badfinger – "Without You"
The Band – "The Weight"
Band Aid – "Do They Know It's Christmas?"
The Bangles – "Manic Monday"
The Bay City Rollers – "Bye Bye Baby"
The Beach Boys – "Good Vibrations"
The Beatles – "I Want to Hold Your Hand"
Beck – "Where It's At"
The Bee Gees – "Stayin' Alive"
Béla Bartók – Mikrokosmos, progressive pieces (153) for piano in 6 volumes, Sz. 107, BB 105
Ben Folds Five – "Underground"
Benjamin Biolay – "La Mélodie du bonheur"
Benjamin Britten – Peter Grimes, opera, op. 33
Beny Moré – "El Canonero"
Bernard Herrmann – *Vertigo*, film score
Bernard Lavilliers – "On the road again"
Les Béruriers Noirs – "L'empereur Tomato Ketchup"
Betty Carter – "Sounds"
The Big Bopper – "Chantilly Lace"
Big Star – "In the Street"
Bill Evans – "My Man's Gone Now" (live, from *Sunday at the Village Vanguard*)
Bill Haley & The Comets – "Rock Around the Clock"
Bill Monroe – "Uncle Pen"
Billie Holiday – "Strange Fruit"
Billy Fury – "Baby How I Cried"
Bing Crosby – "Pennies from Heaven"
Bix Beiderbecke – "Singin' the Blues"
Björk – "Big Time Sensuality"
The Black Crowes – "Hard to Handle"
Black Sabbath – "Paranoid"
Black Uhuru – "Darkness/Dubness"
Blondie – "Sunday Girl"
Blur – "Park Life"
Bo Diddley – "Who Do You Love?"
Bob Dylan – "Like a Rolling Stone"
Bob Marley – "No Woman, No Cry"
Bob Wills and His Texas Playboys – "New San Antonio Rose"
Bobby Brown – "My Prerogative"
Bobby Darin – "Beyond the Sean"
Bon Jovi – "Livin' on a Prayer"
Boogie Down Productions – "The Bridge is Over"
The Boredoms – "Soul Discharge: Bubblebop Shot/52 Boredom"
Boston – "More Than a Feeling"
Bourvil – "Les Crayons"
Brian Eno – "1/1"
Brigitte Bardot – "Initials B. B."
Brigitte Fontaine – "Tanka"
Britney Spears – "Oops... I Did It Again"
Bruce Springsteen – "Born to Run"
Buck 65 – "Square One"
Buddy Bolden – "219 Train"
Buddy Guy – "First Time I Met The Blues"
Buddy Holly – "Oh, Boy!"
The Buggles – "Video Killed the Radio Star"
Buju Banton – "Murderer"
Burning Spear – "Slavery Days"
Burt Bacharach – *What's New Pussycat?*, film score

Bush – "The Chemicals Between Us"
Buzzcocks – "Ever Fallen in Love With Someone You Shouldn't Have?"
The Byrds – "Eight Miles High"
Cab Calloway – "Minnie the Moocher"
Cabaret Voltaire – "Sluggin' fer Jesus"
Caetano Veloso – "Allegria, Allegria"
Cameo – "Word Up"
Camille – "Ta douleur"
Camille Saint-Saëns – Carnival of the animals, zoological fantasy for 2 pianos and ensemble
Can – "Oh Yeah"
Carl Orff – Carmina burana, scenic cantata for soloists, choruses and orchestra
Carl Perkins – "Blue Suede Shoes"
Carla Bruni – "Quelqu'un m'a dit"
Carlos Gardel – "Mi Noche Triste"
Carole King – "Will You Still Love Me Tomorrow?"
The Carter Family – "Keep On the Sunny Side"
Cassius – "Cassius 1999"
Catherine Malfitano – "Ah! Du wolltest mich nicht deinen Mund kussen lassen," from *Salome*
Cecil Taylor – "Enter, Evening"
Cecilia Bartoli – "Ma rendi pur contento," from *6 ariette da camera*
Celia Cruz – "Burundanga"
Chaba Fadela – "Ana Ma H'Lali Ennoun"
Chantal Goya – "Comment le revoir"
Charles Aznavour – "Après l'amour"
Charles Ives – Orchestral set no. 1: Three Places in New England, for orchestra, S. 7
Charles Trenet – "La Mer"
Charles Trenet – "Y'a d'la joie"
Charley Patton – "Screamin' And Hollerin' The Blues"
Charlie Christian – "Solo Flight"
Charlie Parker – "Ornithology"
Les Chats Sauvages – "Twist à Saint-Tropez"
Les Chaussettes Noires – "Daniela"
Cheb Hasni – "Beraka"
Cheb Kader – "Sel Dem Drai (Worries)"
Cheb Mami – "Dellali"
Cheb Mami – "Parisien du Nord"
Cheikha Remitti – "Guendouzi Mama"
The Chemical Brothers – "Music: Response"
Chet Atkins – "Yakety Axe"
Chet Baker – "My Funny Valentine"
Chic – "Good Times"
Chick Corea – "Spain"
Christina Aguilera – "Beautiful"
Chuck Berry – "School Days"
Cibo Matto – "Birthday Cake"
The Clash – "White Man (In Hammersmith Palais)"
Claude Debussy – Prélude à l'après-midi d'un faune, for orchestra, L. 86
Claude François – "Alexandrie Alexandra"
Claude François – "Magnolia forever"
Claude Nougaro – "Toulouse"
Coldplay – "Clocks"
Cole Porter – "I Get a Kick Out of You"
Common – "The Corner"
Compay Segundo – "Amor Gigante"
The Congos – "Fisherman"
The Coral – "Dreaming Of You"
Cornelius – "Star Fruits Surf Rider"
Count Basie – "April in Paris"
Creed – "With Arms Wide Open"
Crosby, Stills and Nash – "Suite: Judy Blues Eyes"
Culture Club – "Time"
Curtis Mayfield – "Move On Up"
The Cure – "Boys Don't Cry"
Cyndi Lauper – "Time After Time"
D'Angelo – "Untitled"
D12 – "My Band"
Daft Punk – "Around the World"
Dalida – "Il venait d'avoir dix-huit ans"
Danny Elfman – *Batman*, film score
Darius Milhaud – Le boeuf sur le toit, ballet for orchestra, op. 58
Dark City Sisters – "Sekusile"
The Darkness – "I Believe in a Thing Called Love"
David Bowie – "Heroes"
David Crosby – "Almost Cut My Hair"
David Guetta – "Fuck me I'm famous"
Dean Martin – "That's Amore"
Debbie Gibson – "Lost in Your Eyes"
Debbie Harry – "I Want That Man"
Def Leppard – "Pour Some Sugar On Me"
Dennis Brown – "Westbound Train"
Depeche Mode – "Enjoy the Silence"
Derek Taylor – "Input #1" (live, from *Outcome*)
Diam's – "Marine"
Dick Powell – "Jeepers Creepers"
Dir en grey – "Cage"
Dizzy Gillespie – "Salt Peanuts"
Doble Filo – "Guarenas Zona Guerrillera"
Dolly Parton – "Jolene"
Donna Summer – "Love to Love You, Baby"
Donny Osmond – "Puppy Love"
The Doors – "L.A. Woman"
Doves – "There Goes the Fear"
Dr. Dre – "Nuthin' But a 'G' Thang"
Duke Ellington – "Diminuendo and Crescendo in Blue" (live, from *Ellington at Newport*)
Duran Duran – "Rio"
The Eagles – "Hotel California"
Echo and the Bunnymen – "The Cutter"
Eddie Cochran – "Summertime Blues"
Eddy Mitchell – "Nashville ou Belleville"
Eddie Palmieri – "My Spiritual Indian"
Edgard Varèse – Déserts, for brass, percussion, piano and tape
Edith Piaf – "Hymne à l'amour"
Edith Piaf – "Je Ne Regrette Rien"
Elis Regina – "Águas de Marçoe"
Ella Fitzgerald – "Air Mail Special"
Elmer Bernstein – *The Magnificent Seven*, film score
Elmore James – "Dust My Broom"
Elvis Costello – "Oliver's Army"
Elvis Presley – "That's All Right, Mama"
Eminem – "Lose Yourself"
Ennio Morricone – *Once Upon a Time in the West*, film score
Eric B. and Rakim – "Paid in Full"
Eric Clapton – "Wonderful Tonight"

Erich Wolfgang Korngold – *The Adventures of Robin Hood*, film score
Erik Satie – Gymnopédie, for piano, no. 1
Ernest Tubb – "Soldier's Last Letter"
Erykah Badu – "Tyrone"
Ethel Merman – "There's No Business Like Show Business"
Etienne Daho – "Week-end à Rome"
Etienne de Crecy – "Liquidation Totale"
The Faces – "Stay With Me"
The Fall – "How I Wrote Elastic Man"
Fantastic Plastic Machine – "L'Aventure Fantastique"
Fatboy Slim – "Goin' Out of My Head"
Faudel – "Tellement je t'aime"
Faust – "Why Don't You Eat Carrots"
Fela Kuti – "Shuffering and Shmiling"
The Flatlanders – "Tonight I Think I'm Gonna Go Downtown"
Fleetwood Mac – "Rhiannon"
Foo Fighters – "There Goes My Hero"
The Four Tops – "Reach Out (I'll Be There)"
France Gall – "Ella elle a"
France Gall – "Les Sucettes"
Francis Poulenc – *Dialogue of the Carmelites*, opera
Françoise Hardy – "Mon amie la rose"
Françoise Hardy – "Tous les Garçons et les Filles"
Frank Loesser – "Luck Be a Lady"
Frank Sinatra – "That Old Black Magic"
Frank Wedekind - "Ilse"
Franz Waxman – *Sunset Boulevard*, film score
Fred Astaire – "Cheek to Cheek"
Fréhel – "La Java Bleue"
Friedrich Hollander – "Ich bin die fesche Lola"
Funkadelic – "Flashlight"
G.G. Allin – "Outlaw Scumfuc"
Gal Costa – "Mamãe Coragem"
The Game – "Hate It Or Love It"
Gang of Four – "To Hell With Poverty"
Garth Brooks – "Friends in Low Places"
Gary Glitter – "Rock & Roll, Part One"
Gene Kelly – "Singin' in the Rain"
Gene Vincent – "Be Bop a Lula"
George Antheil – Ballet mécanique, for pianola, 2 pianos, 3 airplane propellers, siren and percussion, W. 156b
Georges Brassens – "Le Gorille"
Georges Brassens – "L'Auvergnat"
George Clinton – "Atomic Dog"
George Gershwin – Rhapsody in blue, for piano and orchestra
George Harrison – "My Sweet Lord"
George Jones – "He Stopped Loving Her Today"
George Michael – "Freedom '89"
Georges Auric – *Orphée*, film score
Georges Delerue – *Contempt*, film score
Georges Moustaki – "Le Métèque"
Germaine Tailleferre – Overture for orchestra
Gerry and the Pacemakers – "How Do You Do It?"
Giacomo Puccini – *Madama Butterfly*, opera
Gilbert Bécaud – **"Nathalie"**
Gilberto Gil – "Domingo no Parque"
Glenn Gould – Aria from *The Goldberg Variations, BWV 988*
Glenn Miller – "In the Mood"
Gloria Gaynor – "I Will Survive"
Gokh-Bi System – "Xaesal"
Gotan Project – "Tríptico"
Gram Parsons – "She"
Grandmaster Flash and the Furious Five – "The Message"
Grateful Dead – "Dark Star"
Green Day – "Basket Case"
Grinjolly – "Together We Are Many"
Guitar Wolf – "Jet Rock n' Roll"
Guns N' Roses – "Paradise City"
Gustav Mahler – Symphony no. 3 in D minor
Hank Williams – "I'm So Lonesome I Could Die"
Harry Nilsson – "One"
Henri Salvador – "Ma chère et tendre"
Herbie Hancock – "Chameleon"
Hermann's Hermits – "Mrs. Brown, You've Got a Lovely Daughter"
The High Llamas – "Checking In, Checking Out"
Hole – "Celebrity Skin"
Howlin' Wolf – "Smokestack Lightning"
Hüsker Dü – "New Day Rising"
Ibrahim Ferrer – "Mami Me Gusto"
Ice Cube – "Today Was a Good Day"
Ice-T – "6 'n the Morning"
Iggy Pop – "The Passenger"
Igor Stravinsky – Le sacre du printemps, ballet in 2 parts for orchestra
Indochine – "Tes yeux noirs"
INXS – "Need You Tonight"
Iron Maiden – "The Phantom of the Opera"
I-Roy – "Magnificent Seven"
Irving Berlin – "Top Hat, White Tie and Tails"
Isaac Hayes – *Shaft*, film score
The Isley Brothers – "Summer Breeze"
Jackson 5 – "I Want You Back"
Jackson Browne – "Doctor My Eyes"
Jacques Brel – "Amsterdam"
Jacques Brel – "La Quête"
Jacques Dutronc – "Il Est Cinq Heures Paris s'Eveille"
Jacques Dutronc – "Les Playboys"
Jacques Higelin – "Tombé du ciel"
The Jam – "In the City"
James – "Sit Down"
James Brown – "Get Up (I Feel Like Being a) Sex Machine"
James Taylor – "Fire & Rain"
Jamie Cullum – "Lover, You'd Better Come Over"
Jan and Dean – "Deadman's Curve"
Jane Birkin – "Fuir le bonheur de peur qu'il se sauve"
Jane Birkin – "Valse de Melody" (live, from *Arabesque*)
Jane's Addiction – "Been Caught Stealing"
Janet Jackson – "What Have You Done For Me Lately?"
Janis Joplin – "Ball & Chain"
Jay-Z – "Big Pimpin'"
Jean Ferrat – "Que serai-je sans toi?"
Jean-Michel Jarre – "Oxygène"
Jean Sibelius – Finlandia hymn, for chorus and organ (or harmo-

nium), op. 113/12
Jeff Buckley – "Hallelujah"
Jefferson Airplane – "White Rabbit"
Jellyfish – "The King is Half Undressed"
Jenifer – "Ma révolution"
Jerome Kern – "Smoke Gets In Your Eyes"
Jerry Goldsmith – *Chinatown*, film score
Jerry Herman – "Hello, Dolly!"
Jerry Lee Lewis – "Great Balls of Fire"
The Jesus and Mary Chain – "Some Candy Talking"
Jimi Hendrix – "Purple Haze"
Jimmie Rodgers – "Blue Yodel, No. 3" ("T for Texas")
Jimmy Cliff – "The Harder They Come"
Jimmy Reed – "Baby, What Do You Want Me To Do"
Joan Baez – "Diamonds and Rust"
João Gilberto – "Chega de Saudade"
Jobriath – "Take Me I'm Yours"
Joe Cocker – "With a Little Help From My Friends"
Joe Dassin – "À toi"
John Adams – *Nixon in China*, opera
John Cage – 4'33", for any ensemble or number of players
John Coltrane – "A Love Supreme"
John Lennon – "Working Class Hero"
John Williams – *Star Wars*, film score
John Zorn – "Spillane"
Johnny Cash – "I Walk the Line"
Johnny Hallyday – "Je te promets"
Johnny Hallyday - "Noir, C'est Noir"
Johnny Thunders and the Heartbreakers – "Born to Lose"
Joni Mitchell – "Both Sides Now"
Josephine Baker – "J'ai Deux Amours"
Joy Division – "She's Lost Control"
Judy Garland – "Somewhere Over the Rainbow"
Julien Clerc – "Ma préférence à moi"
Juliette Greco – "Le Temps des Cerises"
Juliette Greco – "Je suis comme je suis"
June Carter Cash – "The Heel"
Justin Timberlake – "Cry Me a River"
K.C. and the Sunshine Band – "Get Down Tonight"
Kanye West – "Jesus Walks"
Karita Mattila – "Vissi d'arte," from *Tosca*
Karlheinz Stockhausen – Kontakte, for piano, percussion and electronic sounds
Kate Bush – "Wuthering Heights"
Katie Melua – "Learnin' the Blues"
Keith Jarrett – "Part I" (live, from *The Köln Concert*)
Kenny Rogers – "The Gambler"
Keren Ann – "Jardin d'Hiver"
Khaléd – "Aïcha"
Kid Ory – "Do What Ory Say"
King Oliver's Creole Jazz Band – "Chimes Blues"
King Sunny Ade – "Synchro System"
King Tubby – "King Tubby Meets the Rockers Uptown"
The Kinks – "You Really Got Me"
Kishore Kumar – "Roop Tera Mastana"
Kiss – "Rock and Roll All Nite"
Kluster – "Untitled"
Kraftwerk – "The Robots"
Kris Kristofferson – "Sunday Morning, Coming Down"
Kurt Weill – *Die Dreigroschenoper*, opera
Kylie Minogue – "Can't Get You Out of My Head"
L7 – "Pretend We're Dead"
Ladysmith Black Mambazo – "Izithembiso Zenkosi"
Lara Fabian – "Je t'aime"
Lata Mangeshkar – "Chandni Raaten Pyar Ki Baaten," from *Jaal*
Laurent Voulzy – "Rockollection"
Led Zeppelin – "Whole Lotta Love"
Lee "Scratch" Perry – "Don't Blame on I"
Lefty Frizzell – "Saginaw, Michigan"
Léo Ferré – "Avec le Temps"
Leonard Bernstein – *West Side Story*, musical
Leonard Cohen – "Suzanne"
Lerner and Loewe – "I Could Have Danced All Night"
Les Paul – "How High the Moon"
Lester Young – "Oh, Lady Be Good"
Lil' Louis – "French Kiss"
Limp Bizkit – "Break Stuff"
Little Richard – "Tutti Frutti"
Litto Niebba – "Aguafuertes Portenas"
Liz Phair – "Fuck and Run"
LL Cool J – "I Need Love"
Lorenz Hart – "The Lady is a Tramp"
Lorie – "La Positive attitude"
Louis Armstrong – "West End Blues"
Louis Durey – Sonatina for flute and piano, op. 25
Louis Jordan – "Choo Choo Ch'Boogie"
Louis Prima – "Just a Gigolo/I Ain't Got Nobody"
Love – "Alone Again Or"
Lucky Blondo – "Sur ton visage une larme"
Macy Gray – "I Try"
Madonna – "Express Yourself"
Mahlathini and the Mahotella Queens – "Emthonjeni Womculo"
Malcolm McLaren – "Buffalo Gals"
Maria Callas – "Ah, non tremare," from *Norma*
Mariah Carey – "Fantasy"
Marilyn Manson – "Beautiful People"
Marlene Dietrich – "Falling In Love Again"
Marty Wilde – "Bad Boy"
Marvin Gaye – "Got to Give It Up, Pt. 1"
Marya Delvard – "Lied in der Nacht"
Maurice Chevalier – "Paris Sera Toujours Paris"
Maurice Ravel – *Boléro*, ballet for orchestra (or piano)
Max Steiner – *Gone With the Wind*, film score
MC Paul Barman – "Paullelujah!"
MC Shan – "The Bridge"
MC Solaar – "Nouveau Western"
The MC5 – "Kick Out the Jams"
The Melvins – "Night Goat"
Metallica – "Enter Sandman"
The Meters – "Handclapping Song"
Michael Bublé – "Fever"
Michael Feinstein – " 'S'

Wonderful"
Michael Jackson – "Billie Jean"
Michel Berger – "Chanson pour une fan"
Michel Legrand – *The Umbrellas of Cherbourg*, film score
Michel Polnareff – "L'Amour avec toi"
Michel Polnareff – "La Poupée qui Fait Non"
Michel Sardou – "Le Privilège"
Miklos Rosza – "A Double Life"
Miles Davis – "So What"
Ministry – "Jesus Built My Hotrod"
The Miracles – "The Tracks of My Tears"
Mischa Spoliansky – "Lavender Song"
Missy Elliott – "Get Yr Freak On"
Mistinguett – "Ça c'est Paris"
Mistinguett – "Mon Homme"
Moby – "Why Does My Heart Feel So Bad?"
Mohammad Rafi – "O Dilbar Janiye," from *Hasina Maan Jaayegi*
The Monkees – "I'm a Believer"
Mötley Crüe – "Girls, Girls, Girls"
Muddy Waters – "Mannish Boy"
Mudhoney – "Touch Me, I'm Sick"
Murray Perahia – Etude for piano no. 10 in A flat major, op. 10/10, CT. 23
Mylene Farmer – "Libertine"
***NSYNC** – "Pop"
N.W.A. – "Fuck tha Police"
Napalm Death – "Uncertainty Blurs the Vision"
Nas – "Made You Look"
Nazareth – "Love Hurts"
Les Negresses Vertes – "Sous le soleil de Bodega"
Neil Diamond – "Cracklin' Rosie"
Neil Sedaka – "Breaking Up is Hard to Do"
Neil Young – "After the Goldrush"
Neu! – "Isi"
New Order – "Blue Monday"
New York Dolls – "Personality Crisis"
Nick Cave and the Bad Seeds – "Are You the One I've Been Waiting For?"
Nick Drake – "Pink Moon"
Nikolai Rimsky-Korsakov – The flight of the bumble bee, musical picture for orchestra
Nina Simone – "Mississippi Goddamn"
Nine Inch Nails – "Closer"
Nino Rota – *The Godfather*, film score
Nirvana – "Smells Like Teen Spirit"
Noel Coward – "Mad Dogs and Englishmen"
Noir Désir – "L'Homme pressé"
The Notorious B.I.G. – "Hypnotize"
Oasis – "Live Forever"
Ofra Haza – "Im Nin' Alu"
Orchestra Baobab – "Utrus Horas"
The Original Dixieland Jazz Band - "Livery Stable Blues"
Ornette Coleman – "Free Jazz"
Os Mutantes – "Pannis et Circuses"
Oscar D'Leon – "Hazme el Amor"
Osvaldo Pugliese – "Inspiracion"
Otis Redding – "These Arms of Mine"
Ozzy Osbourne – "Mr. Crowley"
PJ Harvey – "Down By the River"
Parliament – "P-Funk (Wants to Get Funked Up)"
Patricia Kaas – "Il me dit que je suis belle"
Patrick Bruel – "Casser la voix"
Patrick Juvet – "Où sont les femmes?"
Patsy Cline – "Crazy"
Patti Smith – "Rock n' Roll Nigger"
Paul Anka – "Diana"
Paul McCartney – "Maybe I'm Amazed"
Paul Oakenfold – "Southern Sun"
Paul Simon – "Mother and Child Reunion"
Paul van Dyk – "Crush"
Pearl Jam – "Jeremy"
Pet Shop Boys – "What Have I Done to Deserve This?"
Peter Brötzmann – "Machine Gun"
Peter Gabriel – "Sledgehammer"
Petula Clark – "La Gadoue"
Philip Glass – Opening, for chamber ensemble or piano
Pierre Boulez – Le marteau sans maître, for alto, alto flute, guitar, vibes, xylorimba, percussion, and viola
Pink Floyd – "Shine On You Crazy Diamond, pts. 1-5"
The Pixies – "Debaser"
Pizzicato 5 – "Happy Sad"
The Police – "Every Breath You Take"
Positive Black Soul – "Boul Ma Mine"
Prince – "When Doves Cry"
The Prodigy – "Breathe"
Public Enemy – "Bring the Noise"
Puffy Ami Yumi – "Planet Tokyo"
Pussy Cat – "Les temps ont changé"
Queen – "Bohemian Rhapsody"
Quincy Jones – "The Man With the Golden Arm"
R. Kelly – "Fiesta"
R.D. Burman – "Piya To Ab To Aaja"
R.E.M. – "The One I Love"
Radiohead – "Paranoid Android"
Ralph Vaughan Williams – The lark ascending, romance for violin and orchestra
The Ramones – "Blitzkrieg Bop"
Rancid – "Ruby Soho"
Randy Newman – "Political Science"
Raphael – "Caravane"
The Raspberries – "Go All the Way"
Ray Barretto – "El Nuevo Barretto"
Ray Charles – "I Got a Woman"
Red Hot Chili Peppers – "Under the Bridge"
Renaud – "Mistral gagnant"
Renee Fleming – "Gia Nella Notte Densa," from *Othello*
Ria Bartok – "Parce Que J'ai Revu François"
Richard Hell and The Voidoids – "Blank Generation"
Richard Rodgers – "Some Enchanted Evening"
Richard Strauss – *Salome*, opera, op. 54 TrV 215
Rick James – "Super Freak"
Ricky Nelson – "I'm Walking"
Ringo Starr – "It Don't Come Easy"
Les Rita Mitsouko – "Les histoires d'A"
Ritchie Valens – "La Bamba"
Robbie Williams – "Angels"
Robert Johnson – "Hellhound on My Trail"
Robert Shuman – Widmung, song for voice and piano (Myrthen), op. 25/1

The Rolling Stones – "Honky Tonk Woman"
Ronnie Hawkins – "Mary Lou"
Roxy Music – "In Every Dream Home a Heartache"
Rubén Blades – "Buscando America"
Rudy Vallée – "Life is Just a Bowl of Cherries"
Rufus Wainwright – "What a World"
Run-D.M.C. – "Walk This Way"
Ruth Brown – "Teardrops from My Eyes"
Sade – "Smooth Operator"
Saint Etienne – "You're in a Bad Way"
Salif Keita – "Mandjou"
Sam Cooke – "A Change is Gonna Come"
Santana – "Black Magic Woman"
Sarah McLachlan – "Possession"
Scott Joplin – "The Entertainer"
Scott Walker – "The Girls From the Streets"
Serge Gainsbourg – "Je T'Aime ... Moi Non Plus"
Serge Reggiani – "Le Petit garçon"
Sergei Prokofiev – Piano sonata no. 6 in A major (war sonata 1), op. 82
The Sex Pistols – "Pretty Vacant"
The Shangri-Las – "Leader of the Pack"
Shania Twain – "Man! I Feel Like a Woman"
Sheila – "L'ecole est fini"
Sid Vicious – "My Way"
Sidney Bechet – "Summertime"
Silverchair – "Tomorrow"
Simple Minds – "Don't You Forget About Me"
Sinead O'Connor – "Nothing Compares 2 U"
Siouxsie and the Banshees – "Hong Kong Garden"
The Sir Douglas Quintet – "She's About a Mover"
Sister Sledge – "Lost in Music"
The Skatalites – "Guns of Navarone"
Slade – "Cum On Feel the Noize"
Sly and The Family Stone – "Stand!"
The Small Faces – "Itchykoo Park"
The Smiths – "How Soon is Now?"
Snoop Dogg – "What's My Name?"
Son House – "Levee Camp Blues"
Sonic Youth – "Teenage Riot"
Soundgarden – "Spoonman"
Spice Girls – "Wannabe"
Spokes Mashiyane – "Ace Blues"
St. Germain – "Deep In It"
Stan Getz and Charlie Byrd – "Desafindo"
Steel Pulse – "Prodigal Son"
Stephen Sondheim – "Send in the Clowns"
Steppenwolf – "Born to Be Wild"
Steve Reich – "Drumming"
Stevie Wonder – "Superstition"
Sting – "Englishman in New York"
The Stooges – "No Fun"
The Streets – "Let's Push Things Forward"
The Strokes – "Last Night"
Suede – "Animal Nitrate"
The Sugarhill Gang – "Rapper's Delight"
Suicide – "Frankie Starlight"
Sun Ra – "Atlantis"
The Supremes – "You Keep Me Hanging On"
Suzi Quatro – "Devilgate Drive"
The Sweet – "Ballroom Blitz"
Sylvie Vartan – "2'35 de Bonheur"
Sylvie Vartan – "La plus belle pour aller danser"
T. Rex – "Bang a Gong"
Talking Heads – "Psycho Killer"
Teenage Fanclub – "Sparky's Dream"
Téléphone – "Cendrillon"
Television – "Marquee Moon"
The Temptations – "Papa Was a Rolling Stone"
Terry Riley – In C, for unspecified performers
Thelonius Monk – "'Round Midnight"
The Time – "Jungle Love"
Thomas A. Dorsey – "(There'll Be) Peace in the Valley"
Tiffany – "I Think We're Alone Now"
Tindersticks – "Tiny Tears"
Tito Puente – "Oye Como Va"
Toby Keith – "Courtesy of the" Red, White and Blue"
Tom Zé – "Ma"
Tony Bennett – "I Left My Heart in San Francisco"
Tori Amos – "Silent All These Years"
Tracy Chapman – "Fast Car"
Twista – "Slow Jamz"
U2 – "With or Without You"
Uncle Tupelo – "Anodyne"
Underworld – "Born Slippy"
U-Roy – "Wear You to the Ball"
USA for Africa – "We Are the World"
Usher – "Yeah!"
Ute Lemper – "I Am a Vamp!"
Uum Kulthum – "Enta Omri"
Van Halen – "Running with the Devil"
Van McCoy – "The Hustle"
Vanessa Paradis – "Tandem"
The Velvet Underground – "Heroin"
Véronique Sanson – "L'Amoureuse"
The Verve – "Bittersweet Symphony"
Vinicius de Moraes – Cotidiano no. 2
The Vines – "Get Free"
The Waterboys – "The Whole of the Moon"
Waylon Jennings – "Only Daddy That'll Walk the Line"
Wham! – "Freedom"
The White Stripes – "Fell in Love with a Girl"
The Who – "Won't Get Fooled Again"
Wilco – "The Lonely 1"
William Sheller – "Un homme heureux"
Willie Colón – "Plástico"
Willie Dixon – "Spoonful"
Willie Nelson – "Night Life"
Wire – "I Am the Fly"
Wynton Marsalis – "Black Codes (From the Underground)"
X-Ray Spex – "Oh Bondage, Up Yours!"
Yoko Ono – "Walking on Thin Ice"
Youssou N'Dour – "Immigrés/Bitim Rew"
Yves Montand – "Luna Park"
The Zutons – "Zuton Fever"

One Hundred Best Movies That Rock

MOVIES FEATURING A BAND OR MUSICIAN

1. *Jailhouse Rock*
Richard Thorpe, 1957,
featuring Elvis Presley.

2. *King Creole*
Michael Curtiz, 1958,
featuring Elvis Presley.

3. *G.I. Blues*
Norman Taurog, 1960,
featuring Elvis Presley.

4. *Blue Hawaii*
Norman Taurog, 1961,
featuring Elvis Presley.

5. *Girls! Girls! Girls!*
Norman Taurog, 1962,
featuring Elvis Presley.

6. *Kid Galahad*
Phil Karlson, 1962,
featuring Elvis Presley.

7. *Beach Party*
William Asher, 1963,
featuring Frankie Avalon.

8. *Hard Day's Night*
Richard Lester, 1964,
featuring The Beatles.

9. *Viva Las Vegas*
George Sidney, 1964,
featuring Elvis Presley.

10. *Help*
Richard Lester, 1965,
featuring The Beatles.

11. *Head*
Bob Rafelson, 1968,
featuring The Monkees.

12. *Yellow Submarine*
George Dunning, 1968,
featuring The Beatles.

13. *Flame*
Richard Loncraine, 1975,
featuring Slade.

14. *Tommy*
Ken Russell, 1975,
featuring The Who.

15. *Kiss Meets the Phantom of the Park*
Gordon Hessler, 1978,
featuring Kiss.

16. *Rock 'n' Roll High School*
Allan Arkush, 1979,
featuring The Ramones.

17. *The Wall*
Alan Parker, 1982,
featuring Pink Floyd.

18. *Purple Rain*
Albert Magnoli, 1984,
featuring Prince.

19. *Under the Cherry Moon*
Prince, 1986,
featuring Prince.

20. *8 Mile*
Curtis Hanson, 2002,
featuring Eminem.

MUSICALS

21. *An American in Paris*
Vincente Minnelli, 1951.

22. *Oklahoma!*
Fred Zinnemann, 1955.

23. *The King and I*
Walter Lang, 1956.

24. *Gigi*
Vincente Minnelli, 1958.

25. *Porgy and Bess*
Otto Preminger, 1959.

26. *West Side Story*
Jerome Robbins, Robert Wise, 1961.

27. *Mary Poppins*
Robert Stevenson, 1964.

28. *My Fair Lady*
George Cukor, 1964.

29. *The Sound of Music*
Robert Wise, 1965.

30. *Hello, Dolly!*
Gene Kelly, 1969.

31. *Cabaret*
Bob Fosse, 1972.

32. *Grease*
Randal Kleiser, 1978.

33. *All That Jazz*
Bob Fosse, 1979.

34. *Hair*
Milos Forman, 1979.

35. *A Chorus Line*
Richard Attenborough, 1985.

36. *The Little Mermaid*
Ron Clements, John Musker, 1989.

37. *The Lion King*
Roger Allers, Rob Minkoff, 1994.

38. *Hedwig and the Angry Inch*
John Cameron Mitchell, 2001.

39. *Moulin Rouge!*
Baz Luhrmann, 2001

40. *Chicago*
Rob Marshall, 2002.

FICTIONAL

41. *Some Like It Hot*
Billy Widler, 1959.

42. *Nashville*
Robert Altman, 1975.

43. *The Rutles: All You Need Is Cash*
Eric Idle, 1978.

44. *I Wanna Hold Your Hand*
Robert Zemeckis, 1978.

45. *Quadrophenia*
Franc Roddman, 1979.

46. *The Rose*
Mark Rydell, 1979.

47. *The Idolmaker*
Taylor Hackford, 1980.

48. *The Blues Brothers*
John Landis, 1980.

49. *Smithereens*
Susan Seidelman, 1982.

50. *Eddie and the Cruisers*
Martin Davidson, 1983.

51. *This Is Spinal Tap*
Rob Reiner, 1984.

52. *Tapeheads*
Bill Fishman, 1988.

53. *Pump Up the Volume*
Allan Moyle, 1990.

54. *The Commitments*
Alan Parker, 1991.

55. *The Adventures of Priscilla, Queen of the Desert*
Stephan Elliott, 1994.

56. *That Thing You Do!*
Tom Hanks, 1996.

57. *Detroit Rock City*
Adam Rifkin, 1999.

58. *Almost Famous*
Cameron Crowe, 2000.

59. *High Fidelity*
Stephen Frears, 2000.

60. *A Mighty Wind,*
Christopher Guest, 2003.

FAMOUS SOUNDTRACKS

61. *Anatomy of a Murder*
Otto Preminger, 1959.

62. *Breakfast at Tiffany's*
Blake Edwards, 1961.

63. *The Graduate*
Mike Nichols, 1967.

64. *Alice's Restaurant*
Arthur Penn, 1969.

65. *Easy Rider*
Dennis Hopper, 1969.

66. *Midnight Cowboy*
John Schlesinger, 1969.

67. *Harold and Maude*
Hal Ashby, 1971.

68. *Shaft*
Gordon Parks, 1971.

69. *Superfly*
Gordon Parks, 1972.

70. *American Graffiti*
George Lucas, 1973.

71. *Butch Cassidy and the Sundance Kid*
Larry Cohen, 1973.

72. *Saturday Night Fever*
John Badham, 1977.

73. *Heavy Metal*
Gerald Potterton, 1981.

74. *The Big Chill*
Lawrence Kasdan, 1983.

75. *When Harry Met Sally*
Rob Reiner, 1989.

76. *Pulp Fiction*
Quentin Tarantino, 1994.

77. *Il Postino*
Michael Radford, 1994.

78. *Boogie Nights*
Paul Thomas Anderson, 1997.

79. *O Brother, Where Art Thou?*
Joel Cohen, 2000.

80. *Interstella 5555: The 5story of the 5ecret 5star 5ystem*
Leiji Matsumoto, 2003.

BIOPICS

81. *Yankee Doodle Dandy*
Michael Curtiz, 1942,
biography of George M. Cohan.

82. *The Glenn Miller Story*
Anthony Mann, 1953,
biography of Glenn Miller.

83. *Lady Sings the Blues*
Sidney J. Furie, 1972,
biography of Billie Holiday.

84. *Bound for Glory*
Hal Ashby, 1976,
biography of Woody Guthrie.

85. *The Buddy Holly Story*
Gary Busey, 1978,
biography of Buddy Holly.

86. *Coal Miner's Daughter*
Michael Apted, 1980,
biography of Loretta Lynn.

87. *Amadeus*
Milos Forman, 1984,
biography of Wolfgang Amadeus Mozart.

88. *Sid and Nancy*
Alex Cox, 1986,
biography of Sid Vicious.

89. *La Bamba*
Luis Valdez, 1987,
biography of Ritchie Valens.

90. *Bird*
Clint Eastwood, 1988,
biography of Charlie "Bird" Parker.

91. *Great Balls of Fire!*
Jim McBride, 1989,
biography of Jerry Lee Lewis.

92. *The Doors*
Oliver Stone, 1991,
biography of the Doors.

93. *What's Love Got to Do With It?*
Brian Gibson, 1993,
biography of Ike and Tina Turner.

94. *Backbeat*
Iain Softley, 1994,
biography of The Beatles.

95. *Two of Us*
Michael Lindsey-Hogg, 2000,
biography of John Lennon and Paul McCartney.

96. *Little Richard*
Robert Towsend, 2000,
biography of Little Richard.

97. *The Pianist*
Roman Polanski, 2002,
biography of Wladyslaw Szpilman

98. *Beyond the Sea*
Kevin Spacey, 2004,
biography of Bobby Darin.

99. *Ray*
Taylor Hackford, 2004,
biography of Ray Charles

100. *Walk the Line*
James Mangold, 2005,
biography of Johnny Cash.

Copyrights

P. 13: © Rue des Archives; p. 14: © DB Ruhmert DPA/Dalle; p. 15: © Hulton/Getty Images; p. 16: © Time Inc/Time Life Pictures/Getty Images; p. 17: © BPK, Berlin, RMN/Elke Wilford; p. 18: © Swini Ink 2/LLC Corbis; p. 19: © Bettman/Corbis; p. 21: from top to bottom, left to right: © DR, © DR, © Corbis, © Corbis, © DR, © DR; p. 22: © akg-images/British Library; p. 23: © akg-images; p. 24: © Austrian Archives/Corbis; p. 25: © Lorenzo Ciniglio/Corbis Sygma; p. 27: from top to bottom, left to right: © DR, © Rue des Archives, © Rue des Archives, © Rue des Archives; p. 28: © UFA/The Kobal Collection; p. 29: © akg-images; p. 31: © Michael Ochs Archives/Dalle; p. 35: © Shooting Star/Dalle; p. 36: © Rue des Archives; p. 37: © MGM/DR; p. 38: © MGM/The Kobal Collection; p. 39: © Willoughby-Redferns/Dalle; p. 40: (vertical, left) © Getty Images (right): © Getty Images; p. 41 (vertical left): Collection André Tubeuf/DR, (right): DR; p. 42: © GAB-Redferns/Dalle; p. 43: © MGM/The Kobal Collection; p. 44: © EMI/DR; p. 45: © Raoul Benegas; p. 46: (top) © The Frank Driggs Collection/Getty Images, (bottom): © The Condé Nast Publications; p. 47: © The Frank Driggs Collection; p. 48: © Delta copr-Redferns/Dalle; p. 49: (top) © Andy Kinsbury/Corbis, (bottom): © DR; p. 51: from top to bottom, left to right: © The Kobal Collection, © Rue des Archives, © The Kobal Collection, © DR, © The Kobal Collection; p. 52: © DR; p. 53: Hulton Archive/Getty Images; p. 54: © Richard Cummins/Corbis; p. 55: © Beat Goes On/DR; p. 56: © Sony BMG Music/DR; p. 57: © Hustone-Deutch Collection/Corbis; p. 58: © Private collection of André Tubeuf/DR; p. 59: © SAMA/SIPA; p. 61: from top to bottom, left to right: © Sony BMG Music/DR, © Sony BMG Music/DR, © Maverick/DR, © Sony BMG Music/DR; p. 62: © Rue des Archives/le Brecht; p. 63: © Rue des Archives; p. 64: © Henry Horenstein/Corbis; p. 65: © DR; p. 67: © Bettman/Corbis; p. 68: © hansen-hansen.com; p. 69: © Thierry Orban/Corbis Sygma; p. 71: © Jerry Schatzberg/Corbis; p. 72: © DR; p. 73: © MGM/The Kobal Collection; p. 74: (top and bottom) © Rue des Archives; p. 75: © Rue des Archives; p. 77: from top to bottom, left to right: © The Kobal Collection, © Rue des Archives, © DR, © The Kobal Collection, © The Kobal Collection, © Rue des Archives, © The Kobal Collection, © Rue des Archives, © Rue des Archives, © Rue des Archives, © The Kobal Collection, © Rue des Archives, © The Kobal Collection, © Getty Images, © The Kobal Collection, © Rue des Archives, © Rue des Archives, © Rue des Archives, © The Kobal Collection, © Henry Diltz/Corbis; p. 79: © Michael Ochs Archives/Dalle; p. 80: © Polygram Records/DR; p. 81: © Herman; p. 83: (top left) © Corbis, (top right) © Rue des Archives, (center) © Corbis, (bottom left) © Rue des Archives, (bottom right) © Corbis; p. 85: © DR/Courtesy Azzedine Alaia from the book Alaia, Steidl, 2001; p. 87: Marvin Koner/Corbis; p. 88: © Bettman/Corbis; p. 89: © Bettman/Corbis; p. 90: © Mercury/DR; p. 91: © Frank Driggs Collection/Getty Images; p. 93: from top to bottom, left to right: © Sony BMG Music/DR, © Island Records/DR, © EMI/DR, © Collector's choice/DR; p. 94: © DR; p. 95: © Bettman/Corbis; p. 97: © DR; p. 99: © Sony BMG Music/DR; p. 100: © Collectables/DR; p. 101: © Hulton Archives/Getty Images; p. 106: © DR; p. 107: (top) © Michael Ochs Archives/Dalle, (bottom): © DB/DPA/Dalle; p. 109: © Michael Ochs Archives/Dalle; p. 110: © Rue des Archives; p. 111: © Herbert Gehr/Time Life Picture/Getty Images; p. 113: © Warner Music/DR; p. 115: © Corbis; p. 116: © DR; p. 117: © David Reed/Corbis; p. 118: © Courtesy Guy Peelaert; p. 119: (top) © Rue des Archives, (bottom): © kipa; p. 120: © Warner Music/DR; p. 121: © Gysbert Hane Kroot/Sunshine/Dalle; p. 122: © Pierre Fournier/Sygma/Corbis; p. 123: (top) © Rue des Archives, (bottom): © DR; p. 124: © Claude Gassian; p. 125: © Rue des Archives; p. 126: © Bettman/Corbis; p. 127: © Courtesy Guy Peelaert; p. 128: vertical from left to right: © Corbis, © DR, © Getty Images; p. 129: vertical from left to right: © DR, © Time Life Pictures/Getty Images; p. 130: © Philips/DR; p. 131: © Dalle APRF France; p. 132: © Rue des Archives; p. 133: © Courtesy Guy Peelaert; p. 134: © Courtesy Guy Peelaert; p. 135: © Courtesy Guy Peelaert; p. 136: © Getty Images; p. 137: © Courtesy Guy Peelaert; p. 139: © Peter Lindbergh; p. 140: © Courtesy Guy Peelaert; p. 141: © Bettman/Corbis; p. 143: © Bettman/Corbis; p. 147: © Agence Dalle; p. 148: © Rue des Archives; p. 149: (left) © Neal Preston/Corbis (right): © DR; p. 150: © Rue des Archives; p. 151: Neal Preston/Corbis; p. 153: © DR; p. 154: © DR; p. 155: © Claude Gassian; p. 156: © DR; p. 157: © Rue des Archives; p. 158: (top) © Christian Simonpietri/Sygma/Corbis, (bottom): © Inye Yspeert/Corbis; p. 15: © Norman Parkinson Limited/Fiona Cowan/Corbis; p. 160: Archives Olivier Buchet © DR; p. 161: © Rolling Stone LLC 2005 All rights reserved. Reprinted by Permission; p. 162: vertical: © DR; p. 163: vertical: © DR; p. 164: © Condé Nast Archives/Corbis; p. 165: © Shooting Star/Dalle; p. 166: © Pete Saloutos/Dalle; p. 167: McKeourn/Express/Getty Images; p. 169: © DR; p. 171: © Bettman/Corbis; p. 172: © Evening Standard/Getty Images; p. 173: © Van Gelderen; p. 174: © Rue des Archives; p. 175: © Verve Records/DR; p. 176: © Rita Lee; p. 177: © Polygram Records/DR; p. 179: from top to bottom, left to right: © Corbis, © Getty Images, © Corbis, © Corbis, © Corbis; p. 180: © Royalty free/Corbis; p. 181: Shooting Star/Dalle; p. 183: Dalle; p. 184: Neal Preston/Corbis; p. 185: Roger Ressmeyer/Corbis; p. 186: © DR; p. 187: © Bettman/Corbis; p. 189: © DR; p. 190: © Glenn Baker-Shooting Star/Dalle; p. 191: © Corbis; p. 192: (top) © Ammar/Dalle, (bottom): Sunset Boulevard/Corbis/Sygma; p. 193: Courtesy Guy Peelaert; p. 194: © Kobal Collection; p. 195: © Gold/Redferns/Dalle; p. 196: © Gamma; p. 197: Courtesy Guy Peelaert; p. 199: from top to bottom, left to right: © Corbis, © Corbis, © Rue des Archives, © Corbis, © Corbis, © Corbis; p. 200: (top) © Snaoui/Dalle (bottom) © Shooting Star/Dalle; p. 201: © Dalle; p. 202: © Patrick Chauvel/Sygma/Corbis; p. 203: © Shooting Star/Dalle; p. 204: © Rue des Archives; p. 205: © Claude Gassian; p. 206: © ADAGP/DR; p. 207: © Jeff Albertson/Corbis; p. 209: from top to bottom, left to right: © Corbis, © Corbis, © Getty Images, © DR, © Corbis,

© Corbis, © DR, © Corbis; p. 210: © Shooting Star/Dalle; p. 211: © Gold/Redferns/Dalle; p. 212: (left) Warner Music/DR, (right), © Corbis; p. 213: © Henry Diltz/Corbis; p. 215: © Urso Alessandro/Corbis Sygma; p. 217: © Dalle APRF France; p. 218: © Corbis/Sygma; p. 219: © Pillitz/Rapho, Paris; p. 221: © Dalle; p. 226: © Jeff Kravitz/Dalle APRF France; p. 227: © Corbis; p. 228: © Jorgen Angel/Dalle; p. 229: © Knips/Dalle; p. 230: © Henry Diltz/Corbis; p. 231: © Bettman/Corbis; p. 232: © EMI/DR; p. 233: © Arnaud Meyer; p. 235: (1) © Corbis, (2) © DR, (3) © Corbis, (4) D.R., (5) © Corbis; p. 236: © Corbis; p. 237: © Verhorst/Dalle; p. 238: © Neal Preston/Dalle; p. 239: © Sadri/Dalle; p. 240: © Rue des Archives; p. 241: © Lynn Goldsmith/Corbis; p. 242: © Michael Ochs Archives/Dalle; p. 243: © Roger Ressmeyer/Corbis; p. 245: (1) © Scoop, (2) Lee Jenkins/Courtesy Terry Blamey, (3) © Corbis, (4) © Universal/DR; p. 246: (left) © Rue des Archives, (right) © Dalle APRF Dalle; p. 247: © Lynn Goldsmith/Corbis; p. 249: © DR; p. 250: © Dalle; p. 251: (left) © Arnaud Meyer, (top right) © EMI/DR, (bottom right) © Mercury/DR; p. 252: © Tramb/Dalle; p. 253: (top) © Jill Furmanovksky/Idols/Dalle, (center) © Dalle France, (bottom) © Dalle France; p. 257: © Rue des Archives; p. 258–259: © DR/Sony BMG Music; p. 260: ©Abacapress; p. 261: © Abacapress; p. 262: (bottom) © Michael Lavine, (top) © Dalle APRF France; p. 263: © Dalle APRF France; p. 264: © Fabio Nosotti/Corbis; p. 265: © Mute/DR; p. 267: (top left) © Dalle France, (top right) © Rue des Archives, (bottom left) © Rue des Archives, (bottom right) © Dalle France; p. 268: © Barry Schultz/Sunshine; p. 269: © Rue des Archives; p. 270: © Sony BMG Music/DR; p. 271: © Neal Preston/Corbis; p. 273: (1) © Corbis, (2) © Dalle France, (3) © Corbis, (4) © Corbis, (5) © Corbis, (6) © Corbis, (7) © Rue des Archives, (8) © Corbis, (9) © Corbis, (10) © Corbis; 274: © Neal Preston/Corbis; 275: © Bergen/Dalle; 276: © Maverick/DR; 277: © Dalle France; p. 278: © Verhorst/Dalle, p. 279: © Neal Preston/Corbis; p. 280: © DR, p. 281: © Ark 21/DR; p. 283: © Sotheby's image; p. 284: © Dalle, p. 285: © A&M/DR; p. 286: (left) © Dalle APRF France, (right) Clayton/Dalle; p. 287: © UPPA/Dalle; p. 288: (top) © Warner Music/DR, (bottom) © Arnaud Meyer; p. 289: © Caserta/Dalle; p. 290: © Gideon Mendel/Corbis; p. 291: © Nubar Alexanian/Corbis; p. 292: (top) © Getty Images, (bottom) © DR; p. 293: (left) © Sony BMG Music/DR, (right) © Corbis; p. 294: © Youri Lenquette/Dalle; p. 295: © Alexa Brunet-Transit/Dalle; p. 296: © Stefan de Bastelier Idols/Dalle; p. 297: © Baras/Dalle; p. 298: © Getty Images; p. 299: © Piranha/DR; p. 300: © Corbis; p. 301: © Goodacre-Sin/Dalle; p. 302: Gilles Bensimon/Elle; p. 303: © Rue des Archives; p. 304: © Ed Alcock/Eyvine/Dalle; p. 305: © Levy/Dalle; p. 310: © Anthony Mandler-Idols/Dalle; p. 311: ©AnthonyHarnvey/PA/Abacapress; p. 312: © Mazzoni/Dalle; p. 313: © Karl Grant-Idols/Dalle France; p. 315: (1) © David Bowie/1998 Panic in Detroit/Ernst Anger, (2) © CharlElie, 2006 (3) © Astrud Gilberto—All rights reserved, (4) © Dee Dee Ramone/Courtesy Follin Gallery; p. 316: © Gina Miller; p. 317: © DR; p. 318: © Corbis/Sygma; p. 319: © Davies & Davies/Dalle; p. 320: (left) © Piilman/Dalle, (right) © Frank Trapper/Corbis; p. 321: © SIN/Corbis; p. 322: © Nathalie Genet/Dalle APRF; p. 323: (top) © Lucia del Pia/Vanit/Dalle, (bottom) © Sony BMG Music/DR; p. 324: (top left) © Rue des Archives, (top right) ©Corbis, (bottom left) © Corbis, (bottom right) Corbis; p. 326: © Corbis; p. 327: © SIN/Corbis; p. 328: © DR; p. 329: © DR, p. 332: © DR, p. 342: © Assouline; p. 350: © Rue des Archives.

Acknowledgments

The publisher would above all like to thank David Fricke as well as Jean-Jacques Groleau, Thomas Mahler, and Patrick Tchiakpé for their editorial contributions.

The publisher would furthermore like to thank the PR department at Azzedine Alaïa, Olivier Buchet, Rafael Cruzado, CharlElie Couture, Javier Ferrand, Claude Gassian, Bertrand from the Dalle agency and his team, Yvonne Hazens, Gregory Lasorsa at Magya Productions Inc., .Michael Levine, Homero Machry, Arnaud Meyer, Guy Peellaert, Daly Sue at Sotheby's image, and Corbis, Rue des Archives, Gamma, Getty, Scoop, and Abacapress.